SAFE HAVEN?

SAFE HAVEN?

A HISTORY OF REFUGEES IN AMERICA

David W. Haines

Kumarian Press
An Imprint of Stylus Publishing

Safe Haven? A History of Refugees in America

Published in 2010 in the United States of America by Kumarian Press, 22883 Quicksilver Drive, Sterling, VA 20166, USA.

Copyright © 2010 Kumarian Press.

The text of this book is set in 11/13 Garamond

Editing and book design by Aptara

The paper used in this publication meets the minimum requirements of the American National Standard for Information Sciences—Permanence of Paper for printed Library Materials, ANSI Z39.48-1984

Library of Congress Cataloging-in-Publication Data

Haines, David.
    Safe haven? : a history of refugees in America/David Haines.
        p. cm.
    Includes bibliographical references and index.
    ISBN 978-1-56549-331-5 (pbk. : alk. paper) – ISBN 978-1-56549-332-2 (cloth : alk. paper)
    1. Refugees–United States–History.   2. Immigrants–United States–History.   I. Title.
    HV640.4.U54H153 2010
    305.9′069140973–dc22

                                                                          2010011829

All royalties from this book are donated to
organizations serving refugees

Contents

List of Tables

Preface

There are many points at which one could begin the story of refugees in America. One might begin with America as land of refuge for the Pilgrims and note how fundamental to American consciousness has been the idea of flight from oppression to a land that offered freedom of religion. One might contrast that Pilgrim experience with the experience of the rather more economically motivated settlers of Jamestown—perhaps noting in passing that by the time the Pilgrims actually landed in their pursuit of religious freedom, the settlers in Jamestown had already decided on tobacco and slavery in pursuit of their version of freedom.

As an alternative, one might begin the story in Acadia in 1755 as Lieutenant Colonel John Winslow gathered the local men into the church, sealed the doors, and read his proclamation that all their lands were now forfeit and they were to be summarily expelled from their beloved land. Wrote Henry Wadsworth Longfellow of that expulsion:

> Waste are those pleasant farms, and the farmers forever departed! Scattered like dust and leaves, when the mighty blasts of October seize them, and whirl them aloft, and sprinkle them far o'er the ocean.

The American colonies to which the Acadians were sent provided a poor welcome indeed. In particular, the descendants of those Jamestown settlers, now the very prosperous colony of Virginia, refused entirely their requested quota of refugees. The Acadians were thus launched on a sequence of journeys that led some to Louisiana but others back to England, from there to France, and for some yet another trip back to America. This alternative beginning point would yield not America as a land of refuge, but America as a land refusing refuge.

Another option would be to begin with a different expulsion, that of the Cherokee. They, despite their impressive efforts and considerable success in adapting to the ways of the American settlers, were themselves expelled westward. Acknowledged as a sovereign nation by the U.S. Supreme Court, they were then subject to a treaty signed by a small renegade clique and, in

1838, sent on the "Trail Where They Cried" (*Nunna daul Tsuny*). Greed once again held the lead in the American colonies, and the same Andrew Jackson who had fought side by side with the Cherokee became their fatal enemy in their expulsion. This beginning point would yield not America as land of refuge or even as land refusing refuge, but as a land producing refugees.

Such historical precedents help show the mix of motivations for migration (religious freedom, economic gain), the duress of migration (outright expulsion, more discreet discrimination), the responses to migration in general (accepting, rejecting, ignoring), and the specific relation to refugees (being refugees, accepting refugees, rejecting refugees, and creating refugees). Neither the motivations nor the responses are always clear-cut. It is the fate of the dispossessed to be at the mercy of the conflicting humanitarian and self-serving motivations of those whose borders they cross. All of that is very apparent in these early historical precedents.

In this book, instead, I start the story of refuge in America in more modern times. Many dates would serve well. It is now just over seventy years since the Evian Conference of 1938, which showed how very well delay and avoidance can be served by international conferences that propose to help refugees. A just over sixty-year date would yield the Displaced Persons Act of 1948, in many ways the beginning of what we understand as refugee resettlement in the United States. It serves well as a marker of American recognition that some people's movement is indeed forced, and that America has a responsibility to help. A fifty-year date would yield Fidel Castro's rise to power, and the beginning of what would be—until the end of the Vietnam war—America's largest refugee resettlement effort. For a forty-year date, I might pick a personal one, induction into the U.S. Army and the beginning of language classes that would lead me to Vietnam as an army translator and interpreter, and then on to graduate work in Vietnamese history. Although my graduate work ultimately turned in other directions, Vietnam came back to me in the form of refugees. My involvement was initially minimal but, in 1979, my graduate research methods class suggested that we really ought to be looking at this issue of Vietnamese refugees. We did so, subsequently published a few articles, and soon afterwards I found myself working for the U.S. refugee resettlement program. There, I began to understand more clearly the earlier stories about refugees in America, all the places they had come from, all the problems they had faced, and how for many the past would not go away and the future would not arrive—or not easily anyway.

Over the years since then, despite many diversions into different areas, my efforts have often returned to the different facets of the refugee experience in America and to the American experience of giving refuge. There are, after all, two parts to this story of refuge in America. While most of those who help refugees are very modest about their own efforts, or simply recognize that their own need is less, what a nation provides as refuge is indeed a crucial test of what it is. Over its history, the United States has both passed that test and failed it—and will probably do both again. This book aims to make it a little clearer what that test involves and why, despite the distractions of increased security concerns and the surging numbers of other kinds of immigrants, it is still a test to be taken.

Acknowledgments

My major debts are two: first, to the many refugees I have known in different ways over the years: as colleagues, coworkers, friends, students, interviewees, and language teachers; and, second, to the many people I have known as colleagues, coworkers, friends, students, and family who have worked in various ways to provide a haven and new life for refugees in the United States. One of the great benefits of dealing with refugee issues is that it makes you humble and thus one of the great benefits of working with people who work on refugee issues is that they try to put their own egos aside. My former colleagues at the U.S. Office of Refugee Resettlement, for example, were probably the finest set of people I have had the opportunity to work with, and the students in my graduate seminars on refugees are probably the finest students I have known. So, refugees do all of us a great favor by forcing us to be a little more humble about ourselves and a little more honest about our limitations. We know we are never fully equal to the task of providing refuge, that we almost always act too late and with too little, and that we could probably not have endured what the refugees have endured. We also know that the America we provide as refuge may itself bring further pain and loss.

For help on this book in particular, I would like to thank Karen Rosenblum, who has always encouraged me to write on refugee situations and who was coauthor of an article from which Chapter 4 is drawn, to my late parents who were excruciatingly clear about which of my books were readable (and thus useful) and which were not, to Loren Bussert, Shawn Davis, and Leonid Guzman for their help with the data from the federal government's annual survey of refugees (which I helped design some thirty years ago), and to a wide range of people who have read (or heard) and commented on various pieces of this present book in either its current incarnation or in the articles and presentations in which it first emerged, particularly Elliott Barkan, Mary Jane Berman, Linda Gordon, Oliver Mogga—and to the American Studies Association of Korea where I had the opportunity to try out the discussion of Chapter 1 for an international audience. I also have a few special debts to Patrick Thomas and Dorothy Angel Rutherford of that graduate seminar on field methods thirty years ago (with whom I wrote two early articles); to Carol Mortland as my coeditor for *Manifest Destinies* (and who remains for me perhaps the most astute analyst of the refugee/host interaction); and to my coauthors on two pieces about Richmond's refugees (Marilyn Breslow, Dirk Philipsen, and Jan Williamson). Three recent graduate students also deserve particular thanks for stimulating and expanding my thinking on refugees: Elizabeth Murdock Manus for her excellent research on a refugee camp in Ghana; Bethany Burns for her insights on Eleanor Roosevelt's involvement in refugee issues; and Janet Gallay for starting me to think about the Cherokee expulsion as a refugee movement. Finally, I must thank Jim Lance and Erica Flock at Kumarian Press for their support of this project. Publishing this book with an activist press has helped me greatly in conceptualizing how this book can be useful on both academic and practical grounds, for those who seek clarity and those who may seek more specific documentation (which I have often relegated to the endnotes). Thanks also goes to Satvinder Kaur of Aptara for great attentiveness to the editorial and production processes.

For previously published material, I am indebted to NYU Press which published an earlier, shorter version of Chapter 1 (in *From Arrival to Incorporation*, edited by Elliot Barkan, Hasia Diner, and Alan Kraut); to *Identities: Global Studies in Culture and Power* for the major portion of Chapter 3; to the *Journal of Ethnic and Migration Studies* for an abbreviated version of Chapter 4 that I published with Karen Rosenblum; to *International Migration Review* for the discussion of Vietnamese kinship in the second part of Chapter 5; and to the *Journal of Refugee Studies* for an early version of Chapter 6.

For grant support over the years on refugee-related research, I am indebted to the Rockefeller Foundation (for time to review the existing research on refugees in the United States), the Fulbright Program (for a research award looking at resettlement programs in Western Europe), the Social Science Research Council (for support of more historically oriented research on Vietnamese society), and George Mason University's Office of the Provost for both a summer stipend to work on historical materials and a faculty study leave to research general refugee issues.

Refugees and America: Moral Commitments and Practical Challenges

The American experience with refugees over the past seventy years has ranged from acceptance to rejection, from well-wrought program efforts to botched policy decisions, from humanitarian concerns to crass politics. The U.S. Department of State has been both the fabricator of paper walls to exclude refugees and the locus of intense efforts to move them quickly into the United States. Religious and secular voluntary agencies have been lauded for their efforts on behalf of refugees and chided for providing inconsistent services. Refugees themselves have been characterized as true American success stories and criticized as overly dependent on public welfare. The American people, in turn, have often been impressively generous in their welcome of refugees but at other times neglectful, disinterested, and sometimes hostile.

Refugees and America have thus had a long, complicated, and often vacillating relationship. But, throughout, the relationship has been an important one. America has often been the most crucial country of support for refugees, and refugees have often been for America the most visible, challenging, and morally significant of newcomers. Refugees, for example, often receive disproportionate media attention (both positive and negative) and it is often a surprise to people that refugees are such a small numeric segment of overall immigration flows to the United States—about a tenth in recent decades, although much reduced after September 11, 2001.[1] This importance of refugees to America, despite the relatively small numbers of refugees and relatively modest program costs associated with them, has a very strong moral component. On the positive side, refugees represent those whose life experiences most clearly demand humanitarian respect and action. Because of these moral demands, assistance to them often requires practical,

1

incisive actions that are outside the bounds of normal bureaucratic structures and processes. On the negative side, refugees who violate the ideal refugee image by engaging in fraud or even persecution of other refugees are subject to very sharp rejection. The U.S. government itself is subject to censure when it betrays moral standards for political expedience (support of friendly but oppressive regimes; exaggerated claims of security threats) or when it allows bureaucratic ineffectiveness to undermine humanitarian action.

All this makes the American experience with refugees highly complex, but it also makes it useful as a window on how morality, rationality, and expedience interpenetrate in American institutions, attitudes, and social interactions. This opening chapter provides an overview of the relationship between refugees and America over the past seventy years. It deals sequentially with the different moral commitments Americans have toward refugees, some of the practical challenges faced in the domestic resettlement of refugees, and the ways refugees have challenged American thinking about the world. Succeeding chapters will then examine more specific aspects of America as a haven for refugees, including how refugees fare in the United States (Chapter 2), how Americans react to refugees, including what they expect of them (Chapter 3), how refugees fit into existing American social categories, particularly of ethnicity (Chapter 4), how refugees' kin relations affect adjustment to the United States (Chapter 5), and the logic—and occasional illogic—of the programs designed to aid refugees in adjusting to the United States (Chapter 6).

Moral Commitments

There are many points at which to begin the story of refugees and America, but the roots of the U.S. refugee program as it exists today lie especially in the events leading up to the Second World War. Two events in 1939[2] serve as an especially poignant prologue to the American experience with refugees. The first was the ill-fated voyage of the St. Louis. Its passengers were largely German Jews fleeing the now visible threat to them from the Nazi regime. As they attempted to land in Cuba, and then sailed along the east coast of the United States, they were denied the right to land, even though some 700 of them had registered for American visas and had received affidavits of support. Despite their pleas and those of many supporters in the United States, they were rebuffed and thus returned to Europe to face their destinies there (Ogilvie and Miller 2006; Wyman 1985: 38-39). The second event—ultimately a nonevent—was the attempt to pass the Wagner-Rogers bill. That bill was a fairly modest attempt to permit some 20,000 German refugee children to enter the United States. The bill was carefully crafted, nonsectarian in its phrasing (although the majority of those involved would inevitably be Jewish[3]), and with a very broad range of endorsements from organizations and prominent individuals.[4] Yet, even this modest effort to address a well-documented humanitarian need failed. These two examples of the rejection of Jewish refugees set the pattern not only for the denial of new immigration slots, but the construction of additional barriers—"paper walls" in David Wyman's (1985) words—to keep Jews out even when slots were available. It is that combination of the denial of new admissions mechanisms *and* the undercutting of existing admissions mechanisms that buttresses Wyman's more general argument about the full abandonment of Jewish refugees to the Holocaust (D. Wyman 1998).

This *non*program for refugees seen in 1939 provides some important lessons. One is that it matters very much who the refugees of the day are. There was blatant anti-Semitism among many of those opposing humanitarian action for European Jews. There were, after all, special programs for British children during the war, to keep them in the United States and thus out of harm's way in Great Britain. Even after the war, when the United States acknowledged the need to resettle some of the many displaced persons (DPs) in Europe, initial versions of the DP legislation had an anti-Jewish bias—although that was removed in later versions of the legislation (Dinnerstein 1982; M. Wyman 1998). This theme of rejecting or accepting refugees based on their specific identity has been a continuing one in the U.S. refugee program. Those refugees with strong constituencies have fared better. Those who could unite multiple constituencies have fared best of all, for example, by appealing to the humanitarian impulses of the left, the anticommunist impulses of the right, and the communitarian impulses of co-ethnics and co-religionists. The moral commitment to refugees by the United States has thus not been simply a reflection of an abstract humanitarian definition of what a refugee is. Whatever the merits of an internationalist, pan-refugee orientation, the American experience has been—for better and for worse—very much a parochial one of different kinds of commitments toward different refugees based on their circumstances and identity: their class, their religion, their ethnicity, their race, their gender and age (thus the frequent emphasis on women and children), and the existence of any previous connection to the United States.

The U.S. refugee program—from its very *non*inception in 1939—thus provides a useful window on when Americans recognize moral commitments, and when those commitments are strong enough to override direct national interests. The response to refugees since 1939 provides an inventory of why it is and when it is that Americans are willing to reach beyond their borders to bring people within those borders for safe haven. With regular immigrants, much of the policy discussion is quite practical: do immigrants contribute to the country or not. In the more specific area of refugees, however, the core issues are less practical. Instead, the question is whether there is such an overriding commitment to particular people that they should be admitted even if for little practical gain. For the United States, as for many other countries, this provision of safe haven to refugees represents one of the crucial links between humanitarian action abroad and humanitarian action at home.

Reviewing the origins and numbers of refugees admitted to the United States since the Second World War helps indicate something of how commitments to refugees develop. One theme is anticommunism. The United States has been consistently willing to accept as refugees those who flee (or wish to flee)[5] communist regimes. Anticommunism has been crucial to virtually all refugee admissions up until the 1990s (see Table 1.1): the acceptance of displaced persons[6] after the Second World War who might

Table 1.1 Refugees admitted since the Second World War

PERIOD		NUMBER
1948–1952	Displaced Persons Act	415,000
1953–1956	Refugee Relief Act	214,000
1956–1957	Hungarian refugees	32,000
1959–1974	Cubans	656,000
1965–1974	Parolees	78,000
1975–2009	Africa	241,619
	Asia	1,365,683
	Eastern Europe	301,314
	Soviet Union	605,105
	Near East	229,263
	Latin America	105,829
	Other	22,375
Grand total		4,266,188

Sources: The data for arrivals since 1975 come from the U.S. Department of State's Refugee Processing Center. Earlier data are from the actual legislative approvals (for DPs), from special tabulations of Cuban arrivals as presented in Taft, North, and Ford (1979: 67), and from counts of parolees under the 1965 Immigration and Nationality Act from the Congressional Research Service (CRS 1980: 12). Note that asylees and Cuban–Haitian entrants are *not* included but ODP arrivals and Amerasians *are* included. Note also that an additional 6,000 Hungarian refugees were admitted as part of left-over authorized numbers from the Refugee Relief Act. See CRS (1979b, 1980) for more detailed breakdowns of admissions numbers for the pre-1980 period.

otherwise have been repatriated to newly communist countries in Eastern Europe; the entry of Hungarians fleeing the failed uprising there in 1956; the acceptance of Cubans who fled after Fidel Castro's rise to power; the arrival of refugees from Vietnam, Laos, and Cambodia after the collapse of American-supported governments in 1975; and provision for refugees from other communist countries, particularly the Soviet Union. Although the acceptance of refugees from these communist countries has had some very practical political advantages—good press on those "voting with their feet" for freedom—even those advantages rest on a moral commitment: to stand for a particular kind of political and economic system and to recognize in word and deed that people fleeing a competing kind of political and economic system (sometimes even an "evil" system) have every reason to do so, and every right to claim refuge in the United States.

However, the Cuban and Southeast Asian examples go well beyond anticommunism as a general stance and to very bitter relations with two specific communist regimes. Although the acceptance of early Cuban refugees might be construed as simple anticommunism, the dynamics of the Cuban expatriate community and the extent to which many people moved back and forth between Cuba and the United States before 1959, suggest something far more personal. Likewise, those fleeing from Cambodia, Laos, and Vietnam were not simply fleeing communism, but also fleeing situations made worse by American involvement. This was thus not only an ideological commitment, but one that also invoked a moral commitment to help those placed in harm's way by U.S. action. Refugee admissions became a partial restitution for either American inaction (letting Castro achieve power, leaving South Vietnam open to what was ultimately a North Vietnamese invasion), or for actual actions that made things worse (the Bay of Pigs in 1961, collusion in the assassination of Ngo Dinh Diem in 1963).

Although these two commitments, one of ideology and one of responsibility, account for much of U.S. refugee admissions, they do not fully account for all refugee admissions or for the tenacity with which refugee admissions from some places have continued. Another kind of commitment—and also a moral one at least in part—has been for the United States to take a fair share of refugees as part of broader international efforts. That was particularly clear in the U.S. refugee program in the 1990s (especially with the increased numbers of refugees from Africa)[7] but also helps explain earlier flows as well. The United States, for example, came fairly late to the resettlement of displaced persons after the second World War. Other countries had already indicated willingness to accept DPs (although often for reasons more practical than moral).[8] The United States thus needed to do its fair share. Southeast Asian refugee resettlement after 1979 was also part of an internationally based effort to ease pressure on the countries of initial asylum in Southeast Asia, who had begun to forcibly push refugees back to sea or back across land borders—and often to their death. Here, then, the United States was not only meeting its own commitments of ideology and responsibility but also again making a fair share contribution to resolving an international problem. Indeed "fair share" is a recurring theme in refugee policy deliberations from the time of DP programs and legislation onward.

There is another moral commitment: the one reflected in the refugee definition of the United Nations Convention (1951) and Protocol (1967) on Refugees, and of the U.S. refugee program since that definition was incorporated into the Refugee Act of 1980. This commitment is the one with which discussions of refugees often begin: a definition in the realm of international law reflecting a general humanitarian desire to aid people who have been subject to such a degree of persecution that they must flee their home and their country. That definition is helpful in many ways but it is also quite restrictive.[9] The U.N.'s formal designation of refugee status, for example, requires that refugees have crossed an international border (rather than simply being displaced) and that their reasons for flight hinge on five specific kinds of persecution: by race, religion, nationality, belonging to a particular social group, or holding a particular political opinion. Furthermore, the determination of refugee status is an individual one based both on objective events and personal psychodynamics: it is necessarily a fear of persecution standard, not a direct proof of persecution standard.[10] So, in formal legal terms, applying the definition requires a meticulous process for determining status on an individual basis, then considering the right to derivative refugee status of people who may not themselves meet the standard but who are the spouses, siblings, children, parents, or other relatives of those who do. This general humanitarian commitment to refugees thus has a rather complex procedural side, which has often been used to avoid giving refuge.

To return the discussion to the somewhat apocryphal nonbeginning of the refugee program in 1939, it is clear that there was a disavowal of all these kinds of moral commitment: of any ideological reason to save the Jews, of any sense of responsibility for the position in which the Jews found themselves, of any need for a fair share contribution to a broader international problem, or of any need to recognize the situation of individual refugees in terms of a general humanitarian standard. Yet, there is an important caveat to be made to that bleak assessment. If we look at the White House, and a President who was only swayed with great effort to intervene on refugee issues, we also see down the hall another Roosevelt who was assiduously addressing refugee issues and engaged in individual correspondence with refugees. Sometimes she would send notes down the hall to FDR: "FDR, can't something be done?" she noted to him on a denied visa for a man in Portugal. "FDR, something does seem wrong," she wrote about a set of visas that had been approved but not issued (Burns 2002).[11] There is thus an important thread linking Eleanor Roosevelt's correspondence at that time with the broader role she would take after the war on behalf of displaced persons. In that sense, the formal beginnings of the U.S. refugee program, especially the 1948 Displaced Persons Act, lay exactly in the failure to accept refugees nearly a decade earlier that spurred the work of Eleanor Roosevelt and others like her who did see the general humanitarian demands posed by refugees and the extraordinary experiences and needs of individual refugees.

Practical Challenges

The United States, through this thicket of moral commitments, has admitted some four million refugees for resettlement since the Second World War (see Table 1.1).[12] Doing so has raised several persistent challenges. Those challenges are often—as they are again today—very political. Without strong constituencies, the numbers admitted are likely to drift downward. But many of the challenges are more practical, and sometimes simply logistic. Thus, from the time of the DPs on, there has been a concern with "the pipeline" by which refugees can be transported to the United States in a relatively orderly fashion. Sometimes that pipeline has developed additional twists, turns, and holding tanks because of uncertainties at the origin of the pipeline, concerns to regulate and standardize the flow into the United States, and sometimes the desire to regulate health screening, cultural orientation, and language training along the way—as in the refugee processing centers (RPCs) set up for Southeast Asian refugees on U.S. territory in 1975 and then overseas in Southeast Asia after the massive boat exodus of the late 1970s.[13] Even the logistics after refugees reach the United States can be complex. Initial destinations must be chosen and coordinated among resettlement agencies. Those agencies, in turn, must move new arrivals into appropriate housing, through health screening, and toward education and employment.

These practical challenges reflect the scope of what is required by the refugee resettlement process. Refugee resettlement involves a level of social engineering virtually unknown in U.S. public administration. After all, the program aims to take people whose lives have been utterly disrupted, whose kin and community networks—those most elemental of "safety nets"—have been attenuated and ruptured, whose expectations may never have been to come to America, who may know no English and have no exposure to an urban, industrial (or post-industrial) society, and turn them into functioning, successful Americans. It is hardly surprising that refugees sometimes do not make that transition in an orderly or particularly rapid way. It is also hardly surprising that those attempting to assist refugees sometimes drift into quasi-parental views of their charges, for it is perhaps only in parenting that Americans have a model of such broad responsibility for somebody else's social transformation.[14]

This task of social transformation is rendered more difficult by the diversity of refugees coming to the United States. Since there is no uniform set of attributes shared among those entering as refugees, there is likewise no common starting point for this process of social transformation. In recent years, as the U.S. refugee program has become more representative of global refugee flows, the diversity in national and ethnic origin has become impressive. Thus formally designated refugees with more than 10,000 arrivals over roughly the last three decades (see Table 1.2) include Afghans, Bhutanese, Burmese, Cambodians, Cubans, Ethiopians, Hmong, Iranians, Iraqis, Lao, Liberians, Poles, Romanians, Somalis, Sudanese, Vietnamese, and various groups from the former Soviet Union and the former Yugoslavia (especially Bosnians). Furthermore, there are many other smaller groups of refugees, and there is often additional ethnic and religious variation with the larger groups: Iranians include Baha'is, Christians, Jews, and Muslims; Russians include Jews and Pentecostal Christians[15]; the latest group of refugees from Somalia is hardly Somali in an ethnic sense, but rather Bantu people who were trafficked north into Somalia as labor and often as slaves. This range of cultural diversity is in many ways the glory of the refugee program, but it does pose many difficulties in resettlement.

There are other kinds of variation as well. Perhaps most important are issues of age and gender. Those are themselves culturally conditioned, but their effects can be significant even in basic demographic terms. Gender is somewhat unpredictable in its effects, sometimes working to the favor of women and sometimes men, but populations with gender imbalances (lack of young women, lack of older men) face both social and economic challenges. Age has enormous effects in how quickly people adapt to the United States—the younger usually the better. Educational background, occupational background, and English language competence are also crucial—the only clear exception to the language limitation being places (particularly Miami) where Spanish functions as an alternative common language.[16]

Given such diversity, there is no common starting point for this ambitious social transformation. With no common starting point, measuring progress toward resettlement goals has inherent difficulties. To the inevitable and seemingly reasonable program question "how are refugees doing?" there can only be contingent answers because the degree of progress hinges on the starting point.[17] Consider, for example, what is probably the most common measure of progress in resettlement: employment. There is much

Table 1.2 Refugee arrivals by country of origin (1983–2009)

COUNTRY OF ORIGIN	NUMBER	PERCENT OF TOTAL
Afghanistan	34,256	1.68
Albania	3,663	0.18
Angola	416	0.02
Bhutan	18,772	0.92
Bulgaria	2,736	0.13
Burma	52,415	2.57
Burundi	9,051	0.44
Cambodia	71,529	3.51
Columbia	1,357	0.07
Congo	964	0.05
Cuba	75,186	3.68
Czech Republic	7,537	0.37
Democratic Republic of Congo	6,893	0.34
Eritrea	4,065	0.20
Ethiopia	40,912	2.01
Haiti	6,842	0.34
Hungary	5,124	0.25
Iran	82,889	4.06
Iraq	76,401	3.74
Kenya	1,202	0.06
Laos	128,972	6.32
Liberia	32,794	1.61
Libya	364	0.02
Mauritania	401	0.02
Nicaragua	1,536	0.08
Nigeria	1,419	0.07
Poland	28,806	1.41
Romania	34,669	1.70
Rwanda	2,028	0.10
Sierra Leone	8,376	0.41
Somalia	88,948	4.36
Sudan	30,008	1.47
Thailand	4,536	0.22
Togo	1,420	0.07
Uganda	505	0.02
USSR (former)	526,237	25.79
Vietnam	473,443	23.20
Yugoslavia (former)	169,003	8.28
Other/unknown	4,711	0.23
Total	2,040,386	100.00

Source: U.S. Department of State data as reported in annual reports of the Office of Refugee Resettlement for the period 1983–2007. For the years 2008 and 2009, numbers are taken directly from the U.S. Department of State refugee data processing center. Note that this is a "live" database, so numbers change slightly from year to year for previous years. As in the previous table, Cuban and Haitian entrants are *not* included but Amerasians and ODP arrivals *are* included.

quantitative research that addresses refugee employment, for example, annual surveys of refugees that have been conducted,[18] in one form or another, by the federal government since 1975. The last two decades of the twentieth century provide an opportunity to assess this issue of refugee employment. Data from the late 1990s (see Table 1.3) would seem to suggest rather impressive improvement in the situation of the refugees. Whereas in 1995, labor force participation was 49.8 percent for refugees (versus 66.7 percent for the general U.S. population), the figure had risen to 68.9 percent by 1999 (versus a U.S. rate of 67.1 percent).[19] Similarly, refugee unemployment was 15.1 percent in 1995 (versus a U.S. rate of 5.2 percent) but had dropped to 3.1 percent (versus a U.S. rate of 4.2 percent) by 1999.

That seemingly improved portrait in 1999, however, roughly matches the situation far earlier in 1979. At that earlier time, the experience of the 1975 Vietnamese refugees appeared to be rather good. They were employed at higher rates than the general U.S. population and also appeared to be working longer hours (Haines 1985; Marsh 1980; Montero 1979; Stein 1979). Although there was downward occupational mobility, still this

Table 1.3 Refugee employment patterns (1995–1999)

	LABOR FORCE PARTICIPATION RATE			UNEMPLOYMENT RATE		
	ALL	FEMALE	MALE	ALL	FEMALE	MALE
1995						
Refugees	49.8	42.1	57.4	15.1	16.6	14.0
U.S. rates	66.6	59.4	76.7	5.4	5.6	4.6
1996						
Refugees	57.4	49.4	65.4	11.2	12.2	10.4
U.S. rates	66.8	59.3	74.9	5.4	5.4	5.4
1997						
Refugees	58.1	49.5	66.8	7.3	8.9	6.0
U.S. rates	67.1	59.8	74.9	4.9	5.0	4.9
1998						
Refugees	59.1	52.8	66.6	5.2	5.7	4.7
U.S. rates	67.1	59.8	74.9	4.5	4.6	4.4
1999						
Refugees	68.9	63.3	74.4	3.1	3.4	2.9
U.S. rates	67.1	60.0	74.7	4.2	4.3	4.1

Source: Annual reports of the Office of Refugee Resettlement.

Table 1.4 Population employment ratios (1986, 1993, and 1999)

OVERALL EMPLOYMENT RATIO FOR THOSE WHO ARRIVED	1986	1993	1999
This year	23.3	24.9	50.9
One year ago	20.0	28.4	63.2
Two years ago	27.9	30.1	67.7
Three years ago	36.0	37.8	67.8
Four years ago	40.5	39.0	70.9
Five years ago	39.6	25.8	66.8

Source: Annual reports of the Office of Refugee Resettlement.

presented a status report of relative success for the refugees, and likewise relative success for the refugee resettlement program. In between these two dates of 1979 and 1999, however, the employment status of refugees was far less encouraging. If 1986 and 1993, for example, are compared with 1999, the contrast is a sharp one (see Table 1.4).[20] For first year arrivals, the overall employment ratio[21] was 23.3 percent in 1986 and 24.9 percent in 1993, compared with the very respectable figure of 50.9 percent in 1999. That is, in 1986 and again in 1993, the employment ratio for first-year arrivals was less than half of what it was in 1999. For those who had been in the United States for five years, the overall employment ratio was 39.6 percent in 1986, 25.8 percent in 1993,[22] compared with 66.8 percent in 1999.

These data are striking in their contrast of comparatively poor employment outcomes in the late 1980s and early 1990s with comparatively impressive employment outcomes at the end of the 1970s and the end of the 1990s. That is, the employment situation goes from high, to low, to high again. These data could be taken simply to represent the decline and resurrection of the refugee resettlement program. Or the data could reflect shifting economic conditions. That is an especially tempting idea because there was indeed a very deep recession in the early 1980s. Or perhaps the data reflect shifts in the characteristics of arriving refugees. That is certainly the case during the late 1970s and early 1980s, when new arrivals had more limited educational, occupational, and language skills. The effects of such arrival characteristics are crucial. Consider the 1999 survey data, for which the employment situation seemed to vary widely depending on the region from

Table 1.5 Refugee characteristics by region of origin (1999)

REGION OF ORIGIN	EMPLOYMENT RATIO	EDUCATION IN YEARS	PERCENT WITH GOOD OR FLUENT ENGLISH
Africa	59.7	7.5	66.8
Latin America	80.7	11.0	50.4
Middle East	70.8	11.3	74.2
Eastern Europe	74.2	10.9	52.6
Former Soviet Union	50.5	11.8	43.7
Vietnam	74.3	10.1	74.2
Other Southeast Asia	38.0	3.1	50.4
All	66.8	10.6	57.2

Source: Annual report of the Office of Refugee Resettlement.

which the refugees came (see Table 1.5). Those from Asia appeared to be doing fairly well in employment terms, those from the former Soviet Union and Africa far less so. Yet, these were not simply cultural differences, but ones rooted in very elemental issues of demography and human capital. Refugees from the Soviet Union were far older; those from Africa had far less education. Both advanced age and low education are severe obstacles in the U.S. labor market. (Indeed, if those same data are used to look at younger refugees from the Soviet Union and better educated Africans, those refugees were more often employed than the apparently more successful refugees from other countries.)[23]

Refugee resettlement thus aims at an enormous social transformation about which even the most rudimentary measure of progress (employment) indicates more about the starting point of the process and the conditions under which it occurs than about progress per se. Although there are statistical ways to begin to sort out the respective contributions of refugee characteristics, program actions, and resettlement context, they are not easily used even for relatively large populations—such as Cubans and Vietnamese—much less for the wide range of smaller populations and the frequent variability even among the larger populations. There is an even more fundamental problem: the conceptual inadequacy of employment as a program measure at all. Why is immediate employment so crucial? Why not have people go to school so they can get better jobs later on? Why not have parents stay home with their children, keeping them out of trouble, and helping them do their schoolwork, so that in the future, the children can have better jobs or themselves do a better job of helping their own children with their schoolwork?

The U.S. Refugee Act gives mixed guidance on this issue of employment. The actual wording in the act can be taken to mean either a goal of any work now *or* a goal of the best possible work in the future. This ambiguity reflects the failure to resolve the debate that was in process at the time the Refugee Act was passed in 1980. At that time, for example, there were programs for retraining professionals so that they could practice their former profession. "Employment commensurate with existing skills and abilities" did not automatically mean that if a refugee doctor had limited English competence, the only employment option was manual labor. It was only in the context of the new Reagan administration in 1981 that notions of "welfare dependency" began to infiltrate the refugee program, and this notion of appropriate employment came to mean what it usually means now: employment of any kind, and as soon as possible. But immediate employment begs the question of occupational trajectories, of what kind of employment, with what increases in wages and benefits, over the longer run.[24] Only that longer-term data can address a broader notion of employment and how it relates to refugee integration into American society.[25]

This inability to establish even the most rudimentary of program goals, much less any reasonable progress markers toward that goal, helps explain some of the erraticness—even fickleness—of the refugee program over time, and of public opinion about refugees. It is, as noted, fundamentally impossible to give a simple, straight answer to the seemingly reasonable program question: "How are refugees doing?" Any answer is highly contingent. It just depends on which refugees, with what characteristics, having gone through what experiences before arrival, living in what kind of America both generally (economic boom? recession?) and in terms of specific locale (good schools? crime on the streets? helpful employers?). This inability to answer a simple program question poses an overarching practical challenge to the refugee program. It is a terrible frustration to the many people who want to say "refugees are doing great" because they know that on some level that is true. It is likewise a great frustration to those who want to say "they're having serious problems" because they know that is true on some level as well.

There is a brighter side to this dilemma. Much of the difficulty lies precisely with the diversity of the refugee population and the fact that refugees are not selected simply for their preadaptability to the U.S. labor market. This does not mean there are no temptations toward preselection. Much of that early interest in postwar DPs (M. Wyman 1998), for example, was by countries seeking to fill employment needs: Belgium wanted coal miners, Canada's interest lay with farm workers and domestics, Britain needed factory workers and domestics, Iraq requested ten doctors. Furthermore, much of the selection process for DPs was geared for their likely ease in adjustment. There was thus a frequent preference for those from the Baltic countries as well as specific country interests such as Australia's interest in those of British stock and Argentina's interest in Slovenians. Despite such temptations, the moral commitments to refugees suggest that the fit between refugees and the societies that resettle them is unlikely to be smooth—indeed, often the reverse. The diversity of refugee destinies after resettlement thus appropriately matches the diversity of their origins and the tortuous paths by which they reach America.

Conceptual Challenges

The U.S. experience with refugees thus reflects multiple moral commitments that defy easy explanations or decisions about admissions. Instead, the search for the moral underpinnings of the refugee program yields the ebb and flow of a variety of moral commitments to a variety of refugees. That kind of ebb and flow does not make for a very clear and consistent pattern of refugee admissions. Furthermore, the program designed to support refugees in their adjustment after arrival lacks measures of progress that adequately reflect the diversity of refugees and their often difficult experiences before arrival. The result in both cases is a kind of muddle. That muddle, however, provides an opportunity for some thinking[26] about how Americans think about social issues, about programs, and about humanitarian action itself. As an extended example of what the U.S. refugee program provides in lessons about how Americans think about social programs, consider again the issue of diversity among refugees. If arriving refugees are so diverse, with such a range of cultural, social, economic, political, psychological, and spiritual characteristics, tendencies, and connections, then it will be very difficult to categorize them in simple ways. Furthermore, they come from very different places, by unusual and varied passages, and with aftershocks that nonrefugees can probably never fully comprehend. Nevertheless, Americans tend to categorize refugees in relatively simple ways that make their experience understandable in conceptual terms and also addressable in program terms. These attempts to figure out who refugees are reveal a great deal about the categories that Americans use to assign people to their proper place.

The conduct of survey research on refugees must confront this problem of diversity, especially since it is the results of survey research that are crucial to policy development and public discussion. Such survey research is meant to be open; it is not meant to assume who and what people are. Yet, survey research requires some standardization, focuses on individuals (data are sorted as attributes of individuals for the most part),[27] and includes a large number of precoded categories into which respondent answers are sorted, including answers to questions about who the respondent is. The way survey research is structured (both in the questionnaires and in the analysis) reflects the social categories that are assumed to be valid enough and reliable enough (i.e., "real" enough) to use as the structure for research. The "assumed" is the crucial part of the issue and what needs to be examined. The research on Southeast Asian refugees provides a good example.

As a matter of general background, shortly after the influx of approximately 130,000 Southeast Asian refugees in 1975, the federal government began contracting periodic national surveys of these refugees to assess the course of their adaptation to the United States. In 1981, after nine of the surveys, the survey was substantially revamped (including standardized reporting of employment information) and regularized to an annual basis. Somewhat later, the sampling was converted to a panel design and the tracing of respondents was limited to their first five years in the country. There are now some thirty years of these national surveys of refugees with a reasonable degree of consistency in their structure over time. There has been, in particular, considerable stability in the framing of core questions regarding employment, income, and use of public assistance and services since the survey was redesigned in the early 1980s—and these are the source of the employment data provided earlier in this chapter. These surveys are an important resource on substantive grounds,[28] but also provide useful lessons on how people are categorized in survey research. Compared with surveys of more stable populations, refugee surveys are particularly instructive since refugee flows often change rapidly. The history of refugee resettlement in the United States is a chronicle of collapsed governments (as in Southeast Asia), shifting exit restrictions (as in the Soviet Union and its successors), and political fragmentation (as in the Balkans). Refugee flows thus provide good examples of dealing with unexpected and relatively unknown new populations. Refugees are often *not* new members of existing migration flows to the United States but rather "pioneer" flows of entirely new populations. These new populations often speak languages that are new to researchers, with the resulting problems of developing an adequate supply of multilingual interpreters and facing the hazards of translation, which can be severe with noncognate languages.

The refugees from Southeast Asia provides such a good example because the numbers of arrivals generated an unusually broad range of survey research. For the initial surveys of Southeast Asian refugees, this question of "who are they?" seemed fairly simple. The purpose was no more than to survey some refugees from the former French Indochina[29] and see how they were doing.[30] The refugees who arrived in 1975 were largely Vietnamese. Thus the initial surveys were in Vietnamese, of Vietnamese, and by Vietnamese. This was, after all, about Vietnamese refugees. Issues of geographical, national, and linguistic origins seemed self-evident and unitary. However, it soon became apparent that there were also increasing refugee flows from Cambodia and Laos and that more of those refugees would be coming to the United States. Thus the surveys shifted to a tripartite pattern with three separate sections for Vietnamese, Cambodian, and Laotian refugees. Yet the basic logic was the same: national origin was the crucial way to categorize the refugees, and that nationality was assumed to be closely related to social and cultural background. Thus, the implication was that Vietnamese by nationality meant Vietnamese by ethnicity and Vietnamese by language. Cambodians were Khmer and spoke Khmer; Laotians were Lao and spoke Lao.

Unfortunately, that was not the case. By the late 1970s, two major complications had arisen: many of the Vietnamese were ethnic Chinese and many of the Laotians were Hmong—the highland group most involved in the CIA's so-called secret war (although it was not much of a secret). Thus nationality (or, more precisely, national origin) could no longer be assumed to be directly related to ethnicity. However, national background still seemed to imply some facility with the "national" language. It might then be conceivable that a three-language methodological strategy was supportable, at least in terms of formal translations of survey material. Thus the Vietnamese, Khmer, and Lao written translations continued. On practical grounds, however, there was at least occasional need for Hmong and Chinese speakers (usually Cantonese). So the result was a questionnaire in three languages with supplementary on-call help for two other languages.

Despite these changes, the survey results continued to be presented in the three national origin categories: Vietnamese, Laotian, and Cambodian. What was known to be important in the conduct of the research was not yet seen as crucial to the findings. The survey results still failed in providing guidance on how these different ethnic and language groups were adapting. The collapsing of Lao and Hmong into "Laotian" was disastrous in analytic terms; the collapsing of ethnic Vietnamese and ethnic Chinese into "Vietnamese" only marginally less so. In both cases, reporting by national group obscured what were ultimately shown to be very different background and adaptational patterns within those groups. In particular, any statistical analysis (or even descriptive reporting) of almost anything by "Laotian" was, in fact, worse than meaningless since the "central tendency" between the two component populations (Hmong and ethnic Lao) simply did not exist.[31]

Somewhat better were other survey efforts at that time[32] that moved more fully to a five-category model based on ethnicity: Lao, Hmong, Khmer, Vietnamese, and Chinese—with most, but far from all, of the Chinese coming from Vietnam (Haines 2009; Lee 2009). Here, national origin disappeared from the equation. Instead, the criterion was ethnicity, largely overlapping with language.[33] This five-group model was a sharp improvement and proved to be very durable. It remains even today the standard convention for categorizing Southeast Asian refugees. The groups were large enough to be adequately sampled on the national level and large enough to provide ready access to bi- and trilingual interviewers.[34] The limited number of groups permitted a limited number of formal translations and a reasonable degree of stabilization among them. In terms of analysis and understanding, these groupings made good cultural and historic sense. The five-group model was thus workable on technical grounds and defensible on cultural grounds. (It also revealed how comfortable Americans are with standard ethnic categorizations—a topic that receives additional attention in Chapter 4.)

However, the five-group model had limitations. One such problem was the presence of numerous smaller populations. Among the refugees coming from Southeast Asia, for example, there were Chinese from Cambodia and Laos as well as from Vietnam, and they were not always similar to the Vietnamese Chinese. There were a variety of different Chinese dialects spoken even within Vietnam, and with such groups as the Hakka, the argument of a different "ethnicity" is possible. The Hmong were far from being the only highland group coming out of Southeast Asia. Many other highland groups were involved in the war, often through an Army Special Forces arrangement somewhat like that between the Hmong and the CIA. Those highland groups in Vietnam often had great difficulty getting out after the war, but some did.[35] The Mien are another large highland population from Laos who did escape in significant numbers, though far fewer than the Hmong (MacDonald 1998) and they are numerous enough to show up in survey research,[36] although too few in number to be readily analyzable from that survey data. There are other smaller groups who, while readily identifiable on ethnic and linguistic grounds, are so small in number as to challenge the limits of detail possible in survey research.[37]

A further problem is the great degree of variability within particular refugee populations, even when the ethnic designation is appropriate because of shared language, identity, and core cultural beliefs. Differences in educational and socioeconomic background may be sharp. Refugees resettled in the United States are, almost by definition, not representative of the countries from which they came. They may represent only one particular social or political layer of a population. Sometimes they represent two unique layers that diverge in general class background, the divergence between those who are relatively well educated and with an urban background versus those who are rural and often nonliterate. In survey research, this shows up as a bimodal pattern. One classic case involves Cambodians (Rumbaut 1989) because of their differential exodus based on the extent of Khmer Rouge control and proximity to the Thai border. Because of that difference, it makes as little sense to talk of "Cambodian" refugees as a defined population as it does in the cases of "Laotian" and "Vietnamese"—the former for class reasons and the latter for ethnic ones.

Simple regional variation can also be important.[38] For example, a large number of Vietnamese refugees to the United States are actually North Vietnamese in origin—some having come directly from the north, but many having previously moved south in 1954 at the time of the armistice, and fleeing again some twenty years later from South Vietnam. Regional differences may well have language implications. There are, for example, pronounced dialectical differences between the northern, central, and southern parts of Vietnam: the tonal systems are distinct, the shifts in pronunciation of consonants are pervasive, and there are also important variations in diction and phrasing. The sociological meaning of a Vietnamese accent can be fundamental: mutual stereotypes of northerners and southerners are sharp and one's accent may instantaneously create trust or distrust, amity or hostility.[39]

Religion provides a final example of some of the problems in categorizing refugees. For many refugees, religion is the very reason for their migration and is wound deeply into their identity. Indeed, for some, the core of identity may be ethnicity interwoven with religion rather than ethnicity with language.[40] Cambodian Buddhists often say that those who are converted to Christianity are no longer Khmer, for to be Khmer is to be Buddhist. What then of those who do convert to Christianity? For Vietnamese, the division between Catholics and Buddhists is an important one, and was a factor both in flight from South Vietnam and in similar flight from northern to southern Vietnam after the defeat of the French two decades earlier. Although one can easily include Vietnamese as a single linguistic and ethnic group in a survey, the meaning of the responses is hard to interpret when the two really significant historical factors of region and religion are excluded. Thus, even though ethnic and language issues may be resolved for a particular survey, or be clear in a particular public discussion, that does not necessarily mean that the issue of identifying the significant populations has been resolved.

What this extended discussion of categorization suggests is that even in presumptively rational moments, when governments and people attempt to objectively determine what should be done for refugees, knowing exactly who these people are can become a major obstacle. Refugees are not easily categorized through existing notions of nation and ethnicity, much less of race or religion. It may only be with their children, who are acted upon with such force by American society and institutions, that refugees do come to be constructed both externally and internally according to U.S. categories of diversity: nationality and ethnicity, race and gender, age and class, American or foreigner. That, in turn, creates inconsistencies between refugee parents and their children about how people should be classified.

This issue of knowing who people are, and how to categorize them, is partly an intellectual one, and that is extraordinarily useful in highlighting the kinds of identity systems that are central to American society. But the issue is also an intensely practical one. If we do not know how people fit and do not fit into our conventional categories, we may not know what to expect from them and thus whether we can trust them. Thus periodically with refugees, as with other immigrants, comes the suspicion that those who have arrived bring not benefits but problems, not predictable behavior but uncertainties. What if a refugee really isn't a "real" refugee but simply looking for a better life? What if a refugee was a persecutor not someone persecuted? What if the refugee is an anarchist, a communist, or—today—a terrorist?

Then and Now

This chapter began by selecting a particular beginning date for a review of the relationship between refugees and America. The selection of such a date suggests an implicit comparison: of then and now, of how events developed then and how they may develop now. In many ways, the comparison yields sharp differences. There is now, unlike then, a functioning refugee program, a commitment to accept refugees from all parts of the world, and a large, relatively open immigration policy of which refugees are but a minor component. The pervasive discrimination by race and religion (especially anti-Semitism) of seventy years ago stands in sharp contrast to a contemporary refugee program that is responsive to all races and religions.

In other ways, however, the comparison between then and now yields similarities. Now, as then, there is a frequent belief that problems in the world ought to be (and are being) handled "there" rather than "here." Then, as now, there are concerns about the dangers posed by newcomers to the nation's social fabric—even to its security. Finally, then, as now, the result has been both the physical rejection of some refugees and the failure to use available administrative options to admit other refugees.[41] Refugees have not been arriving in the United States as often as they used to. That may change but, for the moment, there is a danger that refugees are becoming the new unseen Americans. That is unfortunate for refugees, especially since the United States is the major country of safe haven for them. But it is also unfortunate for the United States since it is refugees, more than other immigrants, who break down the boundaries between the world as Americans understand it and want it to be and a rather different world: one that is disorderly, resists American preconceptions, and eludes American efforts at control.

It is for that range of reasons that the U.S. refugee resettlement program is so crucial. It throws much light on both the world from which the refugees have come and the world in which they find themselves now. In their experience lies an invaluable story of the world (and its horrors) but also one of America and the ways its moral commitments coalesce into action: how Americans collectively and individually, through private and public sectors, based on secular and religious commitments, set about solving complex social problems—and how Americans are educated about the world in the process. Ebbing away with admissions numbers at the start of the twenty-first century[42] has been not only safe haven for refugees but also much of the very best of what America has been and still can be in terms of humanitarian action.

Notes

1. The U.S. refugee program was effectively shut down for four months after September 11, 2001. When restarted, processing remained very slow, stranding many already approved refugees. Ultimately, only 27,000 refugees entered in FY 2002 (compared with the original ceiling of 72,000), and a similar number entered in FY 2003. In succeeding years, admissions rose to about 50,000, still far below the average numbers admitted throughout the 1980s and 1990s, but again fell in 2006. Figures for 2008 (60,000) and 2009 (75,000) were far better. Note, however, that there is a separate accounting for those people who apply for refugee status after arriving in the United States. The number of what are legally termed "asylees" has been rising—although not enough to offset the decline in regular refugee admissions.

2. As noted earlier in the preface, there would also be good reason to begin this account in 1938 with the Evian Conference (Loescher 1993: 44–45; Wyman 1985: 41–51). I use 1939 instead because of the way the story of the St. Louis has endured as a symbol of the rejection of refugees—even with a movie, Voyage of the Damned, and a meticulous attempt to track the ultimate destinies of all those on the ship (Ogilvie and Miller 2006). That vision of ships pushed back to sea returned in the

late 1970s with the Vietnamese boat exodus and a far more immediate loss of life on the seas. In that sense, the 1942 voyage of the Struma (which was pushed back and sank with only two survivors) was more immediately harrowing in its implications than that of the St. Louis (Wyman 1985: 39). But it was the St. Louis that has lived on in memory. Vice President Walter Mondale, for example, invoked the ill-fated St. Louis as a way to increase public support for the boat people (Loescher and Scanlon 1986: 145). Furthermore, the 1939 pairing of the St. Louis incident with the failure to pass the Wagner-Rogers legislation (Wyman 1985: 75–98) is effective in highlighting the two poles of energizing crisis and plodding legislation that have often characterized the American response to refugees.

3. Certainly the majority of those involved in this proposed legislation would have been Jewish. There was, however, some question of what proportions were Jewish by actual religion and what percent were Jewish simply in the sense of having Jewish forbears. Wyman (1985: 86) estimates that some 50-60 percent of those who would have benefited from the Wagner-Rogers bill would have been Jewish by religion.

4. This effort, unlike some others, was without very strong support from the White House, even from Eleanor Roosevelt (Burns 2002; Wyman 1985: 97).

5. Many refugees have, in fact, been accepted by the United States before they actually fled. "In-country processing" (i.e., processing of refugees in their countries of origin) became increasingly common in the 1980s not only for Vietnamese through the ODP (Orderly Departure Program), but also for those from the Soviet Union (and its successor states) and, in smaller numbers, for other refugees as well. Bill Frelick (1996) provides a useful critique of in-country processing and how it works to the disadvantage of those actually forced to flee and who, because of that flight across borders, more fully meet the international refugee standard.

6. The original Displaced Persons Act of 1948 provided for 205,000 persons, but this was increased to 415,000 when that act was amended in 1950.

7. The broadening of the origins of refugees to the United States is nowhere clearer than in relation to Africa. Although the Refugee Act of 1980 theoretically opened the way to broader geographical representation among refugees admitted to the United States, the entire Africa contingent was less than 3,000 in 1981. But by 2001, the African contingent was nearly 19,000, with Somalis and Sudanese accounting, respectively, for 5,000 and 6,000 admissions. As a percentage of refugee arrivals, Africans increased during that twenty-year period from less than 2 percent to over 25 percent. The aggregate data on refugee arrivals, presented in Table 1.2, underscores the diversity not only in terms of region of origin but also in terms of specific country of origin.

8. Various countries in Europe, and also Australia and Canada, saw the DP camps as sources of needed labor to compensate for postwar labor shortages. The jobs to be filled, of course, were not always ideal. The Belgians, for example, were the first to take a sizable number of DPs from the camps, but that was for 20,000 coal miners. Women were often sought as domestic workers, and many had to be advised to avoid mentioning any higher education since that would make them

overqualified for such jobs and thus unacceptable for placement out of the camps. See, M. Wyman (1998) and Dinnerstein (1982).

9. Figures from the U.S. Committee for Refugees are a standard benchmark. By the early 2000s, the number of refugees had fallen to around 12 million, but by the end of 2006, the collapse in Iraq was again pushing the number of refugees higher, to an estimated 13.9 million. Note that internally displaced persons (IDPs) are not included in these numbers, nor are Palestinian refugees. See UNHCR (2009c) for overall figures on refugees and IDPs.

10. The standard for being a refugee given in international law (and in U.S. law since 1980) is technically a psychological (or at least cognitive) one requiring not proof of persecution but a well-founded fear of persecution.

11. These examples come from Burns's (2002) review of documents at Hyde Park. The nature of these cases is, as she notes, consistent with Lash's notion of the different roles and sensibilities of Eleanor and Franklin Roosevelt, that he often brought up "difficulties, while she pointed out the possibilities" (Lash 1971: 636). But it is also consistent with a distinction between Eleanor's personal, individualized humanitarianism and Franklin's interest group-oriented politicism. The recent publication of the papers of James McDonald has shed a somewhat more positive light on Franklin Roosevelt's attempts on behalf of the Jews but even the editors of that correspondence note how he shied away from public support of the Jewish cause, and that his "willingness to take action varied sharply according to political and military circumstances" (Breitman, Stewart, and Hochberg 2009: 4–5). Robert Rosen provides a more complete defense of Roosevelt on these issues, even chastising David Wyman for his "bizarre charge of American complicity in genocide" (Rosen 2006: 482).

12. Those included in these overall numbers arrived under a variety of specific legal statuses. Many, for example, entered under the provisional parole authority of the Attorney General. Even when their status was regularized, refugee status was not necessarily invoked. Cubans, in particular, have largely been regularized under 1966 legislation (The Cuban Adjustment Act) that does not include the word refugee at all. On the other hand, in government statistics, some kinds of status are counted as "refugee" even though in legal terms they are not: for example, Amerasians, ODP immigrants from Vietnam, Cuban–Haitian entrants, and asylees. In addition, there are a wide range of other legal and illegal immigrants whom many people would consider fully admissible as refugees because all the arguments about moral commitments apply to them as well. The largest numbers were from Central America, arriving in the 1980s (Melville 1985; Rader 1999).

13. Refugee camps have received increasing attention in the academic literature, with the beginnings of some comparative analysis. The nature of camps varies widely with their purpose. Some are unsupervised, ad hoc, places barely across the border, which may provide some security but are themselves often beset by violence and the very politics from which refugees fled. Good examples are the border camps in Thailand (Long 1993; Robinson 1998), camps for Hutu fleeing from Burundi into Tanzania (Malkki 1995b) or those for Hutus fleeing from Rwandan after the

genocide into the Congo (Gourevitch 1999, Ogata 2005). Other camps serve more as refugee-holding centers, with at least rudimentary national and/or international supervision, in which refugees remain until their fate (return, full settlement in place, or resettlement in a third country) can be determined (Mabe 1994; Malkki 1995a, 1995b). Most camps in Southeast Asia were of this kind, although many eventually turned into closed, quite prison–like settings. The range of options from open to closed is perhaps clearest in Hong Kong (Donnelly 1992; Hansen 2009; Hitchcox 1990; Knudsen 1992, 1995). Palestinian camps (Baxter 1997; Peteet 1995; Siddiq 1995) provide examples of what happens when the resolution of that supposedly temporary status never arrives. There are also camps for refugees whose future is certain, but whose processing requires either more time or simply more careful processing. The RPCs for Southeast Asian refugees fit into this category (Reyes 1999; Tollefson 1989) but so as well do refugee camps and "reception centers" within countries of resettlement. The United States used such camps in 1975 (Kelly 1977; Liu, Lamanna, and Murata 1979) and various other countries have done and still do so as well (Haines 1991; ORR 1983b). There is often great variation in refugee camps even within a fairly defined region, whether along the Thai border (Robinson 1998) or in Central America (Phillips 1994). Many refugees arriving in the United States in recent years, whether from Myanmar or Bhutan, have been "warehoused" in such camps for many years.

14. The expectations that refugee adults can adjust rapidly to their new lives in the United States often leads to frustration when the refugees do not make that transformation at the speed or in quite the direction that is desired. That helps explain why those assisting refugees—and those studying them—are prone to skimming over the difficulties of adult refugees in favor of focusing on the faster and more complete adaptation of refugee children.

15. For some useful examples of variability within refugee populations, see Bozorgmehr (1996) and Fahti (1991) on Iranians, Gold (1997) and Whitmore (1996) on Chinese from Southeast Asia, and Garcia (1996) and Grillo (2000) on Cubans. The statistical comparison between Cuban private and public school students in Miami (Portes and Rumbaut 2001) is very helpful in illuminating class issues among Cubans.

16. The pervasiveness of Spanish helps explain why English language competence sometimes is not a crucial factor in statistical analyses of Hispanic refugees and immigrants. For an early example, see Portes and Bach (1985).

17. One might argue that the greater the degree to which the U.S. program is helping refugees most desperately in need, the more difficult will be the course of their adjustment to the United States. Therein lies the rationale for "creaming" from the crop of potential refugees those who will do well after resettlement and therefore make the resettlement program look like it is working well. This dilemma is discussed in some detail in Chapter 6.

18. There are other sources that are more refined in methodology or more expansive in analysis—and are utilized in both Chapters 2 and 6. But they lack the consistent annual iterations of these particular surveys. Census material can also be

helpful even though it fails to distinguish refugees from other immigrants from the same country.

19. These figures relate to the total sampled refugee population, which was limited to arrivals over the preceding five years. The numbers thus refer to the five-year population in each of the years noted. (Longer-term arrivals were removed from the sample each year and replaced by an equivalent number of new arrivals.) This is not, then, simply the improvement in employment rates over time for individual refugees, but an aggregate improvement controlled for length of residence.

20. Because the data for 1979 differ greatly in how they were calculated, the discussion here is limited to years with general consistency in conduct of the surveys and presentation of the findings (i.e., 1986, 1993, and 1999).

21. The population employment ratio (alternately the employment population ratio or employment-to-population ratio) is the percentage of the population that is employed. It thus reflects both labor force participation (looking for work or not) and the unemployment rate (successful in finding work or not).

22. This is clearly an aberrant figure, probably reflecting small sample size for that length-of-residence category. The pattern of data from 1993 is relatively similar to that from 1986 for all other lengths of residence.

23. For analytic purposes, many of these issues are better addressed through multivariate analysis. But these kinds of summary descriptive statistics are the ones usually used in public and policy discussions of refugees.

24. The issue of employment trajectories became of great concern in the 1980s. Not only was there a question of whether refugees could move up, but of whether refugees might be actually moving down. Even with the presumed "success" of Vietnamese refugees, the data were not clear that they were progressing into better jobs (Gold and Kibria 1993; Haines 1987).

25. For reasons of brevity, I omit here the analogous analysis of the Refugee Act's other major goal for refugee resettlement: achieving self-sufficiency. That will be discussed in more detail in Chapter 6, but the gist of the analytic problem with assessing self-sufficiency mirrors that for employment. Is the goal a marginal self-sufficiency now or a more stable self-sufficiency in the future? There are also analogous questions about the degree of self-sufficiency. Self-sufficient to what? To living in a decent neighborhood? To having health care? To raising children with some parental involvement? Rather than addressing those questions, self-sufficiency (like employment) has often been treated at the rudimentary have-it-or-not level, which is then translated operationally into whether or not refugees are receiving public assistance. Self-sufficiency as a program goal also raises formidable method-ological problems. Is self-sufficiency to be construed as an attribute of individuals, of households, of families (which sometimes involve wider nets of people beyond the household), or of some combination of all of these? Self-sufficiency makes most sense as an attribute of households, which in itself makes analysis of the interaction effects of people as individuals, as parts of households, and as conditioned by the totality of the household difficult. Thus even assuming a relatively bounded household as the self-sufficiency unit, the analytic task is staggering.

The Self-Sufficiency Study funded by the federal government in the early 1980s (Caplan, Whitmore, and Bui 1985; Whitmore, Trautmann, and Caplan 1989) was perhaps the most intensive quantitative research on this issue for Southeast Asian refugees.

26. Such issues of understanding how we are understanding issues like diversity is sometimes phrased in terms of reflexivity. At least in anthropology, reflexivity tends to be traced to continental theorists, particularly to Bourdieu (1990) and thus at least implicitly linking backward to Heidegger (1962). The result is, roughly, Heidegger's notion of sense–making underlying Bourdieu's notion of practice. However, since the discussion here focuses on social programs, Dewey may be a more useful anchor. Dewey (1938) was especially clear on the interaction of thought and action. Evans (2001) provides a very nice recent reiteration of Dewey's position and his emphasis on the intermixture of moral and practical goods. Schön (1983, 1987) and Schön and Rein (1994) have carried on that tradition in the emphasis on "design rationality" as part of a reflexive practice of public administration. Whichever be the anchor, this issue of refugee diversity presents a difficult challenge to human "sense-making" on either a personal or a bureaucratic basis.

27. The individual is in many ways a problematic unit for social research. Individuals are, of course, identifiable, trackable, and the unavoidable focus of survey research. But they are not bounded, autonomous systemic units in the social sense. In many ways, they are a less logical unit for social analysis than are families, in general, or the households in which people live, in particular. The discussion in the text about employment and self-sufficiency, for example, requires attention to both the individual and the household. Furthermore, even allocation of employment as an individual variable and self-sufficiency as a household variable is too simplistic since the household influences the employment of its members, and the employment of its members reciprocally influences the household.

28. Data from the first nine of these federal government surveys appear in reports produced by Opportunity Systems, Incorporated (OSI). Beginning with the survey revisions discussed in the text, the findings were reported in the annual ORR reports to the Congress. Linda Gordon (1989) provides a useful overview of the surveys through the mid-1980s. The early surveys were the source of a variety of published articles by those involved with them (Bach 1985; Bach and Carroll-Seguin 1986; Bach et al. 1983, 1984; Haines 1983, 1987; Marsh 1980).

29. There is also an issue of regional labels. The refugees from Cambodia, Laos, and Vietnam were originally identified as from Indochina; thus they were "Indochinese" refugees (and are still sometimes referred to that way). Ultimately, because of the colonial implications of that term, "Southeast Asian" was adopted by the U.S. government, even though that term is more imprecise in focus than the colonially tainted "Indochina." Furthermore, although the refugees were certainly related in a regional sense and as people seeking refuge because of American involvement in that region, the countries are quite extraordinarily different in linguistic and cultural background. The use of a combined category (whether Indochinese or Southeast Asian) was often misleading, encouraging those involved in refugee

resettlement (and the general public as well) to believe erroneously that they would find similar kinds of behavior, beliefs, and social relationships among all these refugees.

30. The theme of this discussion is the unresolvable tension among the three goals of the surveys (as perhaps of all surveys), to adequately represent the population of concern, to standardize the methods and content of questions so that the data can be analyzed, and to understand how these people are actually doing. Achieving a balance among these three (to represent fairly, to standardize effectively, and to analyze meaningfully) is not always easy. More in-depth qualitative research, for example, is far better at meaningful analysis while large-scale surveys are far better at representing the status of the overall population.

31. This was effectively a bimodal pattern by ethnicity (i.e., ethnic Lao versus Hmong), analogous to the bimodal pattern by class (educational level, urban versus rural background) that is discussed later in the text for Cambodians.

32. For overviews of those surveys, see Haines (1989). Of the surveys described in that volume, those by the University of Michigan's Institute for Social Research (Caplan, Choy, and Whitmore 1991; Caplan, Whitmore, and Bui 1985) and Rubén Rumbaut have probably received the widest attention—the latter especially because of its later incorporation into the combined work of Portes and Rumbaut (1996, 2001). The survey by Strand and Jones (1985) is also available in more extended format, and the earlier Bureau of Social Research (BSSR) survey (Dunning and Greenbaum 1982) is particularly rich in its detail on jobs and job histories.

33. These are, indeed, fairly clear ethnic and linguistic divides among some of these groups. The U.S. decennial censuses permit triangulation among place of birth, self-ascribed ethnicity, and language used at home. Thus, the difference between ethnic Vietnamese and Chinese–Vietnamese is very clear, as is the difference between Lao and Hmong speakers among those from Laos. Since the census does not ask about religion, however, many key divisions remain unseen (whether Buddhist and Christian Vietnamese, or Baha'i, Christian, Jewish, and Muslim Iranians).

34. The problem with simultaneously addressing even five groups was severe, and became more onerous the more sophisticated were the survey design and sampling strategies. Thus the noted "Self-Sufficiency Study" of the early 1980s limited itself to Chinese, Lao, and Vietnamese (Caplan, Whitmore, and Bui 1985).

35. In early 2001, for example, a small number of refugees from Vietnam's highlands escaped to Cambodia, setting off an international fracas, one result of which was the resettlement of some of these people to the United States—in addition to a sharply criticized repatriation of others of them back to Vietnam. Interestingly, these people were in almost all press accounts referred to as "Montagnards," a French term for mountain people that is of dubious repute. Here, then, people with a very specific ethnic identity and their own language were effectively consigned to a residual category of "mountain minorities."

36. Mien tend to speak at least some Lao and that is presumably the language in which they were interviewed in the ORR surveys—although language used is not included in the data sets for public use (MacDonald 1997).

37. The problem of including such smaller populations in surveys despite the practical impossibility of doing so has additional complexities when considering refugees, at least during the last two decades. Because of the way they are admitted, there are often many more small religious and ethnic populations among refugee arrivals than among regular immigrants, since their admission is usually based more directly on existing connections to America (e.g., employer sponsors for labor immigrants and family sponsors for family immigrants). The lesson from these national surveys would seem to be that it is often virtually impossible to include such small groups in survey research. One problem is that the researchers may not even know these populations exist. Furthermore, even if it is known that such smaller groups exist, it is not feasible to generate a representative sample of them or to use the survey instrument itself because of language requirements. Furthermore, such small populations are likely to have very different dynamics to their adjustment. Thus, there will not be enough of them to represent themselves statistically (i.e., their own internal variation). Nor it is reasonable to suggest they represent some undifferentiated "other refugees" category, or even a somewhat more precise category like "smaller refugee groups."

38. For Vietnam, class has something of the meaning that it has for more economically developed countries. Nevertheless, there is a well-developed argument that class is not a very great predictor of Vietnamese adaptation to the United States when educational opportunities are widely available (Caplan, Choy, and Whitmore 1991).

39. There are potential problems here for survey research since actual kin terms also vary somewhat by region, although that variation tends to be for relatives (such as uncles and aunts) who are usually clumped together into the "other" category anyway.

40. Even in survey research, religion may turn up explicitly as the answer to the ethnicity question, whether it is Jews from Russia and Eastern Europe or Muslims from Bosnia. That issue receives additional discussion in Chapter 4.

41. The reduction in arrivals after September 11, 2001, was not remedied by any catch-up period. So, even with a gradual return to more normal admissions levels, the net effect was still a permanent loss of at least 50,000 admissions during 1982 and 1983.

42. As the late Arthur Helton put it, efforts on behalf of refugees "should surely be more than the administration of misery" (2002: 290) and driven by something more than the "selective apathy and creeping trepidation" (2002: 29) he saw in the aftermath of September 11.

2

A New Land: Loss, Hope and an Uncertain Future

Safe haven in America is the end of one story—of persecution and flight—but also the beginning of another. That second story of adjusting to a new country is created partly from the capabilities, expectations, values, and experiences that refugees bring with them and partly from the initial situation they find in the United States. It is a story of what refugees bring and what they find. It is also, ultimately, a story of what refugees build: for themselves, for their families, for their communities, and for the United States itself. As they move from the losses they have endured, through the refuge they have found, and toward a new and different kind of future in America, however, they face many problems. Some are practical, some social, and some spiritual. The future toward which they move remains uncertain.

Although the numbers and origins of refugees to the United States have shifted greatly over time, the difficulties of this adjustment to a new society have remained a constant. These difficulties have been, in many ways, similar to those faced by all immigrants to the United States. However, the very nature of the refugee experience, including the dangers of exodus and the relative permanency of separation from home country, has made the adjustment of refugees different in other ways. Furthermore, the nature of refugee adaptation to the United States has been highly variable, as would be expected from the divergent social and cultural heritages that refugees have brought with them and the different situations they have found in the United States. In that sense, the refugee story can only be told fully in the stories of individual people. Nevertheless, there are certain common themes in that refugee adjustment and a generalized overview of them may help provide a framework for better understanding those individual stories.

This chapter attempts that general framework, based on what is now a very extensive body of research.

Refugees as Immigrants

Much of the experience of refugees in America parallels that for other immigrants. As with other immigrants, refugee adjustment to the United States reflects a wide range of cultural, social, and economic factors. Much of that adjustment reflects such simple demographic characteristics as age and sex. Elderly refugees, for example, often lack familiarity with English and with American customs and may find adapting to new ways particularly difficult. Children, on the other hand, adjust more quickly and completely to new customs, often at the expense of their relations with parents. Those in the prime working years—the young and fit—are generally best able to access jobs. In terms of gender, women and men have different experiences and prospects as well. Home country allocation of gender roles may well affect adjustment to the new country. For example, women, by virtue of their roles as wives and mothers, may remain more confined within their homes and thus be set off from experiences that would help them acculturate to the new society. In contrast, women's experience in economic affairs, or relatively high educational background, may make them especially adept at adapting to a new country and, in some cases, more so than men. Women may also simply have a larger accumulation of roles. Hackett, for example, notes from her interviews with refugee women, "the many different persons" a refugee woman is to herself and others both during and after flight (Hackett 1996a: 1). As with other immigrants, then, the relative proportion of the sexes and of particular age groups helps determine the pattern of successes and problems that particular refugee groups experience.

America's refugees have differed markedly in terms of such general demographic characteristics. They have also often differed both from the general U.S. population and from other newcomers. Consider, for example, the ages of refugees in the mid-1970s, when the new Southeast Asian exodus was reshaping refuge in America, adding to the existing numbers of Cubans and Soviet refugees (see Taft, North, and Ford 1979: 18). The U.S. population at that time had a median age of almost twenty-nine, and immigrants arriving that year had a median age of about twenty-four. Cuban refugees who had arrived since the late 1960s were considerably older, with a median age of over thirty-seven; Southeast Asian refugees, who were then becoming the country's new major refugee group, were considerably younger, with a median age under twenty. Soviet refugees, the third largest of the refugee groups at that time, were in between, with a median age two years greater than that of the U.S. population as a whole.

In terms of the proportion of the population under age fifteen, the differences were also striking. Both the U.S. population and arriving immigrants in 1975 had about one-fourth of their members under the age of fifteen, but for both Cuban and Soviet refugees, less than one-fifth of the population was under the age of fifteen. For Southeast Asian refugees arriving in 1975, by contrast, well over a third (39 percent) were under the age of fifteen. Such aggregate numbers thus reflect not only the age of adults but also the numbers and ages of children. The low average age for the Southeast Asian refugee population, for example, reflected large numbers of children, while Soviet (and Eastern European) and Cuban refugees, on the other hand, tended to have fewer children. Such differences have direct implications on virtually all areas of resettlement, from finding housing to obtaining work, to mixing separate incomes of husbands and wives, to planning for the economic future of succeeding generations.

Another crucial set of background factors includes the skills and competencies that refugees bring with them—what is commonly called their human capital. Perhaps the most obvious of these is English language competence. Those refugees with both conversational and writing competence are at a great advantage. Those with more limited English fare worse—unless there is a very large alternative language community in which they can live and work. Faring worst of all are those who are not literate in any language. This became a significant problem in the late 1970s with the arrival of both rural Cambodians and highland Laotians—particularly the Hmong. Such refugees (like more recent arrivals from Myanmar and Somalia) face the double disadvantage of having to learn to read and write per se and also learning to read and write a foreign language. Here too, the basic issue of age at arrival is crucial: those who are younger will have greater success in post-arrival language acquisition.

Language competency—especially in reading and writing—is closely related to educational background. Up until the late 1970s, refugee educational levels tended to be relatively high. An early sample from the roster of the Cuban Refugee Center in Miami in 1963 indicated that more than 14 percent of male refugees over the age of sixteen had completed four years of college. An additional 22 percent had completed high school, with or without subsequent college education. Less than 5 percent had completed no more than the third grade (Fagen and Brody 1964: 392). Data from an early survey of 1,574 Southeast Asian refugee heads of household in Illinois (Kim 1980: 33) presented a somewhat similar picture. Fewer Southeast Asian refugees had completed college (8.3 percent) but more had completed high school (32.8 percent). Only 7 percent lacked any formal education. Data from a 1980 national survey of 1,032 Southeast Asian refugee households gave similar aggregate figures but also illustrated important differences among the three Southeast Asian nationalities.[1] For Vietnamese males, almost 14 percent had completed college and over 40 percent had completed at least the first of the two high school degrees. For the Cambodians and Laotians, the figures were generally lower. Among Laotian males, for example, only half as many had completed college and about one-fourth as many had completed high school (OSI 1981). (These same patterns can also be seen in U.S. census data from 1990 and 2000.)[2] The federal government's major research effort on non-Southeast Asian refugees in the early 1980s also found relatively high educational levels for refugees from Afghanistan, Ethiopia, Poland, and Rumania (Cichon, Gozdziak, and Grover 1986).

Completing this list of crucial background factors is prior occupation. Data for the same three major refugee populations of the 1970s (Cuban, Soviet, and Southeast Asian) suggests relatively high occupational profiles. More than two-thirds of those who had been in the labor force in their country of origin had been in white-collar occupations. For the U.S. population as a whole, by way of comparison, only half of those in the labor force were in white-collar occupations. Perhaps more important are the percentages who were in professional and technical occupations. For the U.S. labor force, the relevant figure was about 15 percent, but for all the refugee populations, the figure was much higher. Of Cuban refugees, one in four had been in a professional or technical occupation; for early Vietnamese refugees almost a third, and for Soviet refugees more than a third, had been in such occupations (Fagen and Brody 1964; HIAS 1980; OSI 1977).

Later groups of refugees have not always had such positive status in terms of this trinity of English, education, and occupation. As the U.S. refugee program has become more globally representative, the result has often been the acceptance of refugees who—precisely because of the situations that force their flight—have been denied basic education, have occupational skills that do not translate well to the United States, lack English competence, and have limited exposure to how American society works. The experience of such special populations (e.g., highland groups from Laos and now Myanmar, Bantu from Somalia) is sometimes matched by refugees from more developed societies who have nevertheless been systematically excluded from educational and occupational opportunities in their home countries, for example, Vietnamese who are Amerasian or are suspected of ties to Americans (Bass 1996; McKelvey 1999; Yarborough 2005). There are thus great variations in English, educational, and occupational backgrounds among refugees overall, and even among refugees from a particular country.

The adaptation of refugees, as of other immigrants, also reflects their social networks in country of origin and their basic beliefs and values—what is sometimes called their social and cultural capital. Those social networks and cultural beliefs and values can both hinder and facilitate adjustment. Extended, strong kin structures, for example, can be invaluable in adjusting to a new country, while fragmented families and single parents face extraordinary pressures. Beliefs and values also matter. Teachers and researchers, for example, have consistently noted the respect and effort they have found among Southeast Asian refugee children, reflecting the near reverence for education in much of Asia (Caplan, Choy, and Whitmore 1991). Traditional Buddhist precepts may help Cambodian refugees come to terms with their holocaust (Mortland 1994b; Welaratna 1993), while Christianity may give them a way to understand their migration—a "theology of immigration" (Ro 2009)—and also an important point of contact with American society and American congregations. Cultural values of reciprocity and gratitude may help refugees interact with those who wish to help them—although sometimes causing them to move away without warning when they believe they can no longer meet such standards. The specific effects of such beliefs and values, whether positive or negative, are difficult to predict, yet are often decisive to the relative success of the resettlement process. Refugees also reflect the specific political systems under which they have lived, and how they adapted to them. Refugees from the Soviet Union and Eastern Europe in the 1970s and 1980s, for example, had spent their lives under planned, socialist economies. The state restricted many of their freedoms, perhaps especially of religion. The state also, however, met many of their basic needs (including employment) without requiring any great individual initiative. These refugees thus had little experience that bore on the self-initiated search for employment that is so crucial in America. Early Cuban refugees, by contrast, had much experience with a free market economy. Aspects of American society, such as entrepreneurship that might have eluded early Soviet refugees thus came naturally to these early Cuban refugees.[3] Cambodians, Laotians, and Vietnamese, in turn, came to the United States having spent most of their lives under a situation of continuing war, itself preceded by a century of French colonial control. Likewise, other refugees, whether Afghan, Cambodian, Ethiopian, Iranian,[4] Iraqi, Rwandan, Somali, or Sudanese, have lives shaped by wars that have often accelerated to the brink of genocide, and sometimes beyond. Those experiences color their expectations about the structure of the American political and economic systems—and about the agencies that aim to help them in their resettlement.[5] It is such experiences that distinguish refugees from other immigrants. Refugees may well be "regular" immigrants in many ways, but they are also quite decisively *not* regular immigrants in other ways.

Refugees as Refugees

While the experience of refugees in the United States in many ways mirrors the factors that affect other immigrants, such as that successful adaptation trinity of English, education, and occupation, the experience of refugees differs in other ways. They are, after all, forced migrants. The distinction between forced and voluntary migration can sometimes be overly sharply drawn. Refugees, for example, are not simply helpless pawns unable to act; indeed, the refugees who escape are often precisely those who could act. Immigrants, for their part, are not always fully in control of their destiny and their "voluntary" choice to migrate may be less than fully voluntary. Nevertheless, this general distinction between forced and voluntary migration remains crucial on humanitarian, legal, and quite practical grounds. Most refugees, for example, have experienced being at risk in their home country because they were different in terms of race, ethnicity, language, religion, class, or politics—and that risk was activated by particular events. The forces that ultimately propelled them to leave have sometimes been diffuse and long term, but have also often been sharp and immediate. Flight is often chosen rapidly, and even when the dangers are not excessive, clandestine action, social and financial losses, and a sharp separation from homeland are almost inevitable. All refugees share this experience to some extent and it conditions their adjustment to the United States. However, there are great variations among refugees as to the precise nature of exodus and the nature and duration of the transit to the United States. For Cubans and Haitians, for example, the United States has usually been the country of first asylum (although they have also come to the United States by way of other countries). For most other refugees, however, arrival in the United States is the result of a long and complex transit. Some of the variations in that transit are worth noting as a reminder of the variability and complexity in the refugee experience after the point of flight and before that of actual resettlement in the United States.

Of the major refugee groups in the United States, Soviet Jews have had perhaps the most orderly transit, but even that involved serious hardship. Up until 1989, all those desiring to emigrate from the Soviet Union had to apply for exit visas to Israel. The time period from application to acceptance varied considerably, as did the overall likelihood of success. During this period, the potential émigré was largely cut off from Soviet society, denied work, and subject to considerable harassment. When exit was approved, the émigré went first to Vienna, and it was only then that any desire to go to the United States could be made known. All Soviet refugees coming to the United States were technically "breakoffs" (*noshrim*) from emigration to Israel. When their desire to not go to Israel was made known, they were then transferred to Rome for processing to the Western countries, including the United States. The entire process, from visa application to arrival in the United States, could be lengthy, and the émigré was likely to be exposed to some material hardship and considerable ideological pressure (Jacobson 1978; Simon 1985). (The process was later changed to permit direct request for U.S. refugee status in Moscow, which greatly simplified transit—see GAO 1991; Lafontant 1990.)

While the exit and transit processes for Soviet Jews were cumbersome and with some risk, for Southeast Asian refugees the experience was far more severe and life-threatening. The initial exodus (largely Vietnamese) from Southeast Asia in 1975 came in the spring with the fall of the American-supported governments and occurred under panic conditions (Kelly 1977; Liu, Lamanna, and Murata 1979). People were caught up in the exodus with little, if any, prior planning. For Vietnamese, flight led almost immediately to camps operated by the United States in the Pacific, then to other camps in the continental United States, and then to resettlement in local communities by the end of the year. For those fleeing Laos and Cambodia, the problems were worse. Those who were able to escape ended in camps of temporary asylum in Thailand where they lingered, rather than moving on directly to resettlement. Camp conditions were frequently poor, with little security, limited supplies, and limited opportunity for planning a future in a country of final asylum.

As these refugees languished in camps, there was a surge in the exodus by boat from Vietnam. This exodus path posed a different set of dangers. Sailing to the south and west from Vietnam was risky. Many refugees lost their lives as boats sank; others experienced thefts, beatings, rapes, and murders by pirates. Approaching land, boats were sometimes pushed back to sea. Those refugees who reached shore found themselves placed in overcrowded camps, also with an uncertain future (Burton 1983; Grant and others 1979; Haines 2009; Robinson 1998; USCR 1984). Those fleeing by boat to the north and east usually faced protracted stays in camps in Hong Kong. Although some camps were open, others were not. In both cases, their freedom was limited; they were exposed to surges of ethnic violence within the camps, and often had no ultimate hope for resettlement (Amer 2009; Hansen 2009).

The boat exodus, and the dramatic pictures of it, led to a positive international response and the resettlement of large numbers of refugees in the United States and other countries. Concerted international response also began to reduce the extent of pirate attacks on refugees, to move people from the temporary asylum camps to resettlement in other countries, and to expand the number of Vietnamese refugees leaving directly from Vietnam without having to flee on their own. The crisis, coupled with concern in the United States about problems in resettlement, also led to the development of special refugee processing centers in Southeast Asia where refugees could receive health care and a variety of training and orientation courses for life in the United States. While this made for a more orderly transit, it also caused its own problems. With such an extended period between flight and resettlement, the camp experience itself came to be a distinct stage of the refugee experience. Many children were born in refugee camps; many others spent important segments of their formative years in camps. In other cases, long stays in refugee camps led not to resettlement, but to repatriation—sometimes forced—to their original country (Donnelly 1992; Hall 1992; Knudsen 1992; Long 1993). Even in 2009, forced repatriation of refugees continued, with some 4,500 Hmong forcibly returned from Thailand to Laos.

In recent years, the very long journeys of many African refugees have been similarly difficult. For many of those from Sudan—especially the so-called "lost boys" (Bixler 2006; Dau 2007; Deng et al. 2005; Hecht 2005; cf. DeLuca 2009)—flight led to life in one refugee camp, then often a move to another refugee camp (particularly from Ethiopia to Kenya), and then further protracted waits before resettlement was possible. Other African refugees languished in Khartoum or in Cairo where they found a very temporary, very insecure refuge, often on the way to nowhere at all (Moorehead 2005). Even by refugee standards, the journey of recently arriving refugees from Bhutan seems torturous. The Bhutanese refugees are actually descendants of people from Nepal who settled in Bhutan in the nineteenth century. Although Hindu in a largely Buddhist country, they were largely tolerated there—and had legal status—until the Bhutanese government in the 1980s launched restrictive measures that, in turn, led to violent confrontations in 1990. Fleeing back to Nepal, these descendants of people from Nepal found themselves in refugee camps, where they remained until an arrangement was finally completed with the Nepalese government that allowed them to leave for resettlement in a variety of countries, including the United States (UNHCR 2006, 2009a).

Welcome to America

Refugees thus come to the United States with varying background characteristics, bringing different skills and abilities, and arriving through a wide range of often harrowing journeys. Those experiences may leave relatively light or horrendously deep scars, both metaphoric and literal. Refugees have also come to the United States at different times and settled in different parts of the country. In essence, they have come to different Americas and must adjust to quite different environments. Indeed, the federal government actively plans their initial location and has, very much unlike the case for regular immigrants, even tried to fashion new ethnic communities in smaller, less "impacted" areas.

The general reception of refugees by the American public has varied greatly. Early Cuban refugees came as exiles from a communist nation strongly opposed by the U.S. government. Their stay was initially viewed as temporary (contingent on the fall of Castro), and they enjoyed strong political support. Southeast Asian refugees also fled from communist governments, but they brought memories of an unpopular war. They arrived when Asian immigration had risen significantly (because of the 1965 revisions to the Immigration and Nationality Act) and they thus became a part of a larger Asian presence and of an even larger and often distrusted "alien" presence. Soviet refugees faced a different set of problems. Having lived their lives in a secular society, they had to come to terms with a Jewish community that supported them extensively but also tended to expect from them a degree of religiosity with which they had little experience. They, like other refugees, thus not only brought their own set of expectations with them, but were also affected by the expectations about them—whether held by American society as a whole or by the individual Americans who interacted with them as sponsors, fellow workers, neighbors, and friends (see Gold 1992; Markowitz 1993; Orleck 1987; Simon 1985).

Refugees have also found, as have immigrants throughout American history, an America at varying stages of economic growth, constriction, and restructuring. Cuban refugees generally fared better in terms of employment prospects in the early 1960s than did Southeast Asian refugees in the late 1970s. The situation became particularly bleak for Southeast Asian refugees during the deep recession of the early 1980s. Although the public might consider that refugees were taking jobs from Americans—then as now—the extent to which refugees were first laid off suggests that this was not generally the case. Case study material from that time indicates the extent to which refugees lacked the necessary seniority to make it through the recession. For example, refugees who had moved into well-paying jobs in the light aircraft industry in Wichita, Kansas, lost those jobs in the recession (Finnan and Cooperstein 1983). The national surveys of Southeast Asian refugees by the federal government that were discussed in Chapter 1 showed relatively high unemployment rates for refugees during that period—24 percent in late 1982 and 18 percent in late 1983 (ORR 1983a, 1984).

The structure of public policy at the time of resettlement also has important effects on refugee adjustment. Different refugee populations, and the same refugee population at different times, have been subject to varying domestic resettlement provisions and regulations—much less varying admissions criteria and overseas training and maintenance. Cubans, for example, were initially allowed to congregate heavily in the Miami area.[6] With Southeast Asian refugees, on the other hand, considerable efforts were made to disperse them throughout the United States. The specific kinds of assistance available to refugees also make a difference. Support to early Cuban refugees was direct and localized in Miami through the Cuban Refugee Center, including open-ended eligibility for cash assistance. After 1980, however, refugees were largely brought into mainstream public assistance programs and subject to the wide variation in how states and localities implement those programs. Assistance—especially cash assistance—was often limited in duration of eligibility.

Finally, the adjustment of refugees is always subject to the particular features of the local communities in which they settle. This is true both in terms of the resources available (jobs, housing) and in terms of more general features of the local environment. Starr and Roberts (Roberts and Starr 1989; Starr and Roberts 1982) demonstrated early on that such general community characteristics as ethnic heterogeneity and median educational levels significantly affected the nature of refugee adjustment. It is also clear that the resources of an established ethnic community make a difference. The lack of an ethnic base has been a problem for smaller refugee groups, and has been the instigating reason for several federal efforts to construct adequately sized clusters of refugees in areas where resources were available for resettlement (Granville Corporation 1982; Kogan and Vencill 1984). Vietnamese had very few compatriots in the United States before the 1975 exodus but were in a better situation than the other Southeast Asian groups, whether relatively large (Lao, Khmer, Hmong) or relatively small (Iu Mien, Thai Dam, Khmu). Even refugees with long-established ethnic communities, such as the Poles and Iranians, have had difficulties in establishing coherent, untroubled relationships with an existing ethnic community that is based on very different socioeconomic and cultural dynamics. Even when there are large numbers of a particular group, the resulting "community" may be extraordinarily complex. Bozorgmehr and Sabagh (1991), for example, have discussed the great diversity within the Los Angeles Iranian community, and Gold (1994a) has shown, also for Los Angeles, how complicated and multi-ethnic the networks of ethnic Chinese–Vietnamese entrepreneurs are.

The variety of possible situations and responses in the United States, coupled with the range of skills and characteristics that refugees bring with them, ensures that the resettlement and adjustment of the refugees is a complex, multifaceted process. It can be smooth but it is more likely to be characterized by a variety of problems. Health deserves special note since the hazards of exodus and the lack of preparation for it are likely to result in serious problems. Even the relatively routinized exit of early Soviet Jewish refugees was attended by a "backlog of medical problems" (Gilison 1979: 24). The health status of Southeast Asian refugees was predictably worse. In the early years, anemia and skin, respiratory, and gastrointestinal problems were often noted, along with more serious conditions, such as malaria, hepatitis, and tuberculosis (Catanzaro and Moser 1982). Concerns about Southeast Asian refugee health led to improved medical screening overseas before refugee entry into the United States and were one factor in the creation of formal refugee processing centers (GAO 1983a). Many of these problems have no complete resolution, and themselves fade into another set of problems that can be characterized more as diseases of resettlement than as diseases of exodus. Rasbridge (1994), for example, has noted the prevalence of hypertension, alcohol-related problems, and gastritis among various refugee groups in Dallas. Yet other health problems exist that are not resettlement-related but may also take their toll on adjustment: Vietnamese men, for example, are notably heavy smokers (Phan 1994). The litany of refugee health problems is a chastening one and the acceptance of refugees from different parts of the world has made the issue more complicated. Thus refugees may have been exposed to a wide range of relatively unknown diseases in their original homes, compounded by additional diseases contracted as they flee, further compounded by exposure in resettlement camps. To that are usually added the effects of malnutrition and general lack of care. The result is a backlog of problems for refugees and a steep learning curve for health care providers (Global Health 2008, 2009; Kemp and Rasbridge 2004; Palinkas et al. 2003).

Housing has been another frequent problem for refugees. There have been problems of affordability, of availability in general, and of availability of appropriately sized housing (Haines 1980). The worst problems probably involve large families seeking to rent. Multi-bedroom apartments tend to be relatively few and official codes about shared bedrooms are often strict. Even when housing has been available, its location has often been less than ideal in terms of employment, schools, or even physical safety. Many refugee families have moved into high-crime areas because of their need for modest-cost, multi-bedroom, rental housing. Although this causes the refugees problems, it has sometimes redounded to the benefit of the neighborhood as a whole, as when Southeast Asian refugees moved into San Francisco's Tenderloin area and helped stabilize a previously transient area (Finnan and Cooperstein 1983).[7] Even then, refugees may be manipulated by landlords who can easily move them out if more profitable options emerge (Conquergood 1992; Hagan and Rodriguez 1992). Quoting Eleanor Roosevelt's comment about "inhabited uninhabitable habitations," Pipher (2002: 95–96) describes her own visits to refugee housing with "snakes, roaches, and rats" in neighborhoods with "meth labs, crack houses, sex offenders, and gangs." But even she ultimately concludes that the problem lies with cost, that "rents are just too high for a family living on minimum-wage salaries while sending money home to relatives."

Another problem area in resettlement has been the interaction between refugees and those seeking to assist them. Many refugees, because of their prior experiences, have little understanding of social services as they are organized in the United States. American social services often emphasize an interventionist, counseling approach that may be alien to refugees. Soviet and Eastern European refugees, for example, spent their lives under governments that supplied a variety of basic material needs but were also relatively unresponsive to demands. Such refugees have been likely to believe that social service agencies in the United States owe them a considerable amount of material aid but that they will be slow and unresponsive unless they are constantly reminded of their obligations to provide that aid (e.g., Gold 1994b; Greenberg 1976). Southeast Asian refugees also had limited exposure to American-style social services and the ideas on which they are based. Such lack of exposure was reflected in refugee perceptions of agency helpfulness. These perceptions were likely to be influenced by class status, with higher status refugees more attuned to the working of service agencies (e.g., Aames et al. 1977: 73). As well, Southeast Asian refugees were attuned to the importance of having ethnic contacts within such service agencies (Mortland and Ledgerwood 1988). Relations between refugees and service providers thus often become quite politicized along ethnic lines. From the service provider perspective, the larger problem has doubtless been the degree to which they must constantly adapt to the cultural expectations of new refugee populations. How can providers reconcile their usual practices with refugees coming not only from different cultures but from very different and sometimes extreme conditions of societal breakdown, for example, from Liberia with rampant violence, breakdowns in family structure, and the very frequent commodification of sex (Murdock 2006; Schmidt 2009).

An Uncertain Future

Once refugees have survived the ordeals of dislocation and relocation, they thus face a second series of challenges. Some of those challenges are immediate: health, housing, education, and that prime issue for all immigrants: employment. Not surprisingly, there is an enormous amount of research on refugee employment that shows (as noted in Chapter 1) that some refugees have done rather well and others not so well.[8] Ironically, the more open and far-reaching is the U.S. refugee program, the more likely there are to be problem cases: adults who are unable to obtain more than low-wage, dead-end jobs and thus families that must have multiple wage earners in those low-level jobs.[9]

Yet there are also longer-term issues. Ultimately, refugees are no longer fully strangers to America, but rather another element in the complex racial, ethnic, and class fabric of American life. They are no longer operating in an unknown environment, but rather trying to assess traditional goals, to utilize this new environment to meet these goals, and often to modify those goals in light of changed circumstances. Although it is possible to argue about the nature or dimensions of assimilation, or about the extent to which refugees retain cultural and political allegiance to their country of origin, it is inarguable that most do become "American" to some extent. Historically, some have done such a good job of becoming American that they have effectively disappeared from view. If they themselves do not do so, then often their children do.

The building of a new life is a complex and difficult process for any newcomer, but it has generally been more so for refugees. Refugees, by definition, are triply disadvantaged in this process. First, they have frequently experienced, and continue to feel the pain of, some of the most brutal events in modern history. Almost all refugees have personally experienced events well beyond the conception of most native-born Americans. Second, refugee exodus involves a rupture of cultural and social relations that is far more severe, and unrecoverable, than the experience of other immigrants. Loss of relatives and friends and of social context is virtually inevitable. Third, the resettlement of refugees usually lacks the advance preparation and preexisting community structures that are often available to immigrants and of enormous help in their adjustment to America. Arriving refugees, by contrast, often know little about the place to which they are going and are often the first representatives in an area of a particular ethnic or national group.

The disadvantages that refugees face affect the course of their longer-term adjustment to the United States, making their frequent successes more impressive and their difficulties more understandable. That longer-term adjustment has somewhat different implications for the refugees themselves and for their children, especially those either born in the United States or who arrive at a very young age. For the parents, the almost inevitable decline in occupational status may never be reversed. For the children, proactive involvement in education may produce a better economic future—although a great deal of research shows that time in the United States tends to reduce the drive of many immigrants. Those different trajectories—of refugees and of their children—may be integrated within the family, or may instead cause schism in the very institution that both parents and children need to prosper in America.

The central importance of the family receives separate attention in Chapter 5, but two other crucial contexts through which the longer-term adjustment of refugees takes place merit attention in rounding out this chapter's portrait of life in a new land. The first is the ethnic community within which refugees usually live and the second is the framework of meaning within which they understand their lives. Given the ruptures of refugee flight, both of these are as often an issue of rebuilding as they are of simply maintaining.

The Ethnic Community

The communities within which refugees live can mediate between them and the wider American society, thus facilitating the adjustment process. These communities are of various kinds, but for refugees with limited linguistic and cultural preparation for the United States, the ethnic community is often of particular importance. It can furnish a wide variety of quite practical support, guiding its members toward the services they need, the personal connections they value, the opportunities they seek, and simply the goods they want to buy. In more general terms, the community provides a set of people with common traditions, goals, and problems. In addition to providing practical support, the community can provide a context within which to understand what is feasible and proper in a new life. Community networks can provide access to jobs and community opinion can provide a rationale for why those jobs are acceptable and even desirable. For example, electronics work was quickly recognized by the Vietnamese community as being clean and good work. Rather than blue collar and repetitive, it was viewed as professional (Finnan 1980). That community determination was essential to the very rapid and very extensive Vietnamese refugee pursuit of such technical occupations, and of the education that would lead to them (Min and Bankston 1994; Penning 1992).

The ethnic community can also directly create jobs. Sometimes this is simply a small economic niche within the community or to market an ethnic product (like food) to the wider nonethnic community. But sometimes the scale is so large that it becomes a full alternative to the existing local economy (Chiswick and Miller 2007). For refugees, the classic case involves

Cubans in Miami (Portes and Stepick 1993; Wilson and Portes 1980). There the combination of sustained Cuban immigration, entrepreneurial skills brought from Cuba, and considerable capital led to benefits for business owners, workers, and the community overall. As described in an early analysis of Cubans in Miami, the "economic expansion of an immigrant enclave, combined with the reciprocal obligations attached to a common ethnicity, creates new mobility opportunities for immigrant workers and permits utilization of their past investments in human capital" (Wilson and Portes 1980: 315).

This Cuban case has spurred great academic fascination with ethnic enclaves (see Model 1992 for an overview of different academic approaches to enclaves and Davis 2004 for a review of Cuban enclaves outside Miami). Such enclaves can draw on their own skills and resources to develop businesses that in the long run benefit both employer and employee. This ability is contingent on community size, but it is also affected by the structure of the enclave, particularly since most national groups of refugees are highly diverse. The Iranian community of Los Angeles, for example, developed in a geographically dispersed way, had a very high educational profile, and comprised four distinct religious groups with diverging interests: Muslim, Baha'i, Christian, and Jewish (Bozorgmehr and Sabagh 1991; Der-Martirosian 2008; Light et al. 1993). The kind of localized ethnic enclave seen in Miami was simply not relevant.

In terms of the overall role of the ethnic community, the situation of refugees is in many ways similar to that of other immigrants. The ethnic community, much like the family itself, can furnish a sense of belonging and the basis for a positive self-identity, as well as making contributions to the economics of a new life in America. Where the refugee experience tends to differ, however, is in the extent to which the ethnic community—again, like the family itself—must be reconstituted and realigned in response to the aftereffects of danger and loss in the home country, danger and loss during exodus, and an unplanned adjustment to a new country. Refugees thus tend to lack exactly the community resources that are needed for such a difficult task. Yet, the rebuilding of ethnic community is often very rapid. Vang (2008: 30–38) chronicles the case of the Hmong in Minnesota: arrival in 1976, public meeting to resolve resettlement problems in 1977, first women's organization established in 1979, affiliation with a national organization in 1980. The chronicle of the first Hmong church in Minneapolis shows that same kind of rapid development: first congregation meets in 1976, incorporated in 1980, building fund started in 1986, building consecrated in 1987. Although for refugees there is much that needs to be rebuilt, the efforts that many refugees bring to the task are impressive indeed.

Making Sense of a New Life

The personal stress points of resettlement are often couched in terms of "psychological" problems or even "mental health" issues. Refugee flight is, after all, a traumatic experience. It may involve a decision made within a few hours that irrevocably changes a person's life. It may occur under panic conditions. Even when longer-range planning occurs, exodus is still usually clandestine, dangerous, and with family members left behind or lost en route. The result is that refugees are left, in the now famous phrase of Egon Kunz, "midway to nowhere" (Kunz 1973). In psychological terms, the results can be severe. Segal and Lourie (1975), for example, reported on the early situation of Indochinese refugees who reached Guam after the fall of Saigon in 1975. They noted "feelings of grief and depression, anxiety about the welfare of separated family members, panic over an uncertain future, feelings of remorse and guilt, confusion, and a growing sense of bitterness, disappointment, and anger." These problems, they noted, resulted "not only in a general sense of malaise, fatigue, and psycho-somatic complaints, but by evidence of lethargy, withdrawal and seclusion, huddling, expressions of melancholy, and crying in private" (Segal and Lourie 1975: 4).

Such feelings do not quickly disappear after resettlement. An extensive literature now exists on such problems and on the ways in which refugees do and do not access services to resolve these problems.[10] But the crucial point is that even the simplest of refugee experiences usually includes great personal loss, and sometimes far worse: horror, holocaust, torture, mass rape.[11] It is also clear that many problems are the effect of the resettlement process itself, whether because of the way in which refugees have been treated as if they were just regular immigrants (Kelly 1977; Tollefson 1989), or because of having simply reached a dead-end in the resettlement process. Rasbridge (1994), for example, has noted how the initial health problems of refugees gradually shift into "chronic and complex diseases of resettlement."[12] Dealing with these "diseases of resettlement," however, requires attention to the very broad range of cultural diversity among refugees, and the often sharp divergence between refugee beliefs about health and illness and American views. For many refugees, the basic concepts of health and illness, much less of physical versus mental health, are inconsistent with American psychological assumptions.[13] Thus, as Fadiman discusses so eloquently, the "condition" of a Hmong child is interpreted as epileptic seizure by American doctors, but spirit possession by Hmong parents. Different refugee populations may share similar general problems in recovering from the trauma of exodus and in adjusting to American society, but the specifics of these problems, their general phrasing, and the resolution of them are likely to differ in their very conceptualization.

What all these paths are likely to share, however, is some negotiation between adherence to traditional beliefs and behavior, on the one hand, and the embracing of American ways, on the other. For refugees, this negotiation involves the multiple assaults on the meaning of their lives: the challenge to their lives that led to flight, the rupturing of their social relations as a result of flight, and the unplanned nature of their move to America. Refugees are thus presented with special problems in constructing the meaning of their lives. These problems appear in many domains of life, but for refugees perhaps the two most difficult involve the political and the spiritual.

In terms of political meaning, refugees are generally people who have lost out in serious political and military conflicts. Whether it is the Vietnamese celebrating national shame day (the anniversary of the fall of Saigon) or Cubans agitating against Castro, refugees face a political situation in the home country with which it is difficult—or impossible—to be reconciled. With the loosening of communist government rule in the 1990s, Southeast Asian and Cuban refugees were particularly torn between the desire to renew ties with the home country, and thus to alleviate the rupture in their social relations, and the desire to *not* lend support to the still-communist governments that ruled the home country. Consider the case of those Vietnamese arriving in the 1990s after being released from "reeducation" camps in Vietnam. They arrived in the United States to find their former colleagues with a two decade head-start on adjusting to the United States and also to find that those same former colleagues were often attempting a partial reconciliation with the home country—a deal with their jailors (Birman and Tran 2008; Nguyen and Haines 1996). The strength and durability of such refugee political views often startles Americans. Even when old animosities seem to have calmed, particular events can easily rekindle them: the 1999 arrival of a young Elián González galvanized the Cuban community in opposition to his return to Cuba; a 1999 photo of Ho Chi Minh in a California shop window brought Vietnamese out in protest; the 2007 arrest of former General Vang Pao in relation to an attempt to topple the Lao government greatly pained the Hmong community, both those who still sought such an overthrow and the many Hmong by then more concerned with life in America.

For other refugees, the initial cause of flight may have partially or completely disappeared. Although communist governments continue in Cuba and Vietnam, in other countries, enough improvement in conditions has occurred to raise questions about exile. The return of President Aristide to Haiti in 1993, for example, was considered by many the end to the rationale for refugee flight from Haiti, although serious instability and reprisals from those associated with the former government continued, compounded further by a devastating earthquake in early 2010. The demise of the communist government in Ethiopia, coupled with Eritrean independence, dramatically changed the home country context for these refugees. The result was a difficult, forced reappraisal of the political significance of exile (Hepner 2009; Koehn 1991; Woldemikael 1996). For Afghans, the Soviet occupation ended in 1989, but the situation in the home country remained unsettled, and the speed of modern communications kept refugees painfully aware of the dangers faced by relatives who remained in, or had returned to, Afghanistan (Lipson and Omidian 1995, 1996; Ross-Sheriff 2006). With the fall of the Taliban in 2001, there was increased return of refugees, but at the end of the decade, the political situation remained uncertain at best. In 2009, for example, the number of returnees dropped from 278,000 to 54,000 (UNHCR 2009b). For Eastern Europeans and Russians, the collapse of the Soviet bloc struck at the issue of their exile—moving it generally from an anticommunist basis to an issue of their status as an oppressed ethnic or religious minority (Gold 1997; Gozdziak 1996).[14] Although the specifics differ, the common element is the constant confrontation with an unstable and often unacceptable political situation in the home country. One result—as discussed in more detail in Chapter 4—is that refugees may avoid using a national identity that would link them to the very people who forced them out. Why, for example, would Jews from the Ukraine identify themselves as "Ukrainian" when it was the Ukrainians who forced their exile?

Refugees also face tremendous challenges to their spiritual lives. Even when the reasons for exodus are religious in nature, and when the United States offers both freedom of religion and an existing religious community that wishes to help the refugees, the challenges can be difficult. Refugees who are Christian or Jewish, for example, may have unique beliefs, traditions, and practices that do not precisely meld with existing mainstream churches or synagogues in America. Many Vietnamese in America, for example, are Catholic, but their particular traditions, coupled with language limitations and frequent rural origin, may require separate services that are impossible except in areas of large refugee concentration—as did happen in New Orleans. Furthermore, Vietnamese Catholics face the concern of Vietnamese Buddhists who question whether Catholics can be truly "Vietnamese" (Rutledge 1985: 61). The problem has been even more severe for Cambodians or Hmong who convert to Christianity since this moves them away from traditional religious practices that are wound very tightly into their ethnic identity (e.g., Capps 1994; Smith-Hefner 1994).

For Russian and Eastern European Jews, it has often been less the difference in traditions than the lack of opportunity in their home country to actively practice their faith that has created a gap between them and the American Jewish community that has been so active on their behalf.

As Gold (1994b: 35) has suggested, their Jewish identity was more secular and nationalistic than religious. The situation of these groups with religious connections in the United States may thus not be so different from that of other refugee (and immigrant) groups who have had to diligently pool resources to recreate their religious institutions. Without a strong community base, this creation of a functioning religious community is not possible. The smaller the community and the smaller the particular religious group, the more serious the practical problems.

These spiritual challenges are to some extent similar to those faced by other immigrant groups. As Peek (2005) has noted so clearly for Muslims, maintaining a religious affiliation often requires considerable work in recreating the meaning of that affiliation. In this effort, refugees generally face additional difficulties since so much of the basic structure of meaning to their lives has been cast into doubt by their experiences before and during exodus. The situation of Khmer refugees is illustrative. They have had to deal with memories of a holocaust that was created by Cambodians themselves. As Usha Welaratna (a Theravada Buddhist herself) has noted, the Khmer Rouge not only "violated every Buddhist precept . . . [and] showed contempt for the first and perhaps most important precept that one should not kill," but "also forced their victims to violate Buddhist precepts in order to survive" (Welaratna 1993: 252, 254). Carol Mortland has also noted how this calls into question the very meaning of life since to many Khmer "to be Cambodian is to be Buddhist" (Mortland 1994a: 6). Although Mortland suggests that Khmer have found ways to describe their experience, including explicit comparison with the Jewish holocaust, they are not truly at rest with those descriptions and "ask a range of questions that continue to bother them, questions most of them would never have thought to ask until their lives were turned upside down" (Mortland 1994b: 90). One result, then, is occasional conversion to Christianity, which may indeed remove these refugees from the general ethnic community, as religion and ethnicity are no longer overlapping. Indeed, it may then be more important that their children marry Christians than that they marry Khmer (Smith-Hefner 1994). That kind of trade-off between religion and life in the United States suggests, as Gozdziak and Shandy put it, that religion operates in "compelling, competing, and contradictory ways . . . as it both facilitates and impedes integration processes" (Gozdziak and Shandy 2002: 131).

Safe Haven?

Overall, then, the refugees who have come to the United States must fashion a new life in America even though they have been witnesses to, and victims of, some of the most chilling events in modern history. Because of that, their adjustment to life in the United States is necessarily a complicated one. As they construct new lives in America, they have to confront persistent, recurring questions about the viability of their political views and the veracity of their spiritual beliefs. They have to recreate relations of kinship and community out of fragmented, ruptured pieces and then attempt to maintain those ties even as their children all-too-rapidly accommodate to American culture. In the process, they have to overcome, or become reconciled to, an often severe loss of social and economic status. They cannot, in practical terms, be who they were and they cannot, in personal terms, be otherwise. This troubled experience of refugees in the United States is important on its own terms. If refuge in America fails to provide a basis for hope for the future, then it is a poor refuge indeed. The experience of refugees in America, however, is also crucial to understanding American society in the second half of the twentieth century, when large numbers of refugees arrived, and now in the twenty-first century, with smaller numbers of refugees hedged in by increased national security concerns—and almost lost within the vast numbers of other immigrants. What has happened to this notion of America as safe haven for refugees? The next chapter turns from the consideration of how refugees adjust to America and considers instead how Americans view refugees and what they think refugees should do and be as newcomers to America. In so doing, it also moves from the national to the local, from the place where policy on resettlement is made to the place where resettlement actually occurs.

Notes

1. As discussed in some detail in Chapter 1, these kinds of breakdown by nationality have serious limitations. Nevertheless, they are used occasionally in this chapter for lack of better data.

2. On educational levels, for example, 5 percent samples (PUMS) from the 2000 census indicate that only .9 percent of those from the Soviet Union lacked any education, followed by 2.1 percent for those from Cuba and 7.2 percent of those from Vietnam. The situation of other Southeast Asian refugees was much worse: 22 percent of those from Cambodia lacked any education and 28 percent of those from Laos. There have also been some shifts over time. In the 1980 census, for example, the percentage of Vietnamese with no education was only 4.6 percent (suggesting that later arrivals had somewhat less education) and the percentage of Cambodians with no education was only 13 percent (suggesting again that later arrivals had less education). All these data refer only to those aged 25–64.

3. For general comments on how the later Cuban arrivals differed, see Eckstein (2006), Gonzalez, Lopez, and Ko (2005), and Henken (2005).

4. The Iranian case is a particularly interesting one. See Bozorgmehr (1996), Mostofi (2003), Behrouzan (2005), and Der-Martirosian (2008).

5. The cultural values and spiritual beliefs of refugees also affect their initial adjustment to the United States. For most of the refugees, for example, individualism per se is less valued than it is by Americans. Rather, the individual is an integral part of ongoing social units, and often appears as less important than the social group, whether that group is based on kinship or unique community or religious traditions. Where they resettle with sufficient density, for example, the minority of Vietnamese who are Catholic, the minority of Hmong who are Protestant, and the minority of Iranians who are Jewish have developed distinctive religious social contexts for their lives in America.

6. There were subsequent efforts to resettle Cuban refugees away from the Miami area. These were successful in the sense of moving many people, but not successful in the sense of diluting the Cuban presence in Miami. This was greatly on the minds of those involved in the initial resettlement of Southeast Asian refugees. That helps explain why there were multiple reception centers created all across the country. To a certain degree, the Southeast Asian program created the opposite problem: refugees in such small numbers that ethnic communities were not viable. Thus, very quickly, there emerged what came to be called "secondary migration" of the refugees, creating an increased concentration of refugees in particular states and localities.

7. The films of Spencer Nakasako deserve particular note. Both a.k.a. Don Bonus and Kelly Loves Tony are available from the VYDC (Vietnamese Youth Development Center) Media Lab in San Francisco and present the Tenderloin as viewed from Vietnamese and Mien perspectives.

8. An extended note on this issue of employment may be useful. The central point about employment is not complicated: refugees must find the financial resources necessary to support themselves and their households. For most, this has required taking jobs that do not match their skills or previous experience. This is the frequently noted downward occupational mobility of refugees—and of many other immigrants as well. Yet, although the wages of refugees may not be sufficient to enable the self-sufficiency of the household, employment of one or more household members is still the necessary first step toward that self-sufficiency. So, employment remains crucial. Despite considerable public concern about refugee employment, most information over the past several decades has provided a relatively optimistic picture of the frequency of employment, if not necessarily of the quality of that employment.

Case-study and small-survey data for Soviet refugees throughout the 1970s, for example, indicated high rates of participation in the labor force and reasonable success in actually finding employment (e.g., Feldman 1977; Gilison 1979; Gitelman 1978). The major early survey effort on Soviet refugees (Simon 1985) had similarly positive findings, as did somewhat later research on Eastern European refugees (Cichon, Gozdziak, and Grover 1986), and Soviet refugees (Gold 1994b). The employment-related success of early Cuban refugees was also very clear. Census data from 1970, for example, showed a labor force participation rate of 84 percent for Cuban-born males, which was the highest rate for any reported group and well above the figure of 77 percent for all men. Cuban-born women had a labor force participation rate of 51 percent, a full 10 percentage points higher than the U.S. average for women at that time (Urban Associates 1974: 102). Data for Cubans arriving in the early 1970s also indicated rapid employment (Portes, Clark, and Bach 1977). Later data sources, particularly the 1990 and 2000 censuses, have confirmed this generally positive portrayal, although the specific argument about the high labor force participation rate of Cuban women has faded as the labor force participation of all U.S. women surged (U.S. Bureau of the Census 1993b).

The employment situation of the initial influx of Southeast Asian refugees in 1975 was similarly positive. By 1977, the refugees (mostly Vietnamese) had achieved labor force participation and unemployment rates similar to the general U.S. population (Marsh 1980; OSI 1977; Stein 1979). By 1980, the data, reflecting the situation of both 1975 and later arrivals, was somewhat less favorable. Interviews conducted with Vietnamese, Cambodian, and Laotian refugee heads of household in 1980 (OSI 1981) indicated labor force participation rates for men of about 60 percent with some variation by country of origin and, for women, from a low of 26.7 percent (Laotian) to a high of 42.4 percent (Vietnamese). Unemployment rates were, at that time, also somewhat high compared to the general U.S. population. However, length of residence was a decisive factor. Later arrivals were likely to have low rates of labor force participation, thus obscuring the gains made by earlier arrivals. Specifically, the combined labor force participation rate (both men and women) for 1975 arrivals was 64 percent—about the national average—whereas for 1979 arrivals it was only 32 percent. Length of residence also had significant effects on unemployment rates. For 1975 arrivals, the unemployment rate was less than 4 percent, compared with 17 percent for 1979 arrivals (OSI 1981).

Later survey efforts have indicated both similarities and differences in the employment patterns of refugees overall. The pattern of improvement with increased length of residence is a continuing one. Annual survey data from the federal Office of Refugee Resettlement indicate how particular entry cohorts continued to make progress from year to year, even if their starting point was relatively low. For example, the percentage of working-age adults who arrived in 1990 who held jobs in 1990 (combining the effects of labor force participation and employment rates) was 14 percent, rose to 25 percent in 1991, and to 29 percent in 1992 (ORR 1993). That 1992 rate, however, was less than half of the equivalent figure (61 percent) for the overall U.S. working-age population. By 2002, however, the refugee employment level trailed the U.S. rate by only about 6 percentage points (60.8 versus 66.6), and even those arriving the year of the survey were already employed at a rate of 40.5 percent. By 2007, it had slipped to an overall rate of 56.8 percent, although the general pattern of improvement over time remained clear, and those in the country a full five years were employed at rates very close to the U.S. average (ORR 2007).

It is difficult to identity all refugees in broader data sources, like the U.S. census, but data on relatively large groups like the Cubans, Vietnamese, Russians, Ukrainians, Cambodians, Laotians, and Bosnians—who have generally arrived with refugee or refugee-like legal status—show a mix of patterns with the relatively well-educated populations having reasonably high employment ratios, and the less educated populations, such as Cambodians and Laotians, not as frequently employed. For 2000, for example, employment ratios (aged 25–64 only) were as follows in order from high to low (again with the female/male figures in parentheses)—Bosnia: 72.9 percent (66.2/79.1); Russia/USSR: 67.7 percent (59.9/77.0); Vietnam: 67.4 percent (60.8/74.1); Ukraine: 64.8 percent (55.9/74.7); Cuba: 62.3 percent (55.9/68.3); Laos: 59.3 percent (51.9/66.5); Cambodia: 58.5 percent (51.4/66.7). For the two largest groups, Cubans and Vietnamese, these aggregate figures actually show considerable stability over the last three censuses. The actual figures for Cubans are as follows with the overall percentage employed (aged 25–64 only) followed by the female/male figures in parentheses—1980: 73.7 percent (61.1/87.9); 1990: 73.2 percent (63.3/82.9); and 2000: 62.3 percent (55.9/68.3). By contrast the figures for those from Vietnam are as follows—1980: 60.9 percent (50.3/72/3); 1990: 68.5 percent (58.0/78.4); and 2000: 67.4 percent (60.8/74.1).

A number of factors affect these employment figures. Age is one. Refugees in the middle years of adulthood have tended to be more frequently in the labor force, and those refugee groups composed mostly of adults in those age groups, such as Soviet and Eastern European refugees, have tended to have the most favorable employment situation overall. Household responsibilities have also been an important factor with women typically in the labor force far less frequently than men. Health problems can also be a factor, as can disadvantageous locations and simple lack of knowledge about the American world of work. One factor that merits particular attention is English language competence. This will be discussed in more detail in Chapter 6 since it is a central refugee program goal, but a few general comments here may be useful. Comprehensive data on Soviet refugees are lacking, but case-study material supports the importance of English for obtaining employment (e.g., Feldman 1977; Gilison 1979; Gitelman 1978). For Cubans, the importance of competence in English has been less clear. Early needs assessments stressed the importance of providing more English language training, particularly for the adult population (Hernandez 1974), although the importance of English for Cubans in Miami is anomalous. That Cuban situation is affected by the strong Cuban ethnic economy and the general prevalence of Spanish. The importance of English language competence for employment has been clearer for other refugee groups. Annual federal surveys, for example, have consistently shown the significance of English language competence for the employment of Southeast Asian refugees. The 1992 survey, for example, showed employment rates rising sharply with higher levels of English language competence (ORR 1993: 55): 5 percent for those with no English, 26 percent for those with some English, and 44 percent for those who spoke English well. A decade later in 2002, the pattern was the same for all refugees, although the net numbers were much higher: 34 percent for those with no English, 58 percent for those with some English, and 71 percent for those with good English (ORR 2002). The figures changed significantly by 2007, when the differential value of English decreased and there was virtually no difference in employment between those who spoke some English and those who spoke it well, although those speaking no English were still less frequently employed (ORR 2007). As a whole, then, the research emphasizes the importance of English for refugees—just as the more general research indicates the same point for immigrants (e.g., Chiswick and Miller 1995; Davis 2004; Evans 2005; Waldinger, Lim, and Cort 2007).

For some refugees, obtaining employment has been a relatively rapid process. They have had the English language facility and the relevant job skills that allow easy entry into the U.S. labor force. For other refugees, obtaining employment has involved overcoming serious job-related obstacles, such as lack of English, or difficult personal circumstances, such as health problems. For yet other refugees, employment has been a nearly unreachable and possibly irrelevant goal. The elderly and those with severe and continuing health problems are unlikely to obtain employment. Many refugees thus have needed and utilized public assistance during their initial years in the United States and sometimes for much longer periods. Almost inevitably, some assistance has been necessary to maintain refugee households through the period when employment is not obtainable, or when its rewards in wages and salaries are insufficient to meet household needs.

This use of public assistance by refugees has been a frequent cause of concern both for the federal government as it has increasingly restricted the extent of public assistance to refugees and for state governments which provide portions of the assistance that refugees receive under mainstream programs. The so-called "dependency rate" emerged as an important policy issue at the very beginning of the first Reagan presidential term in 1981. Such concerns resurfaced in the 1990s as part of more general anti-immigrant sentiment, but were largely quiescent during the immigration debates of 2007 (because of the small number of refugees versus very large numbers of other legal and illegal immigrants). The debate has been a complicated one for a variety of reasons. First, it is extremely difficult to provide a total picture of the contributions that refugees and other immigrants make to the United States either directly through taxes or indirectly through economic growth. It is thus impossible to assess adequately the net costs involved in providing such assistance. Second, refugee (and immigrant) use of assistance is greatly restricted to a few states where the numbers of refugees and immigrant are high and the use of assistance is at a disproportionately high rate. California, for example, accounted for 38 percent of all refugees and immigrants in 1994, but accounted for over half (52 percent) of all the refugees and immigrants receiving reimbursable cash assistance through AFDC and SSI (GAO 1995; cf. Bach et al. 1984). Third, the very reasons for accepting certain refugee groups inevitably led to situations of particular difficulty in resettlement and employment—especially when highly disadvantaged groups with long histories of direct and indirect abuse, and sharply truncated family and community structures, are accepted for admission precisely because of their need for escape and sanctuary.

This is to say no more than that even the initial adjustment of refugees to the United States has been a complex process taking much time and posing serious difficulties for the refugees and for the programs attempting to serve them. The very forces that bring refugees to the United States militate against easy solutions for their adjustment to an American society for which they are often ill-prepared and which is itself often uneasy with their presence—or with the presence of other immigrants with whom they are combined in the public mind.

9. An extended note on the relationship between self-sufficiency and extent and level of employment may also be useful, again drawing in data from the formative years of the U.S. refugee program. This too is discussed in more detail in Chapter 6 as the central goal of the refugee program. But some discussion here may also be helpful in anticipation. To simplify, household economic self-sufficiency hinges on both the number of people employed and the money they receive from those jobs. For refugees, as for the general U.S. population, there is often more than one wage earner per family. If those jobs are at the minimum wage (or lower), there are problems. Even two minimum-wage jobs, for example, are insufficient for large families. While unemployment has been a significant problem for many refugees, it is this issue of underemployment that has probably been the more pervasive problem. Many—although far from all—refugees have come to the United States with relatively high occupational and educational backgrounds. During their first few years in the United States virtually all have had difficulties in obtaining what the Refugee Act of 1980 stipulated as "employment commensurate with their skills and abilities." Barry Stein, in an early, succinct review of research on refugee resettlement (although at a time before the great diversification of refugee admissions), noted the extent of this downward occupational mobility and its implications for refugee adjustment. The achievement of a level of employment consistent with prior occupational status was, he suggested, "of crucial importance to the degree of assimilation and satisfaction a refugee achieves in his resettlement" (Stein 1979: 25). However, such a transfer of occupational status is difficult since "the highly skilled refugees, who represent a majority of most refugee waves . . . have many barriers to successful resumptions of their careers. The major obstacles to the transfer of foreign-acquired skills are nonrecognition of degrees and skills, licensing restrictions by trades and professions, the extensive retraining needed to adjust to national differences, the greater language demands of professional, managerial, and sales work, and the nontransferability of certain skills" (Stein 1979: 39).

The obstacles to finding employment commensurate with existing skills are many, and the extent of the resulting downward occupational mobility has been significant. The initial influx of Southeast Asian refugees, for example, occurred in 1975. That influx included a high proportion of refugees with professional and managerial occupational skills. They had the good fortune to enter a relatively good labor market. About two years later, in the summer of 1977, however, a survey (OSI 1977) indicated that half of those surveyed claimed professional or managerial occupations in Vietnam but less than one in ten had an equivalent occupation in the United States. Specifically, 30 percent had been professionals in Vietnam, but only 7 percent were in professional employment in the United States. For managers, the corresponding drop was from 15 percent to 2 percent. In later years, the proportion of those with professional or managerial occupations in Southeast Asia decreased, but the inability of those with such professional and managerial experience to find equivalent jobs in the United States continued. In 1992, a national survey found that 11.2 percent of Southeast Asian refugees had professional or managerial backgrounds, but only .9 percent had professional or managerial occupations in the United States (ORR 1993: 54). This survey (and other surveys as well) also indicated a corresponding shift away from "white-collar" to "blue-collar work." Extensive research on early Cuban arrivals has indicated a similar pattern of downward occupational mobility (Fagen, Brody, and O'Leary 1968; Portes and Bach 1985; Prohias and Casal 1973; University of Miami 1967). A broad range of research on Soviet Jewish refugees confirms the pattern (e.g., Gilison 1979; Gitelman 1978; Gold 1994b; Markowitz 1993; Simon 1985), as does more limited quantitative research on Eastern European, Iranian, and Ethiopian refugees (e.g., Cichon, Gozdziak, and Glover 1986; Koehn 1991). The net implication is that refugees tend to experience considerable downward occupational mobility during their early years in the United States. Although there is some indication that this process is partially reversed over time, the re-achievement of employment commensurate with existing skills and abilities has been neither a rapid nor inevitable process for most refugees.

This downward occupational mobility has direct implications both for the amounts of income available to households and for the personal satisfaction that refugees find. In terms of income, while refugees have often been quite successful in obtaining jobs, they generally have received relatively low wages. This is particularly the case during their initial years in the United States, but often continues to be a problem throughout their lives. A survey conducted in 1977 of initial Vietnamese arrivals, for example, indicated that almost 85 percent of those working were working forty hours a week or more. Nevertheless, almost a fifth had a weekly income lower than would be expected from working at the then minimum wage (OSI 1977). Similar data emerge from the 1990 Census. Vietnamese participated in the labor force at virtually the same rate as the general U.S. population (64.5 percent versus 65.3 percent) but had much lower per capita income ($9,033 versus $14,420) (U.S. Bureau of the Census 1993c).

Individual wage and salary income does not, however, directly determine the adequacy of household income. One household may do fairly well financially by combining the minimal wages of several working household members, whereas another household may do poorly if a single wage earner making a better salary must support numerous nonworking dependents. Early information on Cuban refugees from the 1970 census is illustrative. Cubans had high rates of labor force participation for both men and women. They also had a rate of intact marriages at about the national rate (Prohias and Casal 1973; Urban Associates 1974). The result was fairly adequate household income.

However, the results are not always so positive. The 1990 census, for example, found Vietnamese with labor force participation similar to that of the U.S. population as a whole, and with a percentage of households with at least two wage earners well above the national level. Yet the percentage of households below the poverty line was almost twice that of the general U.S. population: 25.7 percent versus 13.1 percent (U.S. Bureau of the Census 1993c). The household income situation was much worse for those Cambodian and Laotian households with fewer wage earners, and even somewhat worse for those from the Soviet Union who—despite impressive per capita earnings when they did find work—had relatively low labor force participation rates and relatively few multiple-earner households. Only with a few groups, like those born in Poland and Iran, did the strength of individual incomes outweigh the lack of multiple wage earners within household (U.S. Bureau of the Census 1993a).

In terms of occupational satisfaction, most refugees must accept that they are unlikely to achieve an occupational status in the United States that matches their experience in country of origin. Refugees face barriers of health, age, English language competence, licenses and credentials, and even appropriateness of former employment to the U.S. labor market. Early research on Cuban refugees provided some hope for a satisfactory compromise as "refugees take into account a series of other factors in their subjective comparisons of situations" (Portes 1969: 513), and as a strong ethnic community "can favorably influence the adjustment of its members by providing a comparison reference which does not demean the refugees' sense of worth" (Rogg 1971: 481). Some such compromise may be inevitable over time, but it is likely to be a painful one. That pain is seen in informal research with refugees and in various survey efforts. The job dissatisfaction of Soviet and Eastern European refugees has been widely noted (e.g., Gold 1994b), and the particular problems faced by high-status Southeast Asian refugees have appeared in various survey efforts (e.g., Lin, Tazuma, and Masuda 1979; Starr et al. 1979; Vignes and Hall 1979).

10. For example, see Chung and Lin (1994) for general comments on marital stress and Bhuyan et al. (2005) for the specific case of spousal abuse.

11. One result has been a frequent consideration of the burden on Cambodian holocaust survivors, often couched in terms of clinical posttraumatic stress syndrome (e.g., Abe, Zane, and Chun 1994; Clark, Sack, and Goff 1993; Hinton et al. 2006; Palmieri, Marshall, and Schell 2007). The Bosnian case, including the effects of mass rape, has also drawn considerable attention (Alexander, Blake, and Bernstein 2007; Corvo and Peterson 2005; Mosselson 2007; Schulz, Marovic-Johnson, and Huber 2006; Snyder et al. 2005, 2006).

12. An interesting early indication of the length of time needed for alleviation of alienation comes from a survey of Southeast Asian refugees in Illinois (Kim and Nicassio 1980). The researchers constructed an alienation index on the basis of answers to ten standardized statements about the refugee's life situation in the United States. The results were broken down by ethnic group and by year of arrival. The Hmong had the highest score (indicating most alienation) and the

Vietnamese had the lowest. Furthermore, when respondents were sorted by year of entry, there was a statistically significant and inverse relationship between length of residence and alienation. However, the individual scores showed a rise through the first three years before declining in the fourth and fifth years. Although the declines for those in the fourth and fifth years of residence implied that mental health problems were ameliorated after three years in country, this finding may well reflect the social characteristics of those who arrived in 1975 and 1976.

13. For example, early Cuban refugees, culturally relatively close to Americans in many ways, still had distinctive ideas about what constituted acceptable behavior and therefore a normal "mental health" status. Analysis of value orientations in two separate samples of early Cuban refugees and native-born Americans, for example, indicated significant differences along a number of dimensions. The Cubans tended to prefer lineality (e.g., hierarchical relations within the family), a present-time orientation, and subjugation to nature. The Americans, on the other hand, showed a preference for individuality, mastery over nature, and a future-time orientation (Szapocznik, Kurtines, and Hanna 1979; Szapocznik, Scopetta, and King 1978).

14. For Central Americans, who had been a major focus of public concern about nonlegal refugee groups in the 1980s, the availability of legalization under the Immigration Reform and Control Act of 1986 tended to move them from the status of undocumented refugees to that of undocumented workers (Burns 1993; Coutin 1998, 2000; Hagan 1994; Harmon 1995; Melville 1985; Menjívar 1999, 2006).

3

Perfectly American: Constructing the Refugee Experience

Over the last seventy years, American involvement in refugee resettlement has developed from an ad hoc, largely voluntary agency–managed program to a formal, regulated program with the strong involvement of federal and state governments in addition to voluntary agencies. Over that same period, the numbers of refugees have often changed rapidly, rising precipitously, and then falling again. Origins have also shifted greatly—sometimes representing extensions of earlier immigrant flows (as with Cubans and many Eastern Europeans) yet sometimes representing virtually new populations to the United States (as with many Southeast Asian, Middle Eastern, and African refugees).

The American response to these diverse refugees has been mixed. On the one hand, humanitarian instincts have combined with staunch anticommunist sentiments to produce strong public and governmental support for refugees as individuals who have fled disaster, including "voting with their feet" against the social and economic persecution of communist systems. Since many refugees have been uniquely qualified to discredit communist regimes, they could thus also validate core American political values of freedom and economic opportunity. On the other hand, negative views toward refugees have been far from uncommon. Such negativity is seen in episodic economic competition (Vietnamese fishermen along both the Gulf and Pacific coasts), conflict over other limited resources (perhaps especially housing), and recurring emphasis on the lack of refugee self-sufficiency (including frequent studies of rates of public assistance usage). The negativity is seen in public opinion polls, which show only marginal support for refugees during the second half of the twentieth century, with newer, more "foreign" refugee groups having the least support (Simon 1996; Simon and Alexander 1993; Simon and Lynch 1999). Such public opinion data suggest that Americans have been ambivalent about refugees and about how to perceive refugees, whether as a political category (refugees from communism, refugees from right wing governments), as a religious category (Buddhists, Muslims, animists), as a cultural category (non-English speakers, sometimes nonliterate), as an economic category (sometimes as low-wage manual labor and sometime as high-wage professionals), and as a racial category (particularly in places where their presence is as a new, anomalous group). Refugees are thus not only survivors of some of the most wrenching events of the modern world but also, when resettled in America, find themselves at the locus of American structures of race, ethnicity, class, immigration, economics, politics, religion, and society.

Despite such ambivalence about particular refugees and where they may belong in the grid of American social and cultural categories, the notion of refuge and the imperative toward support and welcome to refugees endures. As an extended example, this chapter considers press treatment of refugees in Richmond, Virginia, during the last quarter of the twentieth century—before the security concerns and surging numbers of undocumented immigrants changed the nature of American immigration, and public opinion about it. Unlike the ambivalent response that emerges in national opinion polls, in this case the construction of refugees is neither negative nor ambivalent, but is instead solidly positive. This positive construction extends across a broad range of refugees of varying racial, ethnic, and national origins.[1]

The discussion that follows focuses, then, not on the actual experiences of refugees but on the way their experiences are constructed by those who are hosts to them as they are resettled in the United States. These constructions of the refugee experience then become elements in the dynamic by which refugees—once exposed to their hosts—construct their own accounts of being refugees. The strength of this refugee construct[2] hinges on the way in which the experience of refugees resonates with core civic and religious values of the localities in which they resettle. In this Richmond case, the result is that the refugees, the city, and the resettlement effort are all rendered as perfectly American.[3] Although the discussion in this chapter is thus predominantly about the idea of refuge—rather than the objective practicalities of refugee resettlement discussed in the previous chapter—some background on Richmond helps set the context for the discussion and also serves as a reminder of the very localized nature of refugee resettlement. Refugees, after all, are not resettled in some abstract America but in distinctive local communities.

Richmond, Immigrants, and Refugees

Over the last two hundred years, this particular locale of Richmond has been sequentially the most "northern" and immigrant-settled city of the South, the almost accidental capital of the Confederacy, a center for the creation of "lost cause" mythology and retreat in minority rights, and a "New South" city with a combination of race-based politics and business-oriented civic leadership. Founded as a trading post at the point at which the James River is no longer navigable, Richmond was at the center of early trade in Virginia, and at the center of the nation's founding. By the time of the Revolution, it was a relatively heterogeneous society, with a range of immigrant populations, free and slave Africans, and continuing relations with Indian tribes (Dabney 1990; Tyler-McGraw 1994). This openness came to an end as slave rebellions in the early 1800s (Egerton 1993) brought a crushing reversal of the relative fluidity that had come to characterize black-white and free–slave relations.

Nevertheless, during the first half of the nineteenth century, while Richmond developed as the premier manufacturing city of the South, its population remained diverse. On the eve of the Civil War, its foreign-born population was substantial, and the mix of free and slave blacks included some who would fight on the side of the Confederacy (Jordan 1995; Tyler-McGraw 1994). During Reconstruction, that diversity continued with increased opportunities for blacks and immigrants—particularly German (Wust 1969: 203–217) and Irish. There was little immigration in Richmond or anywhere in the South after that time. Despite some early contacts with Chinese through the missionary activism of the Episcopalian Virginia Theology Seminary and several Richmond Baptist Churches (Cohen 1984: 11–16), for example, that small effort at importing labor remained limited. The "flood tide of European immigration" that "swept past the South leaving it almost untouched and further isolating it in its peculiarities" (Woodward 1971: 299) largely swept past Richmond as well, with the partial exception (Berman 1979) of some Jewish immigration from Russia and Eastern Europe. By the end of the nineteenth century, the possibilities of Reconstruction had yielded to the disfranchisement of not only blacks but also other groups who stood in the way of the triumph of a new business coalition that, in Richmond as in much of the rest of the South, sought "progressive" development through an enlightened oligarchy of civic and business leaders dedicated to the realization of a "Greater Richmond" (Moeser and Dennis 1982; Silver 1984).

Richmond was, in economic terms, generally successful through the first half of the twentieth century. It was affected relatively lightly by the

Depression, and maintained a strong base in manufacturing and regional finance and trade. As the black population increased, the city made several annexations that retained the status quo of white political and economic control. At the end of the Second World War, Richmond was thus a significant regional city, albeit one that was far removed from any cultural diversity other than the harsh conflicts of race. The refugees who came to Richmond after the Second World War were a minor exception to the pattern. As in other locales, these DPs from Europe generally had some connection to groups in Richmond. Resettlement was largely the province of the Catholic and Jewish communities. Cuban refugees became another minor exception in the 1960s. But, overall, Richmond remained isolated from the changing patterns in immigration that followed from the 1965 revisions to U.S. immigration law. It remained a decidedly black/white community.

With the fall of the American-supported governments in Indochina in 1975, however, that situation changed. Over the last quarter of the twentieth century, a steady number of refugee arrivals gave Richmond new ethnic, national, and racial groups to which it had barely been exposed. The new Asian presence was especially striking. By 1980, the U.S. Census reported some 800 Vietnamese for the Richmond metropolitan area and, by 1990, a combined Cambodian and Vietnamese population numbering nearly 3,000 (slightly over .3 percent of the metropolitan population of 866,000).[4] Along with immigrant streams from India, Korea, China, and the Philippines, Richmond now had a notable Asian presence (of 1.3 percent). The Asian population, though small, increased by a factor of three from 1980 to 1990. In addition, there was resettlement of Cubans, Haitians, and Soviet Jews in fairly sizable numbers, with other, more occasional resettlements from Eastern Europe, the Middle East, and Africa.[5]

There were three key features of the refugee resettlement effort in Richmond that were important for the adjustment of refugees and for the way in which refugees were viewed. The first key feature was that the resettlement effort was almost entirely a religious one, with strong involvement from Catholic, Jewish, and Protestant organizations. Catholic and Jewish organizations, in particular, could trace their involvement in resettlement back to the early days after World War II. "Refugees helping refugees" thus provided an important element of continuity in these religiously based organizations.

The second feature was the considerable diversity in the refugee population in Richmond. Although most refugees in the late 1970s were from Southeast Asia, even there the mixes differed from the aggregate U.S. admissions numbers. For example, there were relatively few refugees from Laos and a relatively large number from Cambodia (reflecting special federal programs directed toward creating Cambodian resettlement clusters). In subsequent years, Richmond received a broad range of refugees from Southeast Asia, Europe, Central America, and Africa. Unlike the situation in some other parts of the United States, the idea of "refugee" remained unanchored to any particular ethnic, national, or racial group. The community and the press could thus continue to maintain a more generalized view of refugees that largely matched the universalistic basis of "refugee" as a moral and legal category.

Finally, the third distinctive feature was that refugees in Richmond generally found employment—even as the general U.S. employment levels of many refugee groups plummeted in the 1980s and early 1990s. This high level of employment was partially the result of restrictive Virginia policies on receipt of public assistance. It was also, however, the result of a strong economy throughout Virginia, a distinctive manufacturing base in Richmond,[6] and the very strong efforts and connections of the resettlement agencies.

On practical grounds, then, the resettlement of refugees in Richmond in the last quarter of the twentieth century resulted in a small, but vastly increased, number of people with new social and cultural characteristics. Many of these were of a decidedly new racial category—Asian—with uncertain meaning in an established black/white social and political structure. Others, such as Soviet Jews, fit well within general established categories, although they often acted in ways that frustrated the resettlement agencies. In some ways, Richmond may be taken as representative of moderate-sized resettlement areas in the United States, particularly those in the South and Midwest (Rasbridge 2001; Rynearson 2001; Wellmeier 2001). For that reason of scale, Richmond is an instructive place for considering a well-organized local community whose notions of service combine civic and religious motivations. The comparison to gateway cities, on the other hand, is sharp. The Richmond experience, for example, contrasts sharply with the experience in the northern part of Virginia (in the orbit of metropolitan Washington) where Vietnamese refugees in particular were a much stronger presence (Hackett 1996b; Haines, Rutherford, and Thomas 1981a, 1981b; Wood 1997).

Other work has outlined the nature of resettlement in Richmond, the general economic patterns for major refugee groups in the city, and the views of service providers and of refugees toward their individual and shared experiences (Breslow et al. 1997; Haines et al. 2001). The remainder of this chapter focuses more narrowly on press accounts about refugees from 1975 through the end of the century. These press accounts shed some light on the resettlement experiences of refugees, but the emphasis here is on what the accounts suggest about American ideas about refugee resettlement, and whether these ideas have been durable over time and applied equivalently to refugees who have differed greatly in terms of class, education, ethnic and national origin, and race.

Refugee Success Stories: American and Universal

In 1975, at the beginning of the Southeast Asian refugee influx, there were two major daily papers in Richmond: the morning *Richmond Times-Dispatch* and the afternoon *Richmond News-Leader.* The two papers were under joint ownership and partially overlapping management.[7] The papers were generally conservative on editorial issues[8] but maintained a separation of editorial and general news policy (Dunford 1995). In 1992, the two papers were consolidated, becoming the *Richmond Times-Dispatch.* From 1975 through 1999, 124 significant articles[9] on refugees appeared in these two papers. The structure of most of this press coverage can be summarized simply as "refugee success stories." The form of these remained relatively unchanged over this quarter of a century. The stories typically begin with a description of the dangers and deprivations that had forced the refugees to flee their home country. The inevitable (and justifiable) flight, often involving the separation from or loss of loved ones, was usually followed by a detailing of the additional losses and hazards during the journey to a place of asylum, often including extended stays in refugee camps. The next stage, permanent resettlement, was usually noted as something of a shock to the refugees since they were unprepared for life in the United States. However, with the assistance of the receiving community, especially the members of a local church or synagogue, the refugees were successfully resettled, finding jobs that were at least sufficient to immediate household needs. This success story format typically concluded with the refugees in a stance of hope toward their future or at least toward the future of their children.

The following examples illustrate this "success story" structure. This set of accounts are abridged, but include direct quotations from the original articles when the specific wording is crucial. Multiple cases are provided to convey the consistency across very different national, ethnic, and religious groups.

A Bosnian couple (White 1994): A Serb married to a Muslim, each of whom has lost one parent to the war, had to flee because of their persecution as refugees and as a mixed-ethnic couple. "With pained expressions, the family recalls the horrors of the war. Branislav remembers the soldiers encircling their home, Alma remembers the running, the hiding, the killing." They flee, and escape with only a suitcase to Spain where they are unable to work. Eventually they are resettled in the United States. Now they must face additional difficulties in finding jobs—especially ones that match their previous high credentials. They "must adjust to a new home, a new country, a new language." The wife's comment to the reporter concludes the article: "We want a normal life and jobs . . . We just want a future for our daughter." Earlier in the article the husband is quoted as saying, "In my opinion, we have a future here."

A Cambodia-born Virginia Military Institute (VMI) student (Meisner 1992): The young man lost both parents in the Pol Pot period. His father was an air force officer who was taken away in 1976; his mother became ill and died shortly thereafter. At age 6, he wandered the Cambodian countryside with a group of Cambodian families who accepted him as one of their own. Eventually, they reached a refugee camp in Thailand, where he remained for several years. He was resettled as an unaccompanied minor in Richmond and placed in foster care. The foster parents encouraged him academically, and when he graduated he was accepted into a variety of good universities, from which he chose VMI for its discipline and connection to military service—a link to his father. Remarks his foster mother at the end of the article: "We have a young man who has become an asset to this country."

A teenage brother and sister who escaped from Ethiopia (Fitzgerald 1991): The pair's parents had been jailed, and they themselves had been questioned and threatened with torture. They escaped, traveling "the back roads and jungles at night . . . slipping past lions and government border patrols." After time in Nairobi, they were resettled as unaccompanied minors in Richmond. Both were reported as adjusting well, with good English skills, and with a variety of extracurricular activities. Their parents were now reported to be out of prison, but the situation was still too tense for them to return.

A 17-year-old Haitian (Johnson 1992). The youth's family moved to Port-au-Prince early in his life. His father was actively pro-Aristide, and after Aristide's ouster he was assassinated. The son was also politically active and "felt it was just a matter of time before a bullet found him." He escaped with no possessions on a fifteen-day sea journey. "Fear hung in the air like a suffocating vapor," but he was picked up by the U.S. Coast Guard and placed in a sequence of facilities before arriving in Richmond. "I was afraid, but not now," he notes.

A Soviet Jew (Slack 1991a). "Nobody's pointing a gun at your head," notes one of the refugees. "Soviet-style anti-Semitism is less violent than that, but more pervasive." Noted another, "For Jewish people in Russia, every day is worse and worse and worse." However, getting out is not easy. The process often takes years, and can be frustrating. Nor is the resettlement process easy. Extensive help, including free housing, is provided for the first few months, but refugees have problems with language and with jobs—particularly finding jobs that match their frequently impressive credentials. But, notes one, "It is necessary to fight. And this is the beginning of the fight, not the end. For sure in America there is a place for you if you can find it." For another, the work situation has not been good, but the move was worthwhile anyway "because we have children."

An 18-year-old Vietnamese (Reynolds 1994). The family escaped from Vietnam because of being ostracized after adopting an Amerasian child. They waited in a refugee camp in the Philippines for about a year before coming to Richmond. The large, ten-member family had particular problems in finding housing and in providing food on a combined income of $300 per week. The wife comments, "I walk three miles to the home of a Cambodian family who sells me vegetables in the summer. Real cheap. A few cucumbers last my family a whole week. I buy our chicken and cakes when they're half-priced and outdated on Mondays. That chicken lasts my family a week." In the meantime, the son is working full-time and giving all his money to his family. But he notes that "after my family is stable, I'd like to go back to school" and America is "better than where we came from."

These refugee success stories—of persecution and flight, an often purgatorial transit experience, resettlement shock, a mixed success in adjustment, and a final stance of hope—were almost entirely about individuals or individual families. The story's journalistic "hook" was often more implicit than explicit. This is largely because the *Times-Dispatch* is a local newspaper[10] and the influx of refugees to the city (and region) has been fairly limited. Thus, the arrival of a single refugee family was a sufficient warrant for a story, as was the anticipation of such an arrival. The story itself thus needed no formal explanation or justification. Yet, although the "hook" might be implicit, it often crossed domains. "Anticipation" stories ("First Cambodian family due this week"), for example, were frequently tied to coverage of international events. Other journalistic hooks were found when the reuniting of a family was tied to such holidays as Christmas, Easter, Thanksgiving, and the Fourth of July. All are holidays when, by American standards, such reunion would be particularly appropriate.

In its coverage of refugees, the local press often appeared unencumbered by the usual requirements of "newsworthiness." An event or holiday, such as Christmas, seemed often more the excuse for a story than the direct reason for it. These accounts of danger and horror, of loss of home and re-creation of home, were treated as of intrinsic and timeless appeal. The life stories of refugees might differ dramatically from the lives of most Americans but would still strike a resonant chord among readers. Refugee stories thus implied a universality of values transcending nationality, race, or religion. This universality was sometimes made explicit, as in a report quoting a poster in a regional resettlement office, "Anyone can become a refugee, and just about anyone can become a sponsor" (Burchstead 1983). But the message of universality was also offered more tacitly in the regular marking of refugee families as middle-class in values, educated (or valuing education), having been in military service for their country, or just concerned about the well-being of their children.

The context for these universalistic refugee stories, however, was very much the specific locale of Richmond, Virginia. An individual refugee or refugee family was usually described as sponsored by a particular church or synagogue, living with a particular family, attending a particular school, and residing at a given address. Reporters sometimes even noted that the resettled refugee had never heard of Richmond before arriving there—an observation that permitted a rediscovery of Richmond through the fresh eyes of the refugees. Throughout these stories, individual, identified Richmonders were described as exhibiting sometimes heroic levels of generosity as they welcomed refugees into their already crowded homes or outfitted new homes for these strangers. The stories thus permitted rediscovery of Richmond and rediscovery of Richmonders.

For example, one story detailed the lives of a Richmond couple with two young children who had opened their three-bedroom house to a family of six Laotians (Gallaher 1979a). The American husband, a veteran of five tours of duty in Vietnam, was himself currently out of work, and they had only recently bought the house after living for ten years in a trailer. They explained their reasons for sponsorship this way:

> Over an occasional dinner watching the news on TV, we commented back and forth, "Gee, wasn't it a shame what's happening. Maybe we can do something, maybe we can do something someday". . . I do feel strongly philosophically about the fact that we were in Vietnam. We probably didn't do that amount of damage in Laos, but if there's any

> way we can repay, if there's any American who can extend a helping hand, I feel that they should... Theologically, I feel it's an absolute must for people to extend their arms and hearts to people in need. (Gallaher 1979a)

Or, consider:

> The Wiseman's had requested six refugees, then they heard they would get nine, and then eleven arrived. All the newcomers had been exposed to tuberculosis. Ley had active malaria. The Americans and Cambodians look back on their adjustments to America with a lot of humor. They remember big conferences on the use of the bathroom... Once when the refrigerator was empty there was another big conference because the newcomers thought there would be no more food. (Gallaher 1979b)

News stories reported on the community environment that Richmonders had created for refugees and they detailed the benefits refugees had received from sponsors, friends, and even strangers. One Richmonder, the manager of an apartment complex, was described as transforming the complex into a coherent neighborhood, complete with neighborhood events, for Cambodians (Adams 1995). A fairly dense Asian settlement was described as "offering a sense of community to the new residents in a strange land" (Kelly 1991), although that sentiment was balanced by another interview with the head of the local Vietnamese Catholic Church who noted the dangers of inward-looking ethnic communities: "I don't think it's good for the foreign people to come here and concentrate themselves. We've learned a lesson from other places, from California and New Orleans" (Wagner 1993).

Through such stories the city constructed itself as a place of generosity and community—an "us" in which religious groups, employers, schools, and individuals were united in the opening of homes and hearts to international needs. These stories celebrated the city and its residents and, in offering a narrative of how "we in Richmond are good," provided at least an implicit contrast with the other Richmond stories of deep and historic division between blacks and whites, homicide rates among the highest in the nation, and increasing economic disparity between the white suburbs and the black urban center. The refugee success story—despite its detailing of the personal loss and horror experienced by refugees—offered a vision of success for Richmond. Thus, the refugee success story was very much also a Richmond success story.

This positive image of Richmond, however, remained secondary to the newspaper's positive treatment of refugees. With a striking consistency, refugees were described as exemplifying the classic American virtues. They were "hard workers," "wanting to work," "ready to work," "dependable workers," "willing to take entry-level jobs," feel themselves fortunate to have a minimum-wage job, "glad to be here," "adjusting remarkably well," "having problems that can be overcome," making every effort to learn English, tolerant of their loss of occupational and economic stature, taxpayers and future business owners, "cheerful, hardworking, and adaptable" (a characterization particularly of Cambodians), not on public assistance, possessing a "family life that should be a model for all of us," with children who are "adjusting very well in school" and sometimes "doing exceptionally well," *and* who send whatever assistance they can to their relatives back home. While there was occasional mention of cultural conflicts, these were more entertaining than substantive, for example in the repeated story of Vietnamese children bringing embryonic chicken eggs to school for Easter. This detailing of the perseverance, energy, and adaptability of refugees,[11] especially when added to description of the horrors they have endured, yields an image of refugees as nothing short of extraordinary Americans who work hard and are even able to bridge entrenched racial divisions:

> Tran Sung came to the United States from a refugee camp in Thailand four years ago. A year later, he was hired as the first Cambodian at Peck's scrap yard on Deepwater Terminal Road in South Richmond. Now he spends his days 30 feet in the air in a 50-ton crane unloading the old bones of American industry that are to be recycled . . . On the ground, a young black man watches closely. He is Louistine Sherrod. "I'm glad I got the opportunity to train" Sung, Sherrod says as he picks up stray scraps of steel. "He's a hard worker and a nice guy". . . "Those two have become a team," says Richard Collins, general manager of the scrap yard. "The only problem I could possibly have with them is separating them". . . Those who work at Peck say there is a camaraderie between the ethnic and religious groups of the 130 employees. "The Cambodians here work so hard, their co-workers have no choice but to accept them," Collins said. "We try to work hard and be easy to get along with," says Ou Sak, who is learning to sort metals into different grades. "The only hurt feelings are from misunderstandings.". . . "They are decidedly reliable. They are conscientious and they are honest beyond reproach" [says Fred Berman, human resources manager for Peck]. (McGehee 1984)

The positive press comments about refugees continued unabated in the quarter century covered here despite, as noted, only marginal support for refugees in national polls (Simon 1996; Simon and Alexander 1993) and even in a *Times-Dispatch* survey of local residents at the time of the Mariel exodus of 1980 showing that "four out of five Richmonders favored more restrictions on the entrance of Cuban refugees," "three of four believe there should be more restrictions on all prospective immigrants, not just the Cubans," "nineteen percent perceive many of the immigrants as prone to crime or violence," and "twelve percent viewing the Cubans as being Communist rather than as those who fled Communism" (Morris 1980). Those negative public attitudes, however, rarely surfaced in the newspaper's regular stories. Even the occasional negative view that made its way into an article was usually paired with something positive. For example, in the story on the *Times-Dispatch* survey, opposition to immigration was explained this way:

> Economic concerns to a major extent explain why they [Richmonders] view the melting pot as having boiled over. "We have enough unemployment," a Chesterfield County man says. The Cubans, a Henrico County woman says, "should not come at all. I am black, and they will only take jobs away from my people. They should stay in Cuba." A Richmond man adds, "We have accepted too many outsiders already.". . . Yet, the typical Richmond area resident won't seem inhospitable when the first Cuban family arrives here, possibly July 4. The consensus seemed to be that since about 114,000 Cuban refugees have already entered the United States, it's only fair that Richmond offer some of them a chance. (Morris 1980)

While there were articles about refugees that could be characterized as predominantly negative, the number was remarkably small: just 8 out of 124. These negative stories included the piece on the 1980 survey (the only negative story of the year), two 1982 articles on the defeat of a federal effort to house an immigrant detention center nearby, two articles (in 1976 and 1983) detailing all the problems refugees face, two stories in April 1986 on tensions between Cambodians and African Americans living in a dilapidated apartment complex, and another April 1986 story on the mental health disorders from which refugees suffer (prompted by the opening of a refugee mental health office). An EEOC (Equal Employment Opportunity Commission) allegation of suspected overrepresentation of Asians at a local Western Electric plant came only at the conclusion of a 1980 story titled "Refugees Are Finding Success" (Dillon 1980). Even confronted with bad news, as in the report of the murder of a refugee woman by her husband, the story reiterated crucial pieces of the refugee success framework: "Both were extremely hard working people who were determined not to accept welfare benefits" (Bowes 1989). In all, then, press coverage was clearly on the side of refugees, who were depicted as remarkable individuals, welcomed into generous and also remarkable Richmond families, all under the auspices of a broad coalition of local churches and synagogues that constituted a remarkable Richmond community.[12]

Global Conversations in a Parochial Context

In the process of discussing refugees, these press accounts touched on a variety of issues of practical and moral significance to the wider Richmond community. Since Richmond resettlement was very much a traditional, ecumenical effort of Protestants, Jews, and Catholics, it was regularly framed in the language of religious service. In a story on arriving refugees, for example, the head of the Protestant resettlement agency noted a need for a "repeat of that [previous refugee] ministry now" (Campbell 1995); another Protestant-resettled refugee family was described as "under the care of Emmanuel Church at Brook Hill" (White 1994). For Soviet refugees, "each of Richmond's six synagogues agrees to accept an equal number of refugees... who are encouraged, though not forced, to worship and to study Jewish customs" (Slack 1991a). Volunteers, notes one article, are "usually from churches or synagogues" (Lemons 1993). Although a broader set of social service agencies provided support to refugees, religious organizations were understood to be at the core of the effort.

Thus, it is not surprising that the newspaper articles often bore the stamp of religious "witness." Some refugee stories actually appeared in the newspaper's religion section, though retaining structure and content similar to articles appearing elsewhere in the newspapers. On occasion, however, there were stories of a religious conversion or evidence of strong religious faith. One 1979 story, for example, described the experience of a Cambodian who converted to Christianity while in a refugee camp in Thailand, was brought to the United States under the sponsorship of a local Baptist church, and was about to take a leave of absence from his job (with the approval of his employer) to return to Thailand to work in the camps as an interpreter "and care for the sick and carry the dead . . . I felt I was helped. So I feel it is now up to me to help others" (Briggs 1979). Another story described a Romanian evangelical Baptist expelled from his home country for his Christian activism, and who was about to embark on a speaking tour sponsored by a Baptist evangelical organization.

Whether in the religion section or other parts of the paper, these detailed personal narratives, told almost entirely from the perspective of the refugees, offered up global events in a manner fitted quite precisely to the unique and parochial context of this city. Refugees were described as readers' neighbors, fellow churchgoers, schoolmates, or part of a local church or synagogue project. Since the stories were told through the eyes of the refugees, the refugees served as the authoritative source on global events. Russians described the functioning of bureaucracies in the Soviet Union and the meaning of the coup against Gorbachev; Cambodians detailed the horrors of the Pol Pot regime; Bosnians provided commentary on the war in the Balkans. Thus, both personal and global histories were presented through the eyes of refugees. The reporter's formal function was thus simply as the recorder of those linked histories, rather than as interpreter or analyst.

Refugees also provided the opportunity for the receiving community to reiterate its key values. A new life in Richmond had many positive features in refugees' eyes, but the concept of freedom was at the core. Refugees noted that people in Richmond can "have their own home" (White 1994); find it "easier to make a living" (Reynolds 1994); can practice their religion; and even that "American teenagers are lucky that they can disagree openly with their parents" (Harvey 1989). Commented another: "I had never heard of Richmond... [but] I am free here. Freedom is very important to me" (Slack 1991a). Although the definition of freedom was far from precise, its importance was clear:

> Luong Minh Anh equates any assessment of his life as a Vietnamese refugee in a Shenandoah Valley community with his concept of freedom. In conversation—managed with a degree of difficulty—Luong's dedication to his concept of freedom comes across as practically total. Whether he is referring to his $3 an hour job in a poultry processing plant in Dayton, or talking about what life was like in Vietnam, he reflects positively or negatively, an overwhelming concern for freedom. (Hamilton 1977)

Linked to freedom, however, was another core value: self-sufficiency. In the urgency toward self-sufficiency, refugees may partially mirror the concern of resettlement agencies, which regularly offer self-sufficiency as their primary goal. Thus, there were such headlines as "Six Years After the Fall, the Trinhs Are Independent" (Marrow 1981). That goal of self-sufficiency hinges on employment and employment, the articles stress, hinges on work, particularly the success-through-effort formula that is well attuned to a regional business city in a right-to-work Southern state. The refugee story seen in these press accounts, after all, is a variant of the American success-through-effort immigrant story. Thus, service providers quoted in these press accounts were unanimous in stressing that refugees must work, even if at low wages in jobs far below their capabilities. Refugees, at least in these press accounts, might have concerns about their current jobs but likewise recognized them as essential. They might hope, however, for better jobs later on for themselves or for their children. "In Virginia, there are jobs" and since "refugees work hard," the American dream can be reconstructed in a Southern city. Noted one refugee: "This country is a very pleasant country. It still has some problems—discrimination, I mean. But if you work hard and try, you can get the things you want" (Green 1995).[13]

These values of freedom and self-sufficiency often expanded into a broader moral review of Richmond and of America. The breadth of this moral framework appeared in particularly full flow in two editorials in the *Times-Dispatch* in the 1990s. The first, written in 1993 as a follow-up to a major newspaper series on Richmond's racial polarization ("Divided We Stand"), noted the presence of race as a central theme in the city's history, but then placed Richmond in a broader context since "its challenges are not unique. Every place on this good Earth has its divisions—its 'twos.'" Then, the editorial switches to a consideration of a particular Vietnamese refugee:

> Newcomers to the nation, the state, the counties, and the city appreciate virtues long timers take for granted. Paul Tran, owner of Asian Imports at Horsepen and Broad, arrived in Richmond without a dime. Why do he and other immigrants come? "Because freedom is here. [Refugees] want to work very hard and to be successful here. They are happy to have freedom." Diversity and unity can co-exist. Happy families also have their disagreements, their fights. Some persons prefer spicy food, others bland. All like to eat. A civil society seeks a union transcending difference, a cohesive civil society. As Tran implies, in the United States—in Richmond—that unifying force includes liberty, opportunity, equality before the law.

The argument made so strongly for Paul Tran emerged again two years later. In this second case, the refugee, a Muslim from Uganda, had applied for asylum on the basis of political persecution. Nevertheless, the editorial consistently referred to him as an immigrant, thus merging the immigrant and refugee stories. But here the implications of the two stories are indeed similar and the concluding reference to the inscription on the Statue of Liberty equally strong:

> If the inscription still means anything, it means always remembering each immigrant has a tale to tell—not all of them as dramatic as Kaabunga's perhaps, but most of them desperate enough to drive the individual to leave everything he loves and knows. It means remembering every immigrant wants only what every American has (liberty) and

what every American wants (a chance for a better life). It means never forgetting that the United States is often a sword against the darkness and a shield for the unconsoled. And, in this particular case, it means understanding that to send a brave and decent young man back into the murderous maw that spat him out—to send him to certain persecution and likely death—would require nothing less than a heart of stone.

At a time when other areas of the United States were witnessing a sharp reconsideration of legal immigration and refugee resettlement (in addition to the broader concern with undocumented immigration), it was encouraging to see a conservative press in a conservative Southern city take such a strong stand. This is a useful reminder that refugee and immigrant settlement in America is not always accompanied by backlash and community "fatigue." Furthermore, it suggests how important refugees can be as the vanguard in expanding the parameters of diversity. Since they have no reasonable choice but to be in America, cultural accommodation to them must be seen in a more positive light than toward nonrefugee immigrant groups who are less inevitably in America—much less toward those living "illegally" in the country (Chock 1991; Coutin 2003; Coutin and Chock 1995; Diamond 1998; Earle 1999; Espenshade and Calhoun 1993; Espenshade and Hempstead 1996; Haines and Rosenblum 1999).

Refugees as Refugees, as Immigrants, and as Americans

As the refugee stories constructed in the press resonate with core views of Richmond as an economic and moral community, the basic notion of "refugee" is imbued with a range of positive meanings that give it its strength and durability. After all, refugees are a direct connection to the outside world along lines of inarguable moral force, whether as the dispossessed to receive a faith-based welcome or as the victims of despotic governments. But refugees are also a metaphorical connection to the essence of the immigrant experience in America. As in the quoted editorial, then, the notion of "refugee" links together America as sword and shield and America as land of opportunity. What refugees represent is thus perfectly American. When Richmonders (and the press as their self-anointed voice) accept refugees, they not only validate the refugees and the refugee experience for which they stand, but simultaneously self-validate themselves as also perfectly American. This conjoint validation and self-validation is in one sense a fiction that only imperfectly represents the reality of refugee resettlement and that may wither before established categories of race, ethnicity, and class. Nevertheless, the existence of this notion of "refugee"—shown as durable here over a quarter century—provides a conceptual mechanism to encompass, bypass, and supplement other identity categories (such as race) and to do so with the imbuement of a broad range of religious and civic meaning. Consequently, the category of refugee provided this Southern city a ready-made moral construct for accepting newcomers and, because the newcomers were so diverse, a ready-made moral construct for accepting Richmond's expanded racial and ethnic diversity.

This kind of localized American-based appreciation of refugees differs from the more international one. In the international arena, "refugee" is a more decisively and abstractly humanitarian category and the views about actual refugees are sometimes more negative and disappointed. Malkki, for example, in discussing "refugee as a singular category of humanity within the international order of things" (Malkki 1996: 378), notes that refugees are often viewed as "unreliable informants" (1996: 384) and as not true refugees because they do not look or act like "real refugees" (1996: 384). Yet her comments describe a situation of long-term camp experience, a transit without resolution, and thus an incomplete version of "the refugee experience" compared to the accounts of resettled refugees in Richmond. To a limited extent, her equation of the conventionalizing and universalizing of the refugee experience with the dehistoricizing and depoliticization of actual refugees might have some corollary in the situation of refugees in the United States, perhaps to the constraining of refugees within the standard multicultural mosaic that Goode (1998) notes as the major alternative to a harsher emphasis on race or class oppositions. Yet, these Richmond newspaper accounts, and the voice they give to at least part of refugees' actual experience (and quantitatively far more voice than they give to the experience of nonrefugee immigrants such as Koreans and Indians), seem to belie that. Where refugees can indeed be said to fail as refugees in the United States is in their failure to succeed as immigrants. These press accounts, in concluding with stances of hope, are, after all, raising the banner of an "immigrant experience" that is characterized by hard work and palpable rewards for it.[14]

A Durable Story

The most obvious implication of this examination of a quarter century of Richmond press accounts is how durable is the notion of refugee and the kind of action required toward refugees. On a conceptual level, that durability reflects two ways in which the label "refugee" is used: as a category of person who requires special legal and humanitarian attention and as a type of person who has survived the ravages of displacement to aggressively create a new life.[15] In this particular locale, the notion of refugee was further stabilized by the availability of employment (thus, refugees can establish that they are hardworking) by a restrictive state benefits system (so that the potential confusion of *non*working refugees can be avoided), by an active resettlement community (that is itself a framework for much of the civic consciousness reflected in the press), and by a relatively limited number of refugees (thus avoiding the potential development of an "impact" mentality).

This durability of the notion of refugee—and of America as land of refuge—is a positive feature of the Richmond press over the last quarter of the twentieth century. However, the very positive qualities of the refugee label can have negative uses. Thus, it is always possible that refugees can be used as a foil in attacking other minorities who may not be as clearly "energetic" and "hardworking" as refugees are portrayed to be. Furthermore, the positiveness and durability of the notion of refugee often require some blindness to contrary information. For example, an Easter morning story (*Times-Dispatch* 1999) reiterated again the dramatic and positive story of Richmond's refugees but on the same front page of the city section was a discussion of the destruction of the major housing development in which many refugees were living, and which had been hailed as the core of Richmond's "veritable United Nations."

The durability and positiveness of the notion of "refugee" thus do not necessarily come without a cost. In particular, there are disquieting efforts to ensure that the notion remains uncontaminated by "false" refugees who do not deserve the legal status of refugees, by unsuccessful refugees who are somehow not properly energetic, or by refugees who may not have the archetypical refugee experience because, for example, they did not actually flee violence but were processed in their own countries of origin (Frelick 1996). Such problems have much to do with the more negative view that emerges periodically in public discourse about refugees in general (McSpadden 1998; Uehling 1998) or about particular refugees in specific locales (Mortland 2001). Yet, precisely because of such problems and potential negativity, retaining the notion of refugee in its full moral sense is important. It is essential, for example, in avoiding fatigue in the receiving community or a confusion that disables even the possibility of active response to refugees and refugee crises. If one believes that the most persistent need in refugee action is to rescue people, one is likely to be sympathetic to efforts to rescue the clarity of the idea of refugee as well.[16] For the press in Richmond, Virginia, much of the durability of the concept of refugee has to do with a particular local vision of the meaning of being both a Richmonder and an American. This is not an unusual situation and is echoed in other medium-sized cities and perhaps in other smaller U.S. communities in general (Benson 2001). Other places, especially larger gateway cities, are likely to have very different anchors for their ideas of the proper roles of refugees. Farther afield in other countries, there may be greater divergence, with contrary assumptions about the meaning of "refugee," the actions to be taken toward refugees, and the research to be conducted about refugees. In Canada, for example, the lack of extensive undocumented labor migration helped avoid some of the negative connotations to "asylum-seeker" that emerged earlier and more strongly in Europe. Asylum-seekers thus had a somewhat better chance of being seen as "true" refugees in Canada. In Europe, a lack of regular (nontemporary) immigration has sometimes shifted the meaning of "refugee" in other directions. Thus, in Germany, a "true" refugee has generally been a returning German rather than an immigrant or even asylum-seeker (Peck 1995). In Palestine, as well, a true refugee is returning, not immigrating, even if that return is to a place in which the refugee—and perhaps even his or her parents—has never lived (Peteet 1995).

There is much work to be done, then, in untangling how people in different places construct and maintain this vital social and humanitarian idea of "refugee" whether in terms of analysis of the people themselves or of the processes by which people are assigned to particular immigration labels. The shift away from refugee to immigrant identification, for example, has been particularly well analyzed for Central Americans in the United States (Burns 1993; Coutin 1998; Hagan 1994; Menjívar 1999). There is also much work to be done in understanding how personal experience filters into how people use these categories. Rumbaut (1999), for example, has suggested the importance of the personal experiences of researchers, particularly whether they are or are not migrants themselves. The same applies to policy and program people.

Overall, then, "refugee" is one crucial part of a broader range of possible labels that are used in different ways, by different people, for different people. Although sorting out those labels can be an arduous task, it is vital in safeguarding the meaning of this particular label of "refugee," which is central on humanitarian grounds and which also, the Richmond experience suggests, is a label that cuts across race, class, religion, nationality, and ethnicity). Perhaps the most benign of those other labels—especially compared to race and class—is ethnicity. However, as the next chapter suggests, the meaning of ethnicity in the United States is far from clear for many refugees. Furthermore, the hazards of ethnic labels in their home countries may well give them a certain wariness about identity labels in general. How, then, do refugees identify themselves beyond simply being refugees?

Notes

1. There are some inherent limitations in this emphasis on the press in one particular city. The resulting view is parochial and a bit one-sided. Yet, there are also some advantages. One is that attitudes toward refugees often are very parochial. Refugee resettlement is very much a localized process. Another advantage is that, while the view may be one-sided, it provides a very good sense of what is durable in that positive view of refugees. This approach might also serve rather well as a way to compare refugee resettlement in different countries, precisely because it forces the discussion toward localities, local issues, and local moral connections.

2. An extended note on the meaning of "refugee" may be needed. It is not a simple concept though it is often treated as if it were. In abstract terms, the coherence and durability of the notion of "refugee" might be best understood as resting on a mutually validating foundation of the categorical (refugee as a jural category), the typological (refugee as a type of person), and the experiential (refugee as a kind of experience and performance). That intertwining of distinct conceptual domains is not without cost, since atypical experiences are often ignored. Yet, the resulting durability of a strong notion of who refugees are and how they should be assisted works well in directing and sustaining efforts on their behalf by service providers and by many academics as well. Indeed, there is a considerable overlap between popular conceptions (and simplifications) of the refugee experience and academic conceptions (and simplifications) of the refugee experience. This is not to suggest that the refugee experience, and the relatively standard accounts of it that are the focus of this chapter, must be judged as either somehow "real" or somehow simply constructed, thus falling prey to what Bourdieu once characterized as "the most fundamental, and the most ruinous" of the oppositions within the social sciences (Bourdieu 1990: 25).

3. This view of refugees is not at all inconsistent with common academic accounts of refugees. At the risk of an overly long detour, some comment on academic views of the refugee experience may thus be of value as a supplement to the text's discussion of Richmonder views.

The U.S. academic interest in refugees largely coincides with the intersection of post–World War II international and U.S. situations. There was limited attention to DPs and Hungarian refugees, but the large Cuban exodus beginning in 1959 generated considerable academic attention, including by a number of very prominent Cuba-origin sociologists. The Southeast Asian refugee flow beginning in 1975, and the flow of Soviet Jews that accelerated in the 1970s, created in the academic world (as in the governmental one) a more general notion of refugee that transcended the specifics of particular groups. One might pair, for example, the reformulation of disparate U.S. resettlement efforts into a unified refugee program in the Refugee Act of 1980 (that will be discussed in more detail in Chapter 6) and the influential 1981 special issue on refugees of *International Migration Review*. A broad-spectrum notion of refugee was thus in play, and one that tended to assume a fairly clear legal definition of "refugee" in accordance with the United Nations Convention and

Protocol on Refugees. Indeed, that formal U.N. definition of refugees was incorporated into the U.S. Refugee Act of 1980.

However, a somewhat different set of issues emerged with the political and moral debates over Haitian and Central American refugees during the 1980s, raising more prominently the interaction of the sociological analysis of what a refugee might be with the jurisdictional, political one. Generally speaking, academics tended to take a broader, more inclusive view, while the U.S. government was more restrictive, questioning refugee motivations for flight and introducing such notions as "economic refugees." The meaning of "refugee" was thus important but variable. By the 1990s, especially with crises in the Great Lakes region of Africa and the general breakdown in Eastern and Southern Europe, academics interested in refugees tended to broaden their sense of refugee populations and the international and transnational fields through which refugees move (and in which they are often stranded). That broadened sense of refugees and refugee programs can be seen by comparing changes in sequentially matched publications over that period, such as the two special issues on refugees of *International Migration Review* (Gallagher 1986; Stein and Tomasi 1981), the Zuckers' two monographs (Zucker and Zucker 1987, 1996); two volumes in which Loescher has been involved (Loescher 1993; Loescher and Scanlan 1986), and my own edited volumes on refugees (Haines 1985, 1996). The general progression was toward viewing refugees as a general category of migrant, as also occurs in general volumes on immigration (Portes and Rumbaut 1996; Reimers 1992). That category tended to follow governmental decisions about legal status. Somewhat oddly, academics tended to think of refugee admissions in terms of their general sense of the right to refuge, but tended to think of refugee resettlement in terms of those with formal refugee status. For example, when perhaps the most eminent of the Cuba–origin sociologists of immigration themselves discuss refugees, they have tended to emphasize not the effects of the refugee experience itself, but the effects of the provision of legal refugee (or refugee–like) status by the U.S. government (e.g., Portes and Rumbaut 2001).

Nevertheless, other academic work—especially by anthropologists—has been attentive not only to the obvious social and economic aspects of refugee flight, but also to the more cultural aspects of life for people who often came from places with little previous U.S. contact. Academics, for example, have now written a wide range of case studies of particular groups of refugees. Although such accounts may tend to overestimate the internal homogeneity and external boundedness of these refugee populations, with many refugee groups there are quite strong reasons for doing so—the Hmong and Khmer come particularly to mind even though the class divisions among the latter raise some of the thornier problems seen with such sharply heterogeneous refugee populations as the Iranians and the Vietnamese. Academics have also been active in collating such accounts of refugees and of immigrants, whether in the format of "groups" in a particular city (Foner 1987), refugees in the U.S. overall (Haines 1996), particular kinds of interactions in selected cities (Lamphere 1992; Lamphere, Stepick, and Genier 1994), or cyclicity in migration itself (Basch, Schiller, and Szanton Blanc 1994). They have also sometimes aimed simply to provide better access to the rich ethnographic resources represented by academics and practitioners (Baxter and Krulfeld 1997; Mortland 1998) and to the extensive survey research on refugees in the United States (Haines 1989).

In that now vast academic literature on the social, economic, and cultural contexts of refugee movement and resettlement, much of the discussion has been couched in a standard account of flight, transit, and resettlement that echoes classic culture change models (especially when the move between countries is also a transition from rural to urban, preliterate to literate, subsistence to market economies), ritual-like separations from one society and post-liminal reincorporation into a new society, and, most generally, a movement out of "place" and a subsequent return to it. Daniel and Knudsen, for example, see the refugee experience as a "crisis of being . . . invariably accompanied by the erosion of trust" which, with reincorporation into a new society, can be "reconstituted, if not restored" (Daniel and Knudsen 1995: 1). Such accounts of refugees, as of other immigrants and displacees, can err in the direction of essentializing on the basis of a constructed ideal type or experience. Though more sophisticated than Oscar Handlin's (1973) classic compression of the earlier immigrant experience, some sociologists continue to emphasize refugees as a clear type of immigrant. Portes (1997), perhaps the most eminent of the sociologists of immigration—and because of his Cuban background therefore also of refugees more specifically—could still in 1997 note the importance of typologies, criticizing only their theoretical limitations in not postulating the causes or consequences of the typological distinctions. Even those who avoid such typifications still use standard structures in their discussion of refugees. Even Malkki (1995a), who has specifically questioned whether refugee studies is a coherent field of inquiry, nevertheless spends considerable effort to demonstrate how vital is the notion of "refugee" both for those who attempt to apply that label from the outside and for those who attempt to claim that label for themselves (Malkki 1995b).

The production of such generalized accounts of the refugee experience by academics—just as by the press in this Virginia city—is a denial neither of the details of specific refugee experiences nor of the social construction of the refugee process. Yet those in an applied context may be excused for understating the way in which "refugee" is a social construction since they must deal with legal categories that directly affect people's lives. Even in a resettlement context, when the life-or-death issue of refugee status has been resolved, the demands of the practical remain. Those demands of the practical tend to favor descriptive material—refugee accounts as testimony not performances—and to relegate more theoretical issues to the side. What is often missing in these approaches is an appreciation of the conceptual frameworks within which refugees, those who aim to help them, and those who aim to understand them, operate. These frameworks are often analyzed on the general national or moral level (Jacobsen 1996; Keely 1996; Plaut 1995), but it is their workings at the local level that define the operations and ultimately results of the resettlement effort.

It is by this roundabout route that this chapter comes to its review of a set of standard accounts of the refugee experience drawn from a particular set of texts (press accounts) in a particular place (Richmond, Virginia). The purpose is not to accept the accounts as simple testimony about refugees, but to look at the way those accounts are structured in order to understand public attitudes about refugees and to look for clues about the logic of the homologous academic and policy discussions of refugees. In this particular Richmond case, there is enormous stability and durability to the standard refugee account wound around a notion of "refugee" that is part jural category (i.e., refugees have met certain legalistic criteria), part cultural typification (i.e., a refugee is a particular type of person), and part experiential account (i.e., a refugee has a certain set of experiences that demonstrate that he or she is indeed truly a refugee). Each of these supports the other. Thus, as the newspaper stories show, discussions of a refugee's experience demonstrate that a person is indeed a specific type of person (honorable, deserving, hardworking), the type of person a refugee is can help explain the basis for persecution (they stood up on the wrong side of an important issue), and their actual legal status not only certifies that they are "true" refuges but also that the efforts on their behalf are appropriate and worthy.

These ways of knowing that somebody is a refugee have their own logics. Their combination and mutual support have implications for the durability of "refugee" at the most general conceptual level. Suffice it to say that the standard press accounts described in the text reflect a consistency among these three assignment regimes, creating a strong and durable way of identifying people. The label "refugee" thus provides an alternative to other primary categories in American society. The attempt here in terms of the label "refugee" thus runs parallel to Ortner's more general goal in "trying to get a fix on the cultural referential range of these [social] categories, on the one hand, and the relationship between that and (varying) academic uses, on the other" (Ortner 1998: 8). Her concerns are with the primary American trinity of categorization schemes: race, ethnicity, and class (which will receive additional attention in Chapter 4). For her, class (particularly her discussion of "middle-class") is a "broadly inclusive class; indeed . . . almost a national category" (Ortner 1998: 8). In an analogous way, the enduring "refugee" label crosses such other categories as race, ethnicity, and class, thus raising the broader question of the autonomy of immigration categories in American society, underlining the need to look at such labels as part of a broader set of options by which people are assigned to social categories.

These press accounts exist in a particular local context, a Southern one with strong strands of regionalism and lost–cause mythology. But Richmond is also a city where the ideologies of Americanness, community, and religion remain explicitly interfused. The Richmond press accounts reflect those values as they include refugees of varying race, ethnicity, and class. As they do so, they bind essential parts of the civic community in terms of national identity (what Americans are like) and community identity (what Richmonders are like), each on both secular (hard work is good) and religious (service is good) grounds. Although the press accounts deal with a universalistic humanitarian category of refugee, they are thus highly localized in their expression and contingent on features of the local community.

4. In this chapter, numbers on population are drawn from the published reports of the 1990 U.S. census and from the online version of the 2000 census. Numbers relating to employment and language for Virginia are drawn from the 5 percent public use sample (PUMS) but the comparative national numbers on the Asian-origin population are drawn from the published census reports.

5. Richmond's experience mirrors the increased diversity of much of the "Old" and partially overlapping "New" ("Sunbelt") South. Perhaps the most impressive aspect of that increased diversity is its variability in different cities (Fairbanks and Underwood 1990; Miller and Pozzetta 1988). Nevertheless, Tindall's (1995: 5–7) evocation of the unrecognized diversity in his home state of South Carolina and in his later location in North Carolina (1995: 43–46) provide a good sense of the way this diversity has appeared in the South—at least until fairly recently—at a relatively leisurely pace and an absorbable volume. That helps explain the surprise about such diversity. It was only in the late 1990s, for example, that *USA Today* would trumpet that the increase in Asians in the South "can no longer be ignored" (Nasser 1998).

6. The positive economic situation of refugees has been vital to their acceptance in Richmond and thus deserves some additional comment. Census data from 1990 are perhaps clearest regarding labor force participation rates for the period being discussed here, although because of overall numbers the data are adequate only to discussing Cambodians and Vietnamese. Nationally, Cambodians had a labor force participation rate of 46.5 percent, but in both Richmond and northern Virginia the rate was far higher (79.0 percent and 86.1 percent, respectively). Nationally, Vietnamese had a labor force participation rate of 64.5 percent, but in both Richmond and northern Virginia the figure was about 78 percent. This is particularly interesting because of the lack of difference in some other characteristics. In terms of English language competence, 70 percent of Cambodians throughout the country over the age of five reportedly did not speak English "very well," whereas in Richmond and northern Virginia the equivalent figures were 45 percent and 59 percent. This might suggest that the better employment situation reflected better refugee language skills. However, for Vietnamese nationally, 61 percent reportedly did not speak English "very well." In northern Virginia, the rate was virtually the same at 60 percent, but was higher in Richmond at 68 percent.

While the pattern of high employment appears as a general characteristic of Virginia, the sharp differences between the kinds of employment in Richmond and northern Virginia are worth noting. Earnings were lower in Richmond than in northern Virginia for Southeast Asian refugees, but the cost of living, particularly housing, was also lower. Northern Virginia had a higher proportion of refugees in technical and sales jobs, but Richmond had a higher number in the craft/repair and laborer/operator categories. The most telling number is the percentage of refugees in manufacturing jobs in Richmond. There the percentage difference between Richmond refugees and those from other parts of the state was sharp, and one that was not found among other immigrants. My sense—from having been on the board of the major local resettlement agency—is that this largely reflected the job placement resources that the resettlement community could provide.

7. Except for one incident, the now defunct *Afro-American* paid limited attention to refugees and is not covered here. The major weekly newspaper, *Style Weekly*, has had several accounts of refugees, similarly positive, but is not included in this discussion.

8. "Conservative" here refers to general national styles of opinion. The Richmond press did, after all, have a long reputation as a progressive voice on a variety of issues, much like the *Atlanta Constitution*, and has often been noted for that (Grantham 1983: 252; Tindall 1967: 552) and for the presence of "university liberals" on its staff (Dunford 1995; Tindall 1967: 632).

9. Short articles were excluded. "Short" had two meanings. For the period from 1975 to 1987, for which this chapter relies on a listing by Virginia Commonwealth University's (VCU's) Cabell Library, it simply means it was not listed. For the later period, for which computerized listings were available, "short" means less than 400 words. (Such short articles were often simply the mentions of community events.) Articles that used the term "refugee" metaphorically were also not included, nor were cases in which the topic was not substantially about refugees—although it bears mentioning that the "refugee" label was often considered important enough to include as an identifier for individuals, whether musical performers or local school athletes. Appreciation is extended to the *Richmond Times-Dispatch* for making available a list of relevant articles for 1988—a year that was not covered either by the VCU list or by the publicly available computer indexes.

10. The paper also considers itself the de facto state newspaper since Richmond is Virginia's capital.

11. Indeed, there was only one story with a "failing to adapt" kind of headline.

12. Although the concern here is specifically with this press construction of the refugee experience, it is important to reiterate that the press view is not at all inconsistent with other sources on the actual process of resettlement in Richmond. Interviews with refugees and service providers, for example, show only modest divergence from the press accounts. Predictably, the press accounts are more likely to gloss over problems, particularly the difficulties in managing multiple jobs for both parents, and some not fully resolvable differences of race and religion (Breslow et al. 1997; Haines et al. 2001).

13. The comment about discrimination raises the question of how this category of "refugee" stands up to entrenched racial divisions. There are two general ways to consider the relation of refugees to race in Richmond, as elsewhere in the South. On the one hand, one can argue that because refugees are generally not black, they become "honorary whites" (Mormino 1986; Rynearson 2001), and that this is a continuing pattern not only for the South but also in the negotiation of race among immigrants groups in the United States in general (Foner 2000; Ignatiev 1995; Roediger 1991; Sacks 1994). Mormino and Pozzetta (1987: 58) note, for example, that the "solid retrenchment of the black community at the lowest end of Tampa's social and economic scale meant the immigrants entered at a level above at least one major segment of the local society, a fact that proved significant in framing the initial reception and mobility of immigrants" (cf. Grillo 2000; Greenbaum 2002).

On the other hand, one can argue that race is not the only defining issue. In Richmond, for example, refugees are of all races, thus suggesting that this category of refugee cuts across, rather than is secondary to, racial categories. Mormino and Pozzetta even conclude their discussion of Tampa by pointing out that the white community's "consistent efforts" to control Latin-origin immigrants induced a closing of the ranks, producing strongly held feelings of "us" against "them." That is, the fact that Latins were not at the lowest rung of the ladder did not preclude their being in a negative and dichotomous relationship with the white community. This and other more quantitative attempts to look at categories of race and class (Foner 2000; James 1988; Roscigno and Tomaskovic-Devey 1994), also suggest that such racial categories are neither immutable nor unaffected by other social categorizations—a point that receives further discussion from the refugee point of view in Chapter 4.

14. The effectiveness of the refugee label within the American context has much to do with the completion of the standard refugee account as the refugee emerges again into the normally constructed world of place, of moving time, of normal political sovereignty, and of trust (Daniel and Knudsen 1995). But it also has much to do, in more abstract academic terms, with the way in which "refugee" is conjointly a jural category, a cultural typification, and a sequenced set of experiences. Roughly speaking, the category is available to those who are stateless by virtue of official persecution, the type of person is most commonly a mix or intermittent alternation of victim and initiator (victimized by fate but with the initiative to flee that fate and seek another), and the experience is one that in one sense creates and molds the person but in another sense demonstrates the appropriateness of the refugee label as a jural category and a personal type. This triplicity of assignment regimes provides consonance and mutual validation. It does so despite the lack of logical equivalence among these three regimes. The jural assignment, for example, may come at various stages of a refugee's personal history, the essence of being a refugee as a type of person is necessarily created at different stages of that personal history, and the exact experiences of any specific refugee may have many elements that do not conform either to the category or to the type. The criteria by which one conforms to a category, a cultural typification, and a typified experience are not only logically different and potentially inconsistent over all, but also perpetually shifting in and out of synchronization as individuals enter (or leave) a category, approach (or diverge) from a type, and go through (or fail to go through) a sequenced set of formative, substantiating experiences.

The durability of the notion of "refugee" within this particular American context also rests on the way it is connected to the transformation of the true (deserving) refugee into the true (successful) immigrant—here by necessity, successful by effort. It also rests on the cross–validation across logically varying and overlapping assign-ment regimes. "Refugee" is such a natural category precisely because it is not just a category but is rather a culturally imbued jural category, just as it is a jurally extrapolated type of person and a conjointly performative and constitutive personal experience. At the very least, there is here a different register to add to those of race, ethnicity, and class in discussing American society—another example of what a "national category" might be.

Perhaps most importantly, the difference between this positive, durable portrayal of the refugee in Richmond and the more negative one internationally (and in some other places in America) lies with the fruition of the refugee narrative—that resettled refugees have indeed successfully completed the "refugee experience." That completed narrative of a completed journey, in turn, benefits from the availability of the notion of immigrant which can retroactively stabilize and disambiguate the refugee experience as it transduces the refugee back (conflating Heidigger, Bourdieu, and Habermas) into the world as it is, a conveniently renationalized habitus—a field of trust, communicative action, and proper belonging.

15. Although many people have noted the tendency to typify refugees as a kind of person—whether or not they thought that was wise—there has been surprisingly little attention to what such typification actually involves. Mallki does important service in showing the duality of perspective in the Burundi refugee situation between the refugees and the international refugee regime. Yet further distinctions within those groups (to avoid the tendency to drift into dichotomal oppositions) are needed as is more attention to how jural categories, cultural typifications, and conjointly constitutive and substantiating experiences interact in providing durability to such notions as "refugee."

16. From a more abstract academic perspective, again, it is hard to avoid noting the effect of inconsistencies in this intermixing of the categorical, the typological, and the experiential. It is easy to understand how strong the notion can become if the three are aligned and why it is that people would want to shore one element up with another. It is also easy to understand why people would be confused and even angry when the three do not align properly: for example, when people who have the identifiable experience of flight are not legally designated as refugees or when the "wrong" people (such as human rights violators themselves) become legal refugees.

4

Ethnicity's Shadows: Dilemmas of Identity

As newcomers to the United States, refugees struggle to recover from the events that forced them to flee and from the many hazards of their journey. They also embark on a new life, on a second story not of flight but of adaptation. That second story has some very practical demands of work, home, and school and some very predictable problems in reconstituting social networks and reformulating webs of meaning, both of which have suffered in exodus. As the last chapter indicated, that longer-term adaptation to a new life requires participation in a durable American notion of what a refugee is, including how a refugee must also meet the expectations for being a "good" immigrant. Part of being a good immigrant is fitting in, and part of fitting in involves the conventional categories that Americans use to identify themselves and others. Some of those categories are "hard" ones and assignment to them is difficult to avoid, hard to escape, and results in serious discrimination. Race is the classic example; the difficulties of refugees deemed to be black are well known, perhaps especially Haitians— who may well have "suffered more prejudice and discrimination than any other contemporary immigrant group" (Konczal and Stepick 2007: 456). Other identity categories seem, at least on the surface, to be more benign: for example, ethnicity. So, where do refugees fit in ethnic terms? And according to whose ethnic categories is that formulation made? In this issue of ethnic identity, once again the experience of refugees is important not only on its own terms but for what it shows of America. This chapter, therefore, examines the way refugees perceive their ethnic identity, but does so with particular attention to what the refugee experience tells us of how Americans use ethnicity as a way to label people. The discussion begins with a review of ethnicity as one of the major identity categories used in the United States, with particular reference to refugees and other immigrants. The chapter then turns specifically to survey data on the ways in which race, religion, and nationality infuse that category of ethnicity—and sometimes replace it. The results suggest that ethnicity is an oddly American notion and that refugees often have difficulties in assessing their place in this American system of ethnicity. Those difficulties, in turn, reflect back on the realities of the refugee experience, especially the extent to which refugees are often escaping exactly this kind of identity categorization.

Constructing Ethnicity

Over the past century, ethnicity has become a core category of identity in Europe and North America, and in contemporary Western social science as well. As a concept, however, ethnicity is neither stable nor unitary. Scholars often struggle with it. Marcus Banks, for example, begins his review of the concept of ethnicity—a concept that "stubbornly resists definition" (Banks 1996: 10)—with a variety of definitions that have been offered for it. Perhaps the most cautionary comment on his list is the Glazer and Moynihan remark that "one senses a term still on the move" (Banks 1996: 4). Certainly, much of the insurgent value of the term in the early twentieth century as a wedge against the biologistic view of race (Omi and Winant 1986) disappeared in the course of the twentieth century as ethnicity became the reason for many of the same kinds of discrimination—and killing—that had characterized racial distinctions. As ethnicity "escaped from the academy and into the field" (Banks 1996: 199), it has developed new uses not entirely consistent with that early progressive challenge to the fixity of racialized differences. That "escape into the field" may also help explain why the concept is so "muddy" (Omi and Winant 1986). It is, to put it simply, used by different people for different purposes.

Despite its limitations, the notion of ethnicity has the general advantage of conveying a people's uniqueness in a way that provides some potential balance between factors of biology and culture—of nature and nurture—and also a balance between what is passed down over time and what is created anew. Compared with race, ethnicity seems to imply a more humane sense of the cultural aspects of people's lives: their beliefs, language, family lives, social relations, and—most emblematically—their cultural expressions. It also usually implies at least some fluidity, some potential for change. Indeed, one distinction sometimes drawn in the academic literature between racial and ethnic identity is that the former is imposed and the latter is chosen.[1] At the very least, most people would probably agree with the idea that ethnicity is as much created as given. This is not to suggest that ethnicity is not sometimes imposed. The label "Hispanic," Oboler reminds us, is "an English-language term coined in the United States and disseminated primarily by mainstream government institutions" (Oboler 1995: 101). It is also a label that served to homogenize a wide range of people with the effect of eradicating the "impact of particular histories and cultural heritage" (Melville 1988: 68). Perhaps the broader point is that there are quite distinct structural contexts within which ethnicity and particular ethnic labels exist. These kinds of settings for ethnicity (complementary, colonial, competitive, and conflictive in her terms) differ greatly in their power relations (Melville 1988: 76).

Ethnicity is thus variable in its definitions and its settings; those settings, in turn, reflect different vectors and levels of power relations. Yet, especially when compared to race, ethnicity does look rather benign. Indeed, overall, ethnicity seems good.[2] The concept serves as a useful compromise between the inherited and the learned and, we might hope, between how a people see themselves and how others see them. Furthermore, compared with mere lifestyle, ethnicity implies something more enduring and profound, something more widely and deeply shared.[3] The notion of ethnicity as a way to categorize people is especially useful in helping to capture the "peopleness" of immigrant populations[4] who—especially like refugees—represent new migration streams.[5] Until it is possible, for example, to know whether people from Vietnam are Vietnamese or Chinese, whether people from Laos are Lao or Hmong, or whether those from the former Yugoslavia are Bosnian, Serb, or Croatian, it is difficult to develop any coherent understanding of them. To reach an appropriate ethnic label for newcomers thus seems a necessary step for both academic and practical purposes.

Ethnicity as a compromise between nature and nurture, and between the maintained and the newly constructed, often functions well in trying to understand refugees (and other immigrants). It helps the native-born develop a rough framework for identifying who these people really are and which ones of them belong together as reasonably coherent groups. As ethnicity becomes a useful marker for the durable "peopleness" of particular immigrant or refugee groups, it is inevitably built into the very structure of survey research. What reputable study of Southeast Asia ("Indochinese") refugees would fail, as noted in Chapter 1, to break down its findings into categories of Vietnamese, Chinese, Hmong, Lao, and Khmer? What reputable study of refugees from the Balkans would fail to distinguish Bosnians, Croats, Serbs, and Kosovars?

There is now a great deal of survey and ethnographic research that addresses the ethnic identity of refugees and other immigrants. Much continues to focus on the way identity shifts toward becoming fully American in the second, third, or succeeding generations. Despite the frequent criticism of models of assimilation—particularly associated with Milton

Gordon (1964)—much of the work of recent immigration scholars continues to emphasize such shifts in ethnic identity. Portes and Rumbaut, for example, in an attempt to assess ethnic self-identity in the second generation (including both immigrant and refugee groups), structure their argument around four trajectories of ethnic identity: national origin, panethnic, hyphenated American, and American (Portes and Rumbaut 2001: 155–191). That set of categories collapses in much of their discussion to the issue of movement "away from immigrant self-identities and toward American identities" (Portes and Rumbaut 2001: 186). Suárez-Orozco and Suárez-Orozco (2001) walk a similar path in their analysis of immigrant children. For them, as well, the crucial issue involves the trajectories of change for the children, whether they will indeed find some way to balance different components of their ethnic identities, will flee from that identity into a mirroring of mainstream American society and "total identification" with it (Suárez-Orozco and Suárez-Orozco 2001: 103), or will develop a more fully adversarial position toward American society.[6]

Yet, Portes and Rumbaut also note something of the internal flux that underlies these categories, especially when juxtaposed to standard racial classifications. Their second-generation interviewees, for example, often substituted national for racial categories (Portes and Rumbaut 2001: 177). Those findings echo Mary Waters' comments on ethnic identity. As she points out, there is indeed considerable flux and choice in ethnic identity. That flux and choice exist, from her perspective, precisely because ethnicity is based largely on beliefs that people have rather than on their actual biological connections. This is despite the fact that Americans generally believe that "ethnicity is primordial, a personal, inherited characteristic like hair color" (Waters 1990: 17). In the nature/nurture tensions within the concept of ethnicity, she thus sees social scientists as tending toward the nurture interpretation of ethnicity (people learn it), and public opinion tending toward the nature interpretation of ethnicity (people inherit it).

Waters also notes that one of the crucial decisions about ethnicity is "whether to apply an ethnic label to ourselves" at all (Waters 1990: 52). There thus appear to be two rather separate questions about ethnicity: first, whether to be ethnic and, second, if so, what kind of ethnic to be. In the historical work on American immigration, the first question (whether to be ethnic at all) has received considerable attention both for its rise and its decline (e.g., Alba 1990). The literature on recent refugees and immigrants, however, has largely continued a focus on the second question: shifts in kind of ethnic identity particularly from some variant of national origin toward some variant of "American." One recent analysis of second-generation Asian-origin young adults (Zhou and Sao Xiong 2005) suggests mostly a "back and forth" shift between national origin categories (e.g., Chinese) and hyphenated categories (e.g., Chinese-American) with very little choice for being "American" or panethnic in identity (e.g., Asian-American). That finding is corroborated by at least one survey specifically of college students (Weisskirch 2005).

The ways ethnicity works for particular refugee and immigrant populations are quite varied. Sometimes the result is fairly consistent with traditional immigrant patterns of assimilation to the United States. The Vietnamese second generation, for example, has moved rather strategically into the Asian-American mainstream (Zhou and Bankston 1999). In other cases, as with Cambodians, there have been sharper internal tensions as the respective meanings of being Khmer and being American have varied by religion, class, and often difficult conditions in the United States (Mortland 2001; Smith-Hefner 1999). In yet other cases, arriving groups must make choices about which part of American society they will join. There are, for example, some practical advantages for Latin American refugees and immigrants who are not Latino and can lay claim to "Native American" status (Wellmeier 2001). There are also constraints. The academic literature is quite uniform, for example, about the hazards of being a distinguishable racial minority whatever one's national, ethnic, or class status (Waters 1999). There is always the danger that ethnicity becomes little more than a cover for race.[7]

The existing research thus indicates that refugee and immigrant ethnic identity does change, just as it also demonstrates that it endures and recreates itself.[8] We also know that the nature and meaning of ethnic identity vary in different situations. The relative importance of ethnicity itself may vary. What were ethnic distinctions in the home country may become racial in the United States (particularly true for African and Haitian migrants), what were class distinctions may become ethnic ones (particularly true for Latin American migrants), what were national and ethnic distinctions may become religious ones (perhaps especially true recently for Muslims), and what were religious distinctions may become ethnic ones (perhaps especially true for smaller religious groups).[9] In all these cases, the relative balance between choice and imposition of identity will vary. In some cases, there may be quite extensive options and fluidity of identity choices; in other cases ethnic identity may be enforced by outsiders. As one example, the contemporary American university is a particularly fluid setting for identity negotiation and reconfiguration of various kinds, including ethnicity. As Lori Peek notes from her study of Muslim identity, the "campus setting provided space and time to explore their identities and make choices about who they wanted to be and how they wanted to live their lives" (Peek 2005: 227). Much of this exploration takes place in the classroom, whether in learning languages

(Jo 2002) or exploring literature (Vasquez 2005).[10] Ongoing research at a large public university[11] also suggests that students find a distinctive measure of freedom in the university to reconsider issues of ethnicity (and other kinds of personal identity) that were relatively submerged at the high-school level. One crucial aspect of this is the ability to navigate differing kinds and levels of identity. As one student noted in a focus group setting, his high school friends were "Asian Americans of different ethnicities" but only at the university level could he find "a Filipino group, a Chinese club, etc." (Haines 2007a; Haines and Rosenblum 2005; Rosenblum, Zhou, and Gentemann 2009). This student was quite conversant with the conventional American category of Asian-American (with its dual ethnic and racial implications) but now was able to deconstruct that label—indeed parry it—with more focused ancestry considerations.

The result of such deconstruction, however, is not necessarily additive or optative. American-born South Asian students and foreign students from South Asia, for example, rapidly discover that "South Asian" or "Asian Indian" has very different implications for those already subjected to American identity regimes and those coming freshly to them (Gunawardena and Findlay 2005; Kurien 2005).[12] That kind of ebb and flow of home country and U.S. ethnic categories is also clear in the broader literature on diversity in American universities.[13] Such information from university settings is helpful in showing how the meaning of ethnicity can be opened up by students who are both removed from the normal flow of many social pressures—that college is a moratorium, as Erikson (1968) would put it, and also a crucible in the formation of personal identity (Haines and Rosenblum 2005). In this environment, then, there is flexibility about both of the ethnic choices originally noted from the work of Mary Waters: whether to be ethnic and what kind of ethnic to be.

Yet, there is also a third and in some ways more primal question about ethnicity. How does this entire American system of ethnic identity mesh—or not mesh—with the ways in which refugees (and other immigrants) identify themselves at arrival in the United States? Here is a fundamental question not so much about the specific ethnic labels in the United States as about the very nature of ethnicity as a category of American identity. As Patel reminds us,[14] categories and identities emerge "hand in hand" (Patel 2000: 4). Without addressing the basic categories of identity that refugees face, we will miss much of the dynamic of their adaptation. Their identity will remain a cipher. We may well be able to document the durability or loss of a generic national origin label, for example, but never know what that label meant to these refugees. We will also miss the opportunity to learn what the refugee experience in America has to say about the very logic and utility of ethnicity as a system of categorization. That is a particular shame since refugees remain among the very keenest observers of American society.

The Data

Most survey sources that can be readily used for refugee research do not have a sufficient level of detail to address this question of the nature of ethnic identity among recent arrivals. In many cases, this reflects the size of the survey, which simply cannot produce useful information for all but the very largest refugee groups. In other cases (especially the decennial U.S. census), there is adequate detail in even the one percent samples to address the experiences of relatively specific groups of refugees. For some groups, the ability to triangulate census data on country of origin, ancestry, and home language provides a solid basis for inferring what are, at least in general social science terms, rather clear ethnic groups (e.g., people who come from Vietnam but speak Chinese and identify themselves as Chinese). Furthermore, the census has been increasingly flexible in letting respondents choose among multiple categories. With some seven million people choosing mixed identifiers in 2000, there was indeed strong indication that "generation mix" had arrived. Yet, the census data on ethnicity are largely derivative to race rather than to cultural heritage per se. They thus reflect, following Mary Waters, public opinion about ethnicity rather than the social science understanding of it. But what about ethnicity on its own terms? What is the fate of this nature/nurture hybrid when it is not explicitly linked to race?

Some answers to this question about ethnicity on its own terms come from the U.S. government's annual surveys of newly arriving refugees that have been noted in prior chapters. These surveys have been conducted in some fashion or other since 1975,[15] and have been used for a variety of analyses of refugee economic status and social change ever since.[16] Although the specific details of each year's survey vary somewhat, they are all drawn as formal national samples from lists of recently arrived refugees, with phone interviews each year of about 1,200 refugee households, yielding information on about 6,000 refugees. For the two survey years that will be discussed in more detail in the following text, for example, there is information on 7,303 individuals for 1995 and 5,774 individuals for 2001. The surveys at that time were set up so that those interviewed for the first time in a particular year were then tracked through an additional four years. That panel design is not particularly crucial for the kinds of analysis here, since the 1995 and 2001 surveys are effectively independent samples, but the continuity in how people identify themselves ethnically over time (which appears in the entire set of surveys) does suggest some durability to notions of ethnicity and helps obviate concerns that shifting standards of implementation in different years might yield shifting results—for example, when there is a change in the contractor conducting the survey or in the staff hired for interviewing and translation.[17]

A methodological warning is in order. These surveys do have limitations. They have tended to be used for relatively basic assessments of refugee economic status: whether refugees are working, going to school, using public assistance, etc.[18] However, for the present purposes, these surveys have two vital advantages. First, they inquire about ethnicity in a particularly open and unscripted way. They have simply asked people for their ethnic identification and then coded the answers that the interviewers were given.[19] (While the interviewers had access to some precoded categories, that did not constrain them to use only those categories.) The results may not have the finesse of more detailed ethnographic material, but they do provide perhaps the best available "fresh take" on how the logic of ethnicity appears to a particularly diverse set of newly arriving refugees. The second key advantage is that the specific question about ethnicity follows two other questions about country of birth and country of citizenship. Although this might tempt respondents to think of ethnicity as different from country of origin and citizenship—that ethnicity is necessarily something more specific or less political, for example—the benefit lies with ethnicity clearly distinguished from the descriptive facts of place of birth and country of citizenship. That clarification is especially reassuring given the potential problems in translation.[20] By the time refugees were asked about ethnicity in the survey, they were at least clear that the answer to the question was not solely a descriptive one about where they came from in either a geographical or legal sense.

Ethnicity as Ethnicity

As a starting point for this discussion, consider the overall responses given to the question about ethnicity in the 1995 and 2001 surveys. Those two years are sufficiently far apart in time so that they are separate samples given the five-year built-in attrition in the longitudinal part of the survey design. Furthermore, those two years represent very different sets of refugees. The 1995 survey, for example, represents the last major wave of Southeast Asian refugees, while the 2001 survey provides information on a far greater number of African arrivals. These are, in effect, two quite different slices of refugee diversity.[21]

The data from the 1995 survey are provided in Table 4.1. Most of the answers given by respondents represent clear and traditional "ethnic" answers: Afghan, Albanian, Cambodian, Chinese, Ethiopian, and so on.

Table 4.1 Reported ethnic origins (1995)

	NUMBER	PERCENT		NUMBER	PERCENT
Refuse to answer	7	0.1	Kurd	25	0.3
Don't know	9	0.1	Kyrgiz	1	0.0
			Korean	1	0.0
Afghan	40	0.6	Lao	60	0.8
Azerbaijani	9	0.1	Liberian	36	0.5
Albanian	4	0.1	Moldavian	20	0.3
American	66	0.9	Mien (Laos)	7	0.1
Armenian	108	1.5	Mordvin	1	0.0
Assyrian	2	0.0	Muslim	41	0.6
Bosnian	116	1.6	Muluba	8	0.1
Burmese	5	0.1	Mexican	1	0.0
Byelorussian	61	0.8	Orthodox	1	0.0
Bulgarian	14	0.2	Polish	1	0.0
Cambodian	12	0.2	Romanian	26	0.4
Chinese	13	0.2	Russian	399	5.5
Chuvash	1	0.0	Rwandan	1	0.0
Croatian	8	0.1	Somalian	136	1.9
Cuban/other Hispanic	150	2.1	Serbian	5	0.1
Ethiopian	55	0.8	Sudanese·	4	0.1
Georgian	4	0.1	Tat	2	0.0
German	5	0.1	Ukrainian	379	5.2
Greek	4	0.1	Uzbek	6	0.1
Haitian	214	2.9	Vietnamese	2,959	40.5
Hmong	441	6.0	White	10	0.1
Iranian	39	0.5	Yugoslavian	5	0.1
Italian	1	0.0			
Iraqi	83	1.1			
Jewish	1,697	23.2	**Total**	7,303	100.0

Note: Percentages do not sum to 100 because of rounding.

Many of these answers might appear to be national labels—yet the respondents had already been asked about their nationality, so their answers to this question would seem to imply some more cultural identification. Furthermore, based on background information about the refugees and other survey responses (e.g., the responses to the prior questions about country of birth and citizenship), many of these labels turn out to stand in contrast to nationality. Thus, there are 13 "Chinese," but review of the data (not shown in the table) indicate that none are from China; rather all are from Vietnam. As another example, there are many refugees from Laos, but the category "Laotian"—the appropriate national label—does not appear on the list at all.

There are indeed 60 "Lao" but that designation is quite specifically an ethnic one for people from lowland Laos who speak Lao as their native tongue. To know the number of refugees from Laos—those who would be Laotian by nationality—requires adding to those 60 ethnic Lao the 441 Hmong (the main Laotian highland group in the United States) and the 7 Mien (another highland group from Laos). Similarly, the 25 Kurds might well like to think theirs is a national label, but the country of birth and origin for all of them in this survey is Iraq. As a final example, the 4 Albanians are not from Albania, but from Kosovo.[22] These cases are hardly surprising. Indeed, they represent ethnicity as conventionally understood, a "peopleness" that may coincide with national labels but is nevertheless distinct from those labels.

Table 4.2 presents the responses from the 2001 survey. Again, there are Chinese who are not from China, but from Vietnam. Again, those from Laos appear in ethnic terms as 22 Lao and 65 Hmong (and no Mien). The 49 Kurds are again all from Iraq. The Albanians (now 100 of them) are all from Kosovo. But the 2001 survey population also has some differences. In particular, there is a sharp increase in African refugees. For many of them, ethnicity is given as nationality. There are some continuing groups such as Ethiopians (104 in this survey compared with 55 in the 1995 survey), but also new populations: 60 Liberians, 4 Nigerians, 18 Rwandans, 8 Sierra Leoneans, 282 Somalians, 130 Sudanese, and 13 people from Togo. In many of these cases, paradoxically, refugees are using a national label in place of what might be expected as an ethnic one. Yet, in other cases, African refugees use exactly the tribal and language identities that would be expected in response to a question about ethnicity. Thus there are 6 Dinka from the Sudan, 2 Gambai and 1 Moosi from Chad, and 1 Kissi and 2 Kono from Sierra Leone.

This African case is particularly instructive since it raises again the issue of options in ethnic identification—that people might well choose nationality as ethnicity even though they have an alternative ethnic label. Or, that they might choose an ethnic or tribal label even when they could use a national one. That kind of choice reflects the dynamics of the home country and the very forces that resulted in their flight as refugees. That choice also reflects refugee perceptions of the nature of the United States and what kinds of label might be most appropriate, or at least acceptable, to Americans. Thus, although the respondents can make a choice, that choice lies at the interstices between two quite different regimes of power: a home country that forced them to leave often precisely because of their identity, and a resettlement country that is imposing on them its own frameworks of identity.

Choices like the above between ethnicity as ethnicity and nationality as ethnicity will be discussed later on in this chapter, but the discussion here

Table 4.2 Reported ethnic origins (2001)

	NUMBER	PERCENT		NUMBER	PERCENT
Refuse to answer	11	0.2	Iranian	97	1.7
Don't know	32	0.6	Iraqi	41	0.7
			Jewish	497	8.6
Afghan	53	0.9	Kurd	49	0.8
Albanian	100	1.7	Kissi (Sierra Leone)	1	0.0
American	11	0.2	Kono (Sierra Leone)	2	0.0
Armenian	118	2.0	Kosovar (Albanian)	157	2.7
Arab	1	0.0	Lao	22	0.4
Assyrian	11	0.2	Lithuanian	4	0.1
Bahai (Iran)	3	0.1	Liberian	60	1.0
Bosnian	1,010	17.5	Moldavian	67	1.2
Burmese	44	0.8	Macedonian	2	0.0
Byelorussian	65	1.1	Moosi (Chad)	1	0.0
Bosnian-Muslim	1	0.0	Muslim	151	2.6
Bulgarian	20	0.3	Nigerian	4	0.1
Cambodian	6	0.1	Romanian	20	0.3
Congo (Zaire)	4	0.1	Russian	339	5.9
Chinese	21	0.4	Rwandan	18	0.3
Chaldean	5	0.1	Sierra Leonean	8	0.1
Christian	3	0.1	Somalian	282	4.9
Creole	4	0.1	Serbian	68	1.2
Croatian	52	0.9	Sudanese	130	2.3
Cuban/other Hispanic	786	13.6	Tatar (Russia)	1	0.0
Dinka	6	0.1	Togo	13	0.2
Ethiopian	104	1.8	Ukrainian	670	11.6
Gagauz (Moldova)	5	0.1	Uzbek	1	0.0
Gambai (Chad)	2	0.0	Vietnamese	472	8.2
German	3	0.1	Yugoslavian	30	0.5
Haitian	21	0.4			
Hmong	65	1.1	**Total**	5,774	100.0

turns first to the use of two other crucial kinds of identity that respondents mentioned when asked about their ethnicity. Those are religion and race. Both are often crucial to how refugees were identified in their home countries and how they will be identified in America.

Religion as Ethnicity

In the 1995 survey (see the top half of Table 4.3), nearly one in four people identified by religion in response to the question about ethnicity. The

Table 4.3 Religion reported as ethnicity (1995 and 2001)

	NUMBER	PERCENT
1995 survey		
Jewish	1,697	23.2
Muslim	41	0.6
Orthodox	1	0.0
Total		23.8
2001 survey		
Bahai	3	0.1
Bosnian-Muslim	1	0.0
Chaldean	5	0.1
Christian	3	0.1
Jewish	497	8.6
Muslim	151	2.6
Total		11.5

overwhelming majority of these were Jews. While there is a long-standing and expansive literature on the unique nature of "Jew" as a religious, ethnic, and racial label in Euro-American society,[23] nevertheless this represents a disjunction with the usual U.S. government-based identity categories that exclude religion and instead anchor ethnicity to race. So, the "ethnic" identities of these 1,697 Jews deserve consideration. These refugees arrived from Russia and other parts of the former Soviet Union. Being Jewish is wound into the reasons for their exodus—and indeed even into the legislative modifications to U.S. refugee law that give them special presumptive claim to refugee status. So, the existence of refugees identifying themselves as Jewish by ethnicity is hardly surprising. However, it is also the case that there were many refugees from that same general region who identified themselves as Byelorussian, Moldavian, Russian, and Ukrainian. At least some of these were probably Jews. This raises again the issue of choice. Religion as ethnicity is not the only option these refugees have, especially given the very mixed degree of religiosity among Jewish refugees from the former Soviet Union.

It is not only Jews, however, who proffer religion as ethnicity. There are also Muslims. For the 1995 survey, 41 of the refugees identified ethnically as Muslim. As it turns out in this case, all these Muslims were from the Balkans and most from Bosnia. The converse, however, was not true. There were also 116 people from Bosnia who identified themselves simply as "Bosnian" by ethnicity (as shown in the prior Table 4.1). Among them were certainly some Muslims. In subsequent years of these annual refugee surveys, a new identity category was actually created for "Bosnian-Muslim." This did not ultimately resolve the ambiguity but merely expanded the number of options. Thus some refugees from Bosnia continued to identify themselves ethnically as "Bosnian" and many continued to identify themselves ethnically as "Muslim." By the 2001 survey (see bottom half of Table 4.3), there was only 1 person using this hybrid category of Bosnian-Muslim, whereas there were 151 people identifying ethnically as Muslim, with 1,010 identifying ethnically as Bosnian (as shown in the prior Table 4.2).[24]

In 2001 overall (see the bottom half of Table 4.3), these two components of religion as ethnicity (Jews from the former Soviet Union and Muslims from the Balkans) continued. Jews were a smaller part of the survey population in 2001 and, as before, there were probably at least some Jews who identified themselves as Byelorussian, Russian, Moldavian, or Ukrainian. Those identifying themselves ethnically as Muslims in 2001 were still largely from the Balkans (although with a single Muslim-identified family from Kenya). In the 2001 survey, however, there were also a few other cases of religion used as ethnicity. There were three individuals identified ethnically as "Christian." (They were members of a single family from Bosnia.) There were also five Chaldean Christians, all from Iraq. Finally, there were three Baha'i from Iran. The cases are not numerous, but they hint at the ways religion filters into ethnic identity. Unfortunately, these data, like those on Jews and Muslims, cannot address the alternative case of when Christian, Chaldean, and Baha'i refugees did *not* filter their religion into ethnic identity. Nevertheless, even these few cases from the survey data suggest the importance of religion and how it occasionally emerges from the shadows of ethnicity to be claimed as ethnicity itself. The historical and sociological bases for that choice are extremely clear in all these cases. For Jews from Russia and Eastern Europe, Baha'is and Christians from the Middle East, and Muslims from the Balkans, ethnicity and religion are intertwined. In all cases ethnicity diverges from nationality, does so based on religion, and that very difference is at the core of why these refugees left their home countries.

Race as Ethnicity

In the U.S. census, as in much other American governmental and social science reporting, ethnicity is technically a subcategory of race—or an extension of being Hispanic/Latino. These annual surveys of refugees raise the intriguing counterpossibility that race for many refugees might be better considered as a subcategory of ethnicity. Table 4.4 provides the cases in which the survey question on ethnicity yielded a clear racial answer. The percentages are not high, but the cases are instructive. In 1995, 10 people identified ethnically as "White." This number grew to 148 in 1996. During

Table 4.4 Race reported as ethnicity (1995–2002)

	NUMBER	PERCENT
1995 survey		
White	10	0.1
1996 survey		
Black	10	0.1
Mulatto	4	0.1
White	148	1.9
1997 survey		
Black	10	0.1
Mulatto	4	0.1
White	143	2.0
1998 survey		
Black	10	0.1
Mulatto	4	0.1
White	131	1.8
1999 survey		
Black	8	0.1
Creole	3	0.1
White	89	1.6
2000 survey		
Black	8	0.2
Creole	4	0.1
Mulatto	2	0.0
White	41	0.8
2001 survey		
Creole	4	0.1
2002 survey		
Black	45	3.0
Creole	3	0.2
Mulatto	1	0.1
White	22	1.6

this same period, some other refugees (although fewer) identified ethnically as "Black." All those identifying themselves as White or Black during this period were from Cuba. These early surveys thus suggest a single country of origin with a racial dynamic so strong as to overtake what would normally be the expected "ethnic" label of Cuban—or possibly "Hispanic/Latino" for those Cubans familiar with U.S. ways of classifying people.

Over the next several years, a somewhat different dynamic emerged in regard to race. There was, for example, a new category of "Creole" used by refugees from Sierra Leone. In addition, the meaning of "White" and

"Black" also changed. This is most clearly seen in the 2002 survey. There were still 22 people identifying ethnically as "White," but only 2 of them were Cuban. The other 20 were from the Balkans. Finally, that year there were 45 individuals identifying ethnically as "Black," but none were from Cuba. Instead, 2 were from Haiti and the other 43 were from the Sudan. All these uses of race as ethnic identifier have clear historical grounding. The importance of race in Cuba, for example, has been widely noted. The identification of those from the Balkans as "White" doubtless reflects shifting categories there, including the very volatile nature of religion as a marker of identity. Race may seem, in contrast to religion, relatively benign.

The number of cases in which race is chosen as ethnicity is small, and rather smaller than the number of cases in which religion is chosen. In particular, "Black" only emerges in the cases of Cuba and the Sudan. For the former, race has much the same meaning as in the United States, although with the twist that it is to be in the economically underprivileged majority rather than minority. In the Sudanese case, to be Black means to *not* be tribal, to *not* be southern, and to *not* be Muslim. These uses of race as ethnicity are thus quite instructive about how complicated a racial classification can be in terms of its underlying regional, class, and religious basis. Race, it would appear, is often a good way to explain who you are in cultural terms (rather than simply physical ones). Race is thus appended to ethnicity rather than the reverse. The small number of cases here, however, suggests that race may be less important as a self-identifier for refugees than is religion—at least outside a North American context in which race is greatly privileged, fortified, and continually reimposed as a primary system of personal identity.

Nationality as Ethnicity

Another kind of identity that can emerge as ethnicity is nationality. After all, many of the ethnic labels that emerge in these surveys can serve dual purposes as nationality and as ethnicity. "Vietnamese," for example, can function both as a national and as an ethnic marker. When national and ethnic markers diverge, however, choice is possible. There may, for example, be important reasons to choose a national label and thereby suppress alternative ethnic, religious, or racial identities. Certainly some of the refugees from Russia and other countries of the former Soviet Union who identify themselves ethnically with a national label are, nevertheless, Jewish and their status as refugees depends on that assertion. This simple survey question about ethnic identity thus requires some cognitive sorting by the respondents of various potential answers to the question. Answering with nationality is thus not a neutral, natural, or inevitable response but a reflexive, optative, and even strategic one. Refugees from the Sudan provide an example. In the 2002 survey, they identified themselves in various ways. One person from the Sudan identified as Nuer and 39 as Dinka. Those are quite conventional ethnic (and tribal) labels.[25] Another 43 were Black, suggesting that they were non-tribal but also not Muslim. (This is an interesting case in which a racial label is more religious and regional in meaning than racial in the standard sense.) But 96 were "Sudanese" in answer to the question about ethnicity. Thus, nationality for these Sudanese was one possible kind of answer when asked about "ethnicity." As another example, refugees from Iran sometimes identified themselves ethnically as "Iranian," but they also sometimes identified themselves as Baha'i, Arab, or Assyrian, drawing on a very broad spectrum of religious, panethnic, and heritage options in assessing the meaning of ethnicity.

One especially intriguing use of nationality as ethnicity can be seen in the cases in which people in these surveys were identified as "American." For the 1995 survey, there were 66 such cases. Perhaps not surprisingly, all these "Americans" were young children. They were, in fact, being identified as ethnically American by their parents.[26] Furthermore, they were all U.S.-born, U.S.-citizen children. Their nationality was thus clearly American. The interesting question, however, is why American nationality was viewed as important enough to override ethnicity. Having already noted in the survey that these children were U.S. born and U.S. citizens, parents continued after those answers to add that the children were also American by ethnicity. Once again, then, nationality assumes priority over actual ethnicity.

This attribution of American ethnicity to young children based on their nationality (by birth and by citizenship) merits some additional attention. To reiterate, in all 66 cases for 1995, those identified as "American" were U.S.-born, U.S.-citizen children. All were under five years of age. However, the reverse was not the case. Not all U.S.-born, U.S.-citizen children under the age of five were identified ethnically as "American." Parents were making a choice. Some were saying U.S.-born/U.S.-citizen means American by ethnicity as well; others were saying U.S.-born/U.S.-citizen does not change a child's ethnicity from that of the parents. The question they were answering—and one that will resonate throughout their children's lives— was, in the Vietnamese case, whether Vietnamese father and Vietnamese mother means Vietnamese child or whether U.S.-born/U.S.-citizen means American child irrespective of the ethnicity of the parents.

In the 1995 survey, this decision about the ethnicity of children was made with differing frequency by different groups (see Table 4.5). Leaving aside populations with very small numbers of U.S.-born children, the proportion of young children identified as "American" (versus those identified as the

Table 4.5 Reported ethnicity of U.S.-born children (1995)

PARENT'S ETHNICITY	CHILDREN ARE SAME AS PARENTS	CHILDREN ARE "AMERICAN"	TOTAL	PERCENT "AMERICAN"
Albanian	2	0	2	0
Armenian	1	2	3	67
Bosnian	1	0	1	0
Bulgarian	0	1	1	100
Byelorussian	4	1	5	20
Cuban/other Hispanic	1	0	1	0
Ethiopian	0	2	2	100
Haitian	3	5	8	63
Hmong	65	1	66	2
Iraqi	2	4	6	67
Jewish	27	3	30	10
Kurd	1	0	1	0
Lao	0	2	2	100
Liberian	0	1	1	100
Moldavian	2	0	2	0
Mien (Laos)	2	0	2	0
Mexican	1	0	1	0
Russian	21	4	25	16
Ukrainian	15	9	24	38
Vietnamese	28	31	59	53
Total	176	66	242	27

same ethnicity as their parents) ranged from over 50 percent for Vietnamese to under 2 percent for Hmong. Aside from Vietnamese, Ukrainians were the only other sizable group with a high proportion identified as "American" (38 percent). However, even the scattered numbers of smaller groups with some children identified as "American" suggests this was not an isolated choice affecting only some groups. Nearly a third of all young U.S.-born children were identified as "American." By 2001 (see Table 4.6), the overall proportion of U.S.-born, U.S.-citizen children identified as "American" had dropped sharply. This partly reflects the decreased number of Vietnamese. However, Ukrainians again had a relatively high percentage (12 percent), although the percentages for both Moldavians (14 percent) and Bosnians (25 percent) were higher.[27]

The attribution of nationality as ethnicity to young children is at the limits of what these particular survey data can be asked to provide. One

Table 4.6 Reported ethnicity of U.S.-born children (2001)

PARENT'S ETHNICITY	CHILDREN ARE SAME AS PARENTS	CHILDREN ARE "AMERICAN"	TOTAL	PERCENT "AMERICAN"
Afghan	2	0	2	0
Albanian	3	0	3	0
Armenian	2	0	2	0
Bosnian	12	4	16	25
Bulgarian	1	0	1	0
Burmese	2	0	2	0
Byelorussian	0	0	0	0
Cuban/other Hispanic	6	0	6	0
Hmong	2	0	2	0
Iranian	1	0	1	0
Jewish	10	0	10	0
Kurd	5	0	5	0
Lithuanian	1	0	1	0
Liberian	1	0	1	0
Moldavian	6	1	7	14
Muslim	3	0	3	0
Russian	0	0	0	0
Somali	11	0	11	0
Sudanese	11	0	11	0
Ukrainian	30	4	34	12
Vietnamese	6	0	6	0
Zairian	1	2	3	67
Total	116	11	127	9

might argue that the number of refugees making this choice of "American by ethnicity" for their children is small. However, at least in 1995, the overall proportion is high (27 percent) and for at least some groups the proportions are quite high across different survey years (particularly Vietnamese and Ukrainians). One might also ask, on a more methodological level, whether these young children might really be "American" in a more standard ethnic sense—that, for example, they might be members of mixed households of children from different marriages that included an actual "American" parent. However, an examination of the full household rosters for these children does not support that view. The children in all cases were living with defined kin links to parents and other relatives, none of whom was identified as "American" in ethnicity.[28] Finally, it might be argued that the identification of these children as "American" in ethnicity is some kind of confusion about the meaning of ethnicity. Yet, that is precisely the point of this chapter's discussion: that there is indeed "confusion" about the meaning of ethnicity and that such confusion is likely to be greatest among the newly arrived. If we are only to allow "appropriate" responses to questions about ethnicity, we will, in effect, be policing ethnicity rather than trying to understand it—just as survey requirements to identify race become part of an overall regime enforcing standard racial conventions on citizen and newcomer alike.

Ethnicity's Shadows

This discussion, based on a rather open-ended survey inquiry about ethnicity to a quite diverse set of relatively new refugee arrivals, has suggested that the U.S. notion of ethnicity overlaps with other key kinds of identity. For these particular refugee newcomers, that overlap is most extensive with nationality, but it also occurs with religion and race. The overlap is extensive enough that nationality, race, and religion are on some occasions substituted for ethnicity as "ethnic identity." These seeming shadows of ethnicity thus often put ethnicity in their own shadow. That they do so has much to do with their intrinsic importance. It also has much to do with the limitations of ethnicity as a concept and with the dangers that occur when ethnicity becomes all too salient as a category—when it becomes viewed, following Waters, as "primordial." One final set of findings from these surveys illustrates these points.

In these surveys, as in almost all surveys, respondents sometimes did not answer questions. Sometimes refugees did not answer the question about ethnicity. There was thus "missing data." For these surveys, there were two categories of missing data. The first of these was generated by the response of "don't know." That particular nonresponse suggests that the notion of ethnicity was not clear in general to the refugees, or at least not clear in relation to their specific situation. Those responding "don't know" were at least partly contesting the logic of the question. Looking at the 1995 data (see again Table 4.1), it appears that the number of those responding "don't know" is very small. The figure might not merit attention if this were just an occasional response by refugees from many different countries. But it was not. Instead, those saying "don't know" were uniformly from the former Soviet Union and Yugoslavia. In subsequent years, the numbers in this "don't know" category were much higher (35 in 1996; 37 in 1997; and 32 in 1998).[29] These "don't know" responses might suggest some confusion about what ethnicity means when nationality and religion clash, but they also reflect a natural confusion attendant on the collapse and shift of national borders. "Don't know" is thus a reminder that such categories of identity as ethnicity are subject to flux, and that such flux may be so severe as to render the category ambiguous, and perhaps even meaningless.

Perhaps even more instructive is the second kind of missing data. Some survey respondents simply "refused to answer." Why would anyone refuse to identify themselves according to this quite sanitized American notion of ethnicity? The answer again involved those from the former Soviet Union and Yugoslavia. The number doing so in 1995 was small but in succeeding years was high (43 in 1996; 39 in 1997; and 38 in 1998). In this case, Bosnians represent the major segment of the "missing" data. It is thus useful to reframe these numbers in terms of all responses about ethnicity given by Bosnians. Thus, of those from Bosnia in 1996, 63 identified themselves as Bosnian, 182 as Bosnian-Muslim, 4 as Muslim, and 15 as other Balkan (Croatian and Serbian).[30] In addition, 31 refused to answer and 10 "didn't know." Thus, overall, 13 percent of those from Bosnia either refused to answer or "didn't know." "Missing data" thus became a significant response category. That represents the ambiguity of the categories—their inadequacy to the complex interplay of elemental social categories of nationality, religion, and even race. Ethnicity for Bosnian refugees echoes with the collapse of Yugoslavia. These "missing data" reflect very well the malign face of ethnicity as it spreads to the point of "ethnic cleansing."

This Bosnian refusal to answer may be the most extreme statement in these surveys about ethnicity, but it is hardly the only set of survey responses that challenges the logic, utility, or even courtesy of using ethnicity as a way to categorize people. Clearly, race and religion can substitute for conventional social science notions of ethnicity. Frequently, nationality can also do so. The attribution of "American" ethnicity to some U.S.-born, U.S.-citizen children is particularly instructive. For those who know the research on Vietnamese in America, it will be very easy to appreciate how some Vietnamese parents would see their children as "Vietnamese" and others would see them as "American." The Vietnamese refugee influx was, after all, profoundly political and the homeland has been both culturally primal but politically reprehensible (Nguyen and Haines 1996). To label a child as "American" does not merely reflect a desire to have them belong to the new country, but to also put them beyond the reach of a detested political regime. To label them as "Vietnamese" might imply national sovereignty rather than cultural connection. Likewise, those who know the research on Jews from Eastern Europe or Muslims from the former Yugoslavia would readily appreciate why some parents would designate their children as "American" and for themselves reject the very notion of ethnicity, seeing it as inexplicable, objectionable, or dangerous. There were actually a few cases in the survey of parents who identified themselves as Jews but who identified their children as ethnically American. This makes good sense if one recognizes that in seeking to avoid a religious label for their children, they might well find home country national labels unacceptable since they invoke the very states responsible for their persecution. Thus, the only available neutral choice would be "American." It is also very much a choice for the future over the past.

While much of the information provided in this chapter is consistent with the broader ethnographic literature on refugee identity formation in the United States, it is nevertheless helpful to see these very differently situated refugee stories reflected together in surveys that capture both the patterns of identity and even something of the cognitive dimensions of identity choice. The data provide a reminder of how arbitrary is the sanitized semi-cultural, semi-racial Euro-American notion of ethnicity. That, in turn, serves as a warning that preconceived notions of ethnic identity may undermine the ability of refugees to tell us who they are and how they mix and match, reject and absorb, ignore and modify the identity labels and categories that so readily ensnare the native-born—including, inevitably, their own children. As refugees operate conceptually in the spatial and temporal interstice between the countries that forced their departure (and challenged their very identity) and a United States that seeks to impose its own identity categories, they are in a unique position to tell us something about the logic and force of two very different identity regimes. In the survey data used here, they have the opportunity to speak from the breach as much by accident as by design. Their varied choices about ethnic identity serve as a warning that those who try to understand the refugee experience may sometimes drift toward becoming the enforcers of orthodox identity categories rather than questioning the meaning and utility (and courtesy) of those categories. We may then effectively be interrogating the people on behalf of the categories rather than interrogating the categories on behalf of the people. For the refugees themselves, the imposition of such social categories—or the imposition of the melded notion of refugee as successful immigrant discussed in the last chapter—is likely to have broad effects. Sometimes those effects will be positive and sometimes negative. Sometimes the effects will vary even within a household, with parents identified as refugees (or refugees from a particular country) but the children identified as members of more conventional ethnic or racial groups. The very certainty and durability of these American ways of labeling people often produce for refugees yet additional uncertainties in their lives in America. Against those uncertainties, their major fortification is the family, the focus of the next chapter.

Notes

1. Jenkins (1997: 44–50) provides a useful sequential discussion of these two separate polarities of culture and biology, and the primordial versus the instrumental (distinctions that he sees as homologous to some degree), and for the specific point about race as imposed and ethnicity as chosen.

2. Jenkins (1997: 49) also supports the notion that "the anthropological celebration of ethnicity is a 'good thing.'" Hirschman (2004), as another example, makes the same argument from the inverse perspective that even at its very worst as ethnocentrism, it is still positive in comparison to racism. Nevertheless, the critique that ethnicity (and ethnocentrism) may effectively recreate race (and racism) also has its supporters—for example, Grosfoguel (2004).

3. On the one hand, then, ethnicity seems humane, flexible, and certainly not racist, even though the enduringness of ethnicity almost always hinges on both cultural and biological transmission. Culture, after all, travels especially well along bloodlines. On the other hand, ethnicity conveys a quite durable notion of a "peopleness," even though we also know how often ethnicity is created, shaped, reshaped, invented, denied, imposed, rejected, negotiated, argued, and sometimes just ignored.

4. Omi and Winant (1986) stress the importance of an immigrant analogy in the very development of the concept of ethnicity, for it was immigrants who initially raised the questions of the possibility of change and thus the need for a kind of identity that was mutable.

5. Ethnicity often carries the sense of "peopleness" that used to be adduced by the word "nation" (before that notion was wedded to the state). As an example, refugee law says nothing about persecution for "ethnicity," but only for race, religion, *nationality*, political opinion, or membership in a particular social group.

6. Karakayali (2005) provides a useful critique of the long-standing tendency to frame problems of the second generation according to a notion of children living in "two worlds." His own work on early immigrant autobiographies suggests that this notion of two worlds—although not corresponding particularly to the experience of children—was nevertheless absorbed into their writing due to its pervasiveness as a concept in the society at large.

7. Consider, for example, the phrasing of a recent review of ethnic relations that begins with "Throughout its history, the United States has been inhabited by a variety of interacting racial or ethnic groups" (Frederickson 1999: 23). The "or" at the end of the sentence quite diffuses the difference between what might lead to a diatribe on slavery and what might lead to a paean to cultural diversity.

8. The literature is also clear that ethnic identity can have a positive transforming effect as well as a more negative and limiting one.

9. For examples of these four cases, see Grosfoguel (2004); Baker-Cristales (2004); Peek (2005); and Hussain and Bagguley (2005).

10. One of the interesting findings from both these studies is the tendency of people on the outside of the ethnic category to respond as if issues are universal to all people, while those within the ethnic category construe them as representing specific ethnic cultural tendencies.

11. This discussion is drawn from Benson (2005); Sanchez and Thorp (2005); Gentemann and Zhou (2005); Gunawardena and Findlay (2005); Haines and Rosenblum (2005); and Rosenblum, Zhou, and Gentemann (2009). The more general impact of immigrants on higher education has also received broad attention (Gray, Vernez, and Rolph 1996; Grubb, Badway, and Bell 2003; Harklau 1999; Musil et al. 1995; Smith 1997), including the effect of immigrants on other minorities (Hoxby 1998).

12. A more general example of this divide is provided by Tsai, Ying, and Lee (2000). It is worth noting that the General Ethnicity Questionnaire, which they use for this particular piece of research, is framed toward ethnicity as culture and language. That is, "Chinese" is effectively stripped of its specifically national implications. It is thus *not* an issue of national origin in the strict sense. Nevertheless, as with an emphasis on national origin, ethnicity is here constructed as a single bounded dimension of identity, rather than a kind of holding place for multiple dimensions of identity.

13. See, for example, Schwartz and Montgomery (2002) and Tanaka (2003). This is an issue not only of identity, but of interaction (Chen et al. 2001), and of forging new paths to college for those who have not previously attended for various reasons, including gender (Bankston 1995; Lee 1997; Simmons and Plaza 1998; Yiv and Secombe 1999; Zhou and Bankston 2001).

14. Patel's specific reference is to the Indian census, but it applies rather well to the U.S. case as well.

15. As noted in an earlier chapter, these annual surveys had their origin in 1975 with what had become by 1979 a set of nine surveys of Southeast Asian refugees conducted and subsequently published by Opportunity Systems Incorporated. In 1981, the survey was substantially redesigned and in 1984 transformed into a panel design (Gordon 1989). These surveys were influential in early discussions of the economic adjustment of Vietnamese refugees (Stein 1979). The redesigned surveys were also used extensively for discussions of general adaptation (Bach et al. 1983, 1984; Haines 1983), and for more specific issues of household composition (Bach 1985), continuities in the labor force activities of women (Haines 1987), the effects of type of sponsorship (Bach and Carroll-Seguin 1986), and the degree of continuity in household formation between Vietnam and the United States (Haines 2002). Over time, and with changes in the U.S. refugee program, these surveys have expanded to include a very wide range of countries of origin. They thus provide data not only on the Southeast Asian refugees for whom the surveys were first designed (still crucial in the 1995 survey to be discussed in the text) but also the surge in arrivals from Eastern Europe and the former Soviet Union (well represented in both the 1995 and 2001 surveys), and also the greatly increased number of Africans (who are particularly apparent in the 2001 survey—and some of the more illustrative data used from the 2002 survey).

16. More descriptive reports of the survey's methodology and findings are provided in the annual reports of the Office of Refugee Resettlement. The data presented here are calculated separately from the public use data files for the 1993–2002 surveys.

17. There are two kinds of translation involved: formal written translation of the instrument into a foreign language for the largest of the refugee language groups (e.g., Chinese, Lao, Hmong, Khmer, and Vietnamese for the 1995 survey) and ad hoc translations by staff when that is necessary during actual survey calls for less common languages.

18. The surveys were conducted by phone based on lists of refugees resettled. Those lists include initial addresses. Although there are some potential problems with phone interviews, they do have some advantages in general (ease of having multiple interpreters available) and possibly some advantages for this particular topic, for example, by taking statements about ethnicity out of direct visual encounter. The answers that will appear about race, for example, might have been different if conducted in person rather than by phone.

19. This is partially an artifact of the situation at the time these surveys were redesigned in 1980. As part of the team that did that redesign, I would note the strong commitment at that time to move away from nationality as a classifier and toward a set of Asian ethnic categories not terribly different in concept from those used in the contemporary United States. The two driving forces in that process were the presence of large numbers of Chinese among those from Vietnam, and the arrival of numerous highland groups from Laos (especially Hmong). The mixing of these populations with ethnic Vietnamese on the one hand and lowland Lao on the other had truly bizarre effects in statistical reporting. Any statement about how "Laotians" were doing simply ignored the very different situations of ethnic Lao and Hmong. The differences were less sharp for ethnic Vietnamese versus Chinese from Vietnam, but still significant (Haines 2009; Lee 2009).

20. Concepts of ethnicity and actual linguistic codes for ethnicity are related. Whether interviewees are faced with an English word whose parameters are unclear to them or whether a written or verbal translation actually shifts the meaning of "ethnicity" is not always clear. Whether it is the translator or the interviewee who makes the "translation," the same problem (and potential) remains in the research to show a divergent notion of the term "ethnicity." This is not always, however, a serious problem. As an example, in the Vietnamese case, "ethnicity" is usually translated formally as *dan toc*—roughly "people-lineage." That is a reasonably good gloss for ethnicity, though it actually rings more with the spirit of the late nineteenth or early twentieth century European notion of "nation" (in its original sense of peopleness) rather than with the current link of that term to the state apparatus of governance.

It may also be worth reiterating more generally that refugees are a particularly crucial set of immigrants in terms of this issue. They are arguably the most diverse segment of contemporary U.S. immigration and the one least preadapted to the United States whether in terms of economic roles or the identity categories under discussion here. The degree to which refugees are unexpected immigrants from new source countries along often extremely disorderly migration routes suggests that they are likely to have the freshest, least acclimated views of the United States. Their reactions to this American system of ethnicity categories can thus be very helpful in analyzing those categories.

21. Even with groups that continue to arrive over time, and thus would appear to represent continuity in admissions, there are often shifts in the numbers or in their individual characteristics.

22. These ethnic labels are not always fully self-explanatory. One might wonder, for example, how many Eritreans were among the Ethiopians, or how many Chinese-Vietnamese might have (for a variety of reasons) identified themselves as Vietnamese. That is, the ethnicity options *not* taken are unavailable in these surveys. Here, decennial census data are more reliable since minority status (e.g., Chinese-Vietnamese) can be triangulated among country of origin, self-described race, ancestry, and home language.

23. See Gilman (1991) for the specific issue of Jews, but see also Roediger (1991) and Jacobson (1998) for the more general issue of being white in America and Takaki (1989) for a good review of the stages by which white and Asian were ever more carefully distinguished in American federal and state law. Despite the general intransigence of race (as compared with ethnicity), it is worth reiterating that race can change: Jews became white (Sacks 1994) and Latinos became people of color (Melville 1988: 74). That is a reminder that race is a system of categories attributed to biological differences, not a system that is based on biological differences.

24. In interim years, the number of responses for the hybrid category of Bosnian-Muslim was, in fact, quite large. In 1996, for example, it was the most frequently used ethnic identity option for those from Bosnia.

25. The terms "ethnic" and "tribal" have different connotations here with tribal specifically meaning linked by kinship. In common discussion, however, very strong ethnic consciousness in a group might well be noted as "tribal" and certainly a tribal identity would meet any of the (less restrictive) criteria for shared ethnicity.

26. Qian (2004) provides a very interesting analysis of a similar issue: how the race of biracial children is assessed by their parents in response to census questions.

27. This decline is gradual over time, not sudden. The 2001 survey was in fact conducted during Fall 2001, and that might have affected how some people responded. But the pattern itself was already established.

28. The only other people in the family identified as "American" were their other young U.S.-born, U.S.-citizen siblings.

29. The numbers for "don't know" were higher both before 1995 and after. The survey in 1995 thus appears anomalous in this regard.

30. There were also thirteen people identified ethnically as Burmese. They were from Bosnia both by birth and citizenship.

5

Binding the Generations: Households and Refugee Adaptation

T he adaptation of refugees to the United States reflects their experiences before arrival and the conditions that they find in America after arrival. For refugees, the interplay of background factors and current conditions is particularly difficult for they, unlike most other immigrants, arrive with the aftereffects of harrowing exodus and transit experiences and with relatively little preorientation to the life they will lead in America. For them, the bridging of the old and the new, prior lives and new lives, is likely to be more difficult than it is for other migrants.

Although the United States has a resettlement program that attempts to alleviate that abruptness of transition (discussed in Chapter 6), the burden on refugees remains heavy. There are the many losses of exodus: loss of property, of kin, of personal security, and simply of time spent in intermediary camp situations. There are also the effects of refugee policies: what kinds of people are accepted, which relatives are included, how they move to their new country, and where specifically they are settled. The legal status they are given is also crucial. Many who might seem to be refugees are not granted formal refugee legal status and thus must navigate America with more temporary legal statuses or even with no legal status at all—they melt into the general "illegal immigrant" population.[1]

The background characteristics of refugees—as of other migrants—are conventionally placed into two general categories: cultural and socioeconomic. On the cultural side, for example, the success of particular refugees is often associated with such features as a strong work ethic or a high valuation of education.[2] Such cultural characteristics are usually described in a national, ethnic, or sometime religious context. On the socioeconomic side, virtually all analyses of refugee and immigrant adaptation examine the effects of such background variables as education, language competence, and occupation. These are particularly easy factors to examine in survey and census work and their importance has been amply documented in the research on both refugees and immigrants.

Between these cultural and socioeconomic factors, however, lies a third kind of background factor that applies not so much generally to a culture or specifically to an individual. Rather, it involves the social groups and networks through which people organize and interpret their lives. Most important of these is the family. The formation, durability, and structure of families are inseparable from the daily lives of refugees whether in the home or new country. The very emphasis on economic self-sufficiency in resettlement programs, for example, underscores the importance of the family since the measurement for success—self-sufficiency—is based on the joint status of families rather than directly on the individuals within them.

Families: Households and Networks

The individual is embedded in a web of many social relationships, but the most crucial part of that web is what we generally call "the family." Families vary greatly in structure and function in different cultures. Roughly speaking, "the family" has two main components: an actual living group, the household, and an extended set of kin beyond the household—what Americans tend to call the immediate (or nuclear) family and the extended family. Depending on the cultural group and the specific sociohistorical circumstances, the division between the two may be fairly sharp or it may be quite blurred. For example, when related households live side by side, the physical boundaries of the house do not preclude daily interactions between households.

Despite such potential blurring between the household and the wider set of kin, a focus on the household has the practical advantage of emphasizing those people who most closely interact on a daily basis. Those people in the household are not necessarily a family grouping. Single refugees may live together for both social and economic reasons. In some cases, they may well become "like family." However, for the great majority of households, the ties among people are those of kinship. The household is thus a very practical unit that is easily defined (those who regularly live together) and also a vital social unit that has both practical and symbolic importance.

The general nature of the household stems to a large degree from demographic considerations, particularly fertility. Southeast Asian refugee families, for example, have had more children than mainstream American families; Soviet refugees have had fewer. Automatically, then, Vietnamese refugee households have been larger, included more children, and experienced especially acute problems: housing has been difficult because of the relative lack of rental properties for large families; education has required parental interaction with children in multiple schools; and household incomes have been strained by the needs of those multiple children. Groups with even larger families and with adults less well "capitalized" with English, education, and occupational skills—such as the Hmong and Somali—have faced even more severe problems. Because of such elementary demographic considerations, the household becomes the crucial stage on which the economic destiny of refugees is played out.

The household functions as a primary arena of economic strategy but also one of social identity. The structuring of roles within the household has important social as well as economic effects. For example, early Cuban refugee women entered the labor force in relatively large numbers, despite cultural conventions that had often restricted them to the home in Cuba. This shift reflected considerable flexibility in women's roles as wives and as mothers. Specifically, employment was seen as a way to contribute to the family without sacrificing rights and obligations within the home (Boone 1980, 1994; Ferreé 1979; Perez 1986; Prieto 1986). Similar flexibility in the role of wives has often been noted for the Vietnamese (Benson 1994; Haines 1986; Hoskins 1975; Kibria 1990) both in the United States and in Vietnam itself. If refugees bring with them to the United States the belief that women's work outside the home is both acceptable and important, then the household has an additional wage earner and enhanced flexibility in achieving economic self-sufficiency in America.

Analysis of the economic and social effects of household structure, however, has often been stymied by the extraordinary social and cultural diversity of the refugees who have come to America. That diversity applies to families considered both at the household and wider kin levels. Even within the same general geographical region of origin, the variations may be extensive. Refugees from Southeast Asia provide an example. On the one hand, both Vietnamese and Hmong kinship is organized patrilineally. This does not necessarily mean that the family itself is patriarchal, but rather that blood relations between males are used to extend the family back to distant ancestors and laterally to include distant cousins. For both the Hmong and the Vietnamese, these sets of relatives can be quite extensive. The resulting kin groups can function as units for a variety of social, political, economic, and ritual activities. In Vietnamese villages, for example, a particularly large kin group could act as the framework for the economic and political life of the entire village (Hickey 1964). For the Hmong, the extensions of the kin group and the multiplicity of functions are even greater. Leadership, for example, may be the result of belonging to a particular lineage and is likely to be validated through a series of polygynous marriages to women of other clans or family alliance groups (Dunnigan 1982; Geddes 1976; LeBar, Hickey, and Musgrave 1964; Vang 2008). For the Hmong and Vietnamese, then, the family extends directly into what in the United States would be characterized as "the community." This is particularly so for the Hmong and helps explain how they can continue quite traditional patterns of mass migration even after arrival in the United States—and why they are sometimes more proactive in community organization and action (Hein 2006; Vang 2008).

The Lao and Khmer are rather different in terms of kinship. Both show a tendency toward relatively small nuclear family households, rather than the extended ones that are common for Hmong and Vietnamese. Khmer kinship terminology and residence patterns, in particular, show considerable similarity to those of the United States. One result is that, for the Khmer, "community" may be quite similar to the American notion of a group that complements family life rather than being a direct extension of it. This may help explain both why the Khmer worked so hard to recreate community after arrival in the United States (building Buddhist temples, for example) and why, when lacking a residential community with a religious center, their adjustment to the United States has often been rather difficult (Ebihara 1985; Hein 2006; Mortland 2001; Ong 2003; Pho, Gerson, and Cowan 2007; Smith-Hefner 1999).

This diversity in refugee kinship makes generalizations about the role of the family in adjustment very difficult. Refugee populations coming to the United States have differed from each other and, by and large, from American society in the interactions among kin within households and beyond. In some cases, particular household and kin structures have eased adjustment. Strong marital relationships, for example, may facilitate effective dual-wage earning strategies. Strong emphases on extended families may facilitate effective multigenerational strategies for achieving economic success, if not now then over time. In other cases, distinctive household and kin practices may have less desirable results in a new American environment. Strong patriarchal patterns, for example, may result in spousal friction and abuse under the pressures of resettlement. Continuing moves within the United States by refugees after arrival, often to reunite families and recreate extended kin structures, may undermine resettlement efforts as refugees move away from the programs designed for them. The exact effects are often unpredictable. For example, refugees whose background includes large, strong, and formally defined kin groups might be expected to suffer greatly when those groups are disassembled. Yet, such refugees have often shown great flexibility in creating alternative social bonds when those wider kin groups are missing.

Young Nuer refugees from the Sudan, for example, have forged strong lateral ties with other refugees whom they met in camps in Africa or later on in the United States (Holtzman 2000; Shandy 2007). One of the great lessons from kinship studies is that one never knows what a kinship system is actually capable of until it is seen in times of stress and disruption.

The Nuer case, nevertheless, is a reminder that discussions of kinship in the abstract cultural sense often require reassessment because refugees simply do not have the full range of components of their kinship systems. They lack the actual people to match the potential slots in the kinship system. Discussions of cultural patterns in marriage, for example, make limited sense when people have lost their spouses or when an imbalance in the number of men and women makes marriage impossible. The American proscription of polygamy in itself has caused problems for some refugees when secondary wives must be denied (at least formally). For some groups—like the Hmong—polygamy is common and makes good sense given the very high mortality of men from war. It provides an opportunity for women to marry and remarry even if the number of men is limited. For the Khmer, in contrast, the emphasis on the nuclear household may have dealt a harsher blow for widows than it would have in a kinship system with more extended households—or which were more accepting of polygamy.

The lack of spouses reflects a prime gap in conjugal ties, but there is also much generational loss among refugees. Older people may well be left behind in refugee flight, or be subject to greater loss of life if they do attempt to flee. Very young children may also be left behind, especially if there is uncertainty about whether return will be possible. Instead, it is likely to be young adults who are best able to flee and to survive the journey. Indeed, they may be pushed to leave by their parents. The more dangerous the flight, and the more extended the journey, the more likely that it will be they who make the trip, and that they will tend to be male. The Sudanese boys who fled on their own are well known now in the United States as the "lost boys" (Bixler 2006; Dau 2007; Deng et al. 2005)—but see DeLuca (2009) for comments on the "lost girls."

Sometimes, however, even young children are sent away. Some 14,000 unaccompanied Cuban children, for example, were resettled in the very early 1960s under Operation Pedro Pan (Conde 1999; Torres 2004; Triay 1999). Operation Babylift in April 1975—marred by a fatal plane crash—brought out a few thousand unaccompanied Vietnamese children for adoption as the Republic of Vietnam was collapsing. The children were supposed to all be orphans, but some parents sent their own children out through the program (Peck-Barnes 2000; Sachs 2010). Refugee children may also be cut off from family for other reasons. Amerasian children from Vietnam, for example, are likely to have fragmented family relations in Vietnam and subsequently in the United States (Ashabranner and Ashabranner 1987; Nguyen 2001). For them too, a special program was eventually instituted (under the Amerasian Homecoming Act of 1988) that provided support because of their special connection to the United States. All these programs echo exactly the purpose of the failed Wagner-Rogers legislation of 1939: to create a special flight path for those least able to flee on their own. Whatever the merits of such programs—and they are often criticized—one result is usually children who lack their own family resources in the United States.

The Family in Adaptation

Given that variability in cultural background and historical circumstances, it seems almost nonsensical to talk about "the family" and its role in refugee adaptation. Yet to not acknowledge this most elemental social setting would be even more so. So a few general comments about how the family operates in adjustment may be of some use before providing a more extended case example for one particular group of refugees.

Overall, refugee adjustment is a function of individuals but also of social groups. The effects of household structure on self-sufficiency and general income levels provide one crucial practical example. Having more wage earners in a household is generally good for self-sufficiency; large numbers of small children generally pose problems. Being divorced or widowed with a large number of small children is usually disastrous.[3] Within the household, there are thus two distinct sets of issues: those involving conjugal ties and those involving generational ones. Each has potential importance in easing— or complicating—adjustment to the United States. Consider again the high labor force participation rates of Cuban women and how they contributed substantially to the economic progress of the families in which they lived. In her early analysis, for example, Ferreé (1979: 48) noted that "there is no necessary conflict between traditional standards of female behavior and women's paid employment. Since the Cuban woman is working for her family, her employment is not seen as an expression of her independence or the loosening of traditional controls and restraints... Because female employment is needed to maintain standards of respectability for the family, daughters are counseled to prepare for a lifetime career, and parents are willing to invest in such preparation." Boone (1980, 1994) has noted a similar contribution to the family among Cuban women in the Washington, DC, area. Wives and mothers there as well not only fulfilled traditional roles within the family, but also directly contributed to the family's economic adjustment.

Somewhat similar conjugal patterns emerged among Southeast Asian refugees, particularly those from Vietnam, where the traditional role of women was also flexible enough to include management of the home and participation in the labor market (e.g., Haines 1986, 2006; Hickey 1964; Hoskins 1975). Ironically, similar patterns among Lao refugees were sometimes discouraged by Americans who had been indoctrinated to the idea of stereotypical Asian wives who deferred to their husbands in all matters beyond the household (Rynearson and DeVoe 1984). Although such conjugal economic cooperation is perhaps the most obvious source of the multiple incomes that are so crucial to the economic progress of refugees (and other immigrants), other kin relations can also be important. Adult siblings among the Vietnamese, for example, not only provide mutual emotional support, but also cooperate in economic activities (Haines 2006: 187–189; Haines, Rutherford, and Thomas 1981a) while extended family alliances among the Hmong have been active in bridging the distance between refugees and U.S. service providers (Dunnigan 1982; Fadiman 1997; Goodkind 2005; Vang 2005). There can, however, also be problems. The rearrangement of conjugal roles, for example, is not always easy. The incorporation of wives (and mothers) into the labor force may facilitate the family's economic adjustment, but it may burden domestic relations. Again, the early research on Cuban refugees is instructive. The positive contribution of the family is clear (e.g., Perez 1986), but so are the strains. On the basis of research with Cuban women in Miami, for example, Gonzales noted that "conflicts between the economic pressure to work and the social need to maintain the domestic role have strained the smooth running of the traditional Cuban family" (Gonzales 1980: 2). One result was the frequent use of tranquilizers (e.g., Page and Gonzales 1980; cf., Martinez 2006).

Janet Benson (1994) has portrayed analogous strains on Southeast Asian refugee families in Kansas, where the dictates of both parents working alternate shifts at meatpacking plants left no time for spousal interaction or much parental supervision of children. Refugees could initially view this work as easy money and a good opportunity to accumulate capital, but the costs for family life were soon apparent. As Benson (1994: 122–123) notes: "Even if workers escape serious injury or disability, families inevitably pay a price in terms of domestic stress, inadequate health treatment, substandard housing and child care, and other problems resulting from their incorporation in a labor system that places overwhelming emphasis on productivity."

Conjugal ties thus present both opportunities and challenges. So too with generational ties. Just as parents are tripped up by shifting roles, so too are children tripped up by the dual demands of traditional culture (represented by their parents) and American culture (represented by schools, peers, and the media). This can easily lead to conflict. An early assess-ment of the needs of Southeast Asian refugee youth (IRAC 1980: 1), for example, suggested that childhood and adolescence are the "battlefields over which and in which the most severe cultural conflicts emerge. Children are the key to any group's survival as a distinct cultural unit. As 'New Americans' immigrant children find themselves charged by their elders with maintaining what often appears to be an increasingly remote and irrelevant cultural heritage." Children's competence in the new culture thus tends to put them at odds with their parents. By contrast, if they adhere to tra-ditional cultural values, as represented by their parents, they are likely to be in conflict with American culture and its educational system. In that sense, they are similar to other immigrants. However, for many refugee children, there are also the strains of the refugee experience itself. Whether in families or on their own, they thus face problems as children, as immi-grants, and as refugees. As Mosselson (2006: 184) notes from her study of Bosnian adolescents, the identity development of refugee children is distinct in being linked to "coping mechanisms utilized in response to their refugee situations."

At the other end of the spectrum, the senior generation may be cut off from the new world of work and from their usual social interactions and social status. The elderly are often far more isolated in the United States than they were in the home country. This aspect of generational tension seems best resolved when the elderly have access to their own activities in addition to steady family interaction. That kind of option is perhaps clearest in places like Miami with its dense residential areas of Cuban resettlement (Hernandez 1974; Portes and Stepick 1993). An analogous situation emerged for Vietnamese in New Orleans—where the cultivation of Vietnamese style gardens (often on public land along the levees) became the special domain of the elderly, combining well with the clustering of residences and an active Catholic parish (Airriess and Clawson 1991, 1994).[4]

These benefits and stress points, changes and continuities, in conjugal and generational ties are at the core of refugee adaptation to a new country. But, again, discussion of the role of "the family" in refugee adaptation can skip too easily over the specific social patterns and cultural beliefs embedded in different kinship systems, and also skip too easily over the losses of actual kin to separation and often death that, in turn, require modification of those kinship-related patterns and beliefs. As a partial remedy, the remainder of this chapter addresses the specific case of the Vietnamese, illustrating in more detail how kinship operates in both the past and the present, often with a clear aim on the future. It is only with this kind of specific cultural and historical account that one can begin to see how the frequent changes in family life under the pressures of refugee flight and resettlement are at least partly counterbalanced by continuities.

A Vietnamese Example

The specific discussion of Vietnamese household dynamics that follows is in three parts. The first part is a review of the existing sociohistorical data on household formation and structure in southern Vietnam during the period from the end of French control in 1954 until the fall of the Republic of South Vietnam in 1975, a collapse that led directly to the influx of Vietnamese refugees into the United States. Southern Vietnam is the geographical area from which most—although not all[5]—Vietnamese refugees fled and the period of the Republic is the time period in which the reasons for leaving are generally—although not always[6]—anchored. Two specific household characteristics that appear in this historical period are relatively high proportions of young adults who remain unmarried and relatively high proportions of young adults who reside with their parents. The result is that "children" experience living with their parents both as children *and* as adults. One economic result is that households have several potential wage earners.

The second part of the discussion is a brief comparison of these data from southern Vietnam during the Republic with more recent data on southern Vietnam and on northern Vietnam. This segment of the discussion suggests that the southern Vietnamese experience is distinctive in its own right and is durable over time. The analysis also indicates that this combined pattern of delayed marriage and continued residence with parents is *not* representative of Vietnam overall. This is a useful reminder about the need for specificity in looking at the cultural and social characteristics of refugees. They are, almost inevitably, *not* typical representatives of the countries from which they come.

The third part of the discussion is a consideration of Vietnamese refugee households in the United States based on the federal government's 1999 annual survey of refugees and the 2000 U.S. census. Although the census data are cumulative, the 1999 survey reflects the experience of the very last of the cohorts of Vietnamese refugees to the United States, thus providing a good test over several decades and across the migration experience itself of the durability in these characteristics of Vietnamese households. That 1999 survey also includes a broad range of other refugees and thus permits a statistical examination of whether these issues of marital timing and co-residence with parents are as distinctive to Vietnamese refugees as they appear to be from the historical material. The 2000 U.S. census provides equivalent data on other Asian migrant groups and thus permits a quantitative comparison of the uniqueness of Vietnamese with other Asian-origin immigrants.

There are obvious limitations in using this kind of specific example to anchor a broader discussion of refugee resettlement in the United States. The Vietnamese are hardly typical refugees, and their household arrangements are hardly typical either. Yet, the Vietnamese are, with the Cubans, the largest of the refugee groups to the United States, and their experience merits attention on that basis alone. There are also some theoretically interesting features of the Vietnamese case, including a rather long history of prior migration in Vietnam—a reminder again that refugee flight is often a continuation at a greater distance of previous internal migration. On more practical grounds, this kind of detailed comparison requires some depth in both the U.S. and country-of-origin situations. It is thus not easily taken on for more than a single set of refugees, and not very easily even then. The discussion that follows builds on a mix of U.S. and Vietnam material with which I have been working for nearly forty years—including having worked in Vietnam with both ethnic Vietnamese and minority internal migrants (see especially Haines 2006).

Vietnamese Kinship, Vietnamese Households

The literature on Vietnamese kinship has rapidly expanded over the last two decades providing a much more detailed portrait not only of its central cultural tendencies, but of its empirical variation and change under shifting social and economic conditions. Work by Vietnamese and Nordic social scientists on northern Vietnam has been especially helpful (Gammeltoft 1999; Le Thi 1999; Liljestrom and Tuong Lai 1991; Nguyen 1998; Norlund, Gates, and Vu Cao Dam 1995; Pham Van Bich 1999; Vu 1998). Such fresh research and analysis supplement the classic Vietnamese sources (Phan Ke Binh 1983; Toan Anh 1966, 1968); earlier American efforts on southern Vietnam (Haines 1990; Hickey 1964; Jamieson 1986a, 1986b); and a variety of other attempts to extract information on kinship from more distant historical sources (Haines 1984; Whitmore 1984), from secondary analysis of the greatly improved survey data on contemporary Vietnam (Bélanger 2000), and from the language itself (Cooke 1968; Luong 1990; Nguyen Dinh Hoa 1956). This combined work suggests a kinship system that has strong patrilineal elements, pervasive attention to seniority, but nevertheless some measure of equality among those of different genders and generations. The relatively favorable position of women has received frequent comment, particularly in analysis of early Vietnamese legal codes (Do Thi Binh 1999; Haines 1984; Ta Van Tai 1981, 1984; Thanh Duy 1998; Yu 1990).

Central to this kinship system in a practical sense is the household. The importance of the household is evident even in the terminology. The vernacular Vietnamese word for house (*nha*) is also used to describe the family and even one's spouse. It thus evokes place, a marital relationship, and the kin group that derives from both. The more formal term (*gia dinh*) invokes not only the family but the image of the village communal hall with its plaques indicating imperial investiture of the village—much as the altar to the ancestors provides the same formal investiture for the household.

Although it is difficult to document very much about households in earlier historical periods, there are data for the period of the Republic of Vietnam (1954–1975) that provide a baseline for considering the general structure and formation of households in at least the southern part of the country. To summarize a broad range of demographic, census, and survey data, the southern Vietnamese population was growing during the period, fueled by a "baby boom" after the end of the French war in 1954 (Ng Shui Meng 1974; VQGTK 1957, 1958, 1959, 1960a, 1960b). However, by the late 1960s, there was—at least for urban areas—a distinct delay in the age at marriage (VQGTK 1963, 1968). Data on fertility are not conclusive but suggest that, as might be expected, the delay in marriage was associated with a decrease in the total number of children that women were having. The very large households that can be seen in survey data for the period are thus not necessarily "typical" of Vietnamese society but may well represent an interlude from the relatively small households in Vietnam that are noted for historical periods (Whitmore 1984) and that emerged again with a sharp decline in fertility over the last two decades of the twentieth century (CCSC 2000).

One particularly useful source is a survey by the South Vietnamese government conducted in Saigon in 1967. The data are especially valuable because of the detail of the published findings (VQGTK 1968). Tables 5.1 and 5.2 present data from that survey on marital status and current activities by age group. The general patterns are predictable ones: the percentages married and working increase with age up until about the age of fifty-five, when both the percentages married and working start to decline. The differences between men and women are also predictable: lower percentages working for women than for men and a large incidence of widowhood among older women.

What is more interesting than the general pattern, however, is the specific timing of these transitions to marriage and to work. For men aged 20–24, only 20 percent were married although 69 percent were already working (with 29 percent still in school). For men aged 25–29, 55 percent were married although 90 percent were working. Even for men aged 30–34, only 81 percent were married—this in a society that is usually described as having "universal" marriage. For women, a similar pattern emerges.

Table 5.1 Men's marital status and current activities; percentages by age
(Saigon, 1967)

	MARITAL STATUS			MAJOR ACTIVITIES			
	SINGLE	MARRIED	DIV/WID	WORK	HOME	SCHOOL	RETIRED
Age group							
15–19	96.8	3.2	0.0	35.7	4.0	58.5	0.0
20–24	80.3	19.7	0.0	69.1	1.1	28.6	0.0
25–29	44.9	55.1	0.0	90.3	1.6	7.1	0.0
30–34	18.3	80.8	.9	97.5	.6	.7	0.0
35–39	10.4	88.5	1.1	98.2	1.0	.2	0.0
40–44	5.3	93.8	.9	97.1	1.3	.3	.1
45–49	3.6	92.4	4.0	94.9	.7	0.0	2.5
50–54	3.0	92.2	4.8	93.8	1.6	0.0	3.6
55–59	3.2	88.4	8.4	77.0	1.6	0.0	20.3
60 and over	3.6	77.5	18.8	45.3	1.4	0.0	51.6

Source: VQGTK (1968: 17).

Notes: "Div/wid" means divorced or widowed; there was no separate category in the survey for separation per se. For major activities, work means in the labor force (i.e., working as well as "unemployed" in the normal sense); unemployment so defined was quite rare among respondents—only 2.6 percent for all males of age 14 and older. The categories for current activities will not sum to 100 percent because of the deletion of several small categories in the original, none of which accounted for even one percent of the total population.

For those women aged 20–24, only 38 percent were married. For those aged 25–29, the figure was 66 percent, and for those aged 30–34, the figure finally rose to about the same as for men of that age: 80 percent. The data thus indicate there were large proportions of adult men and women in their twenties who were not married, and a substantial number of those in their early thirties as well. These people were, in the great majority, working and thus not "dependents" either in the general sense or in the more restricted sense of being students.

Tables 5.3 and 5.4 portray the life sequences of these men and women from another perspective: their relationship to the head of household in which they lived. Again, the overall patterns are predictable, at least for a very kin-oriented society. Both men and women were, in the great majority, continuing to reside in their parents' households during their early adult years, gradually moving into the status of head of household or spouse of head. As they aged, they then ultimately moved into the status of parent

Table 5.2 Women's marital status and current activities; percentages by age
(Saigon, 1967)

	MARITAL STATUS			MAJOR ACTIVITIES			
	SINGLE	MARRIED	DIV/WID	WORK	HOME	SCHOOL	RETIRED
Age group							
15–19	92.6	7.3	.1	30.4	22.3	46.4	.1
20–24	61.0	37.6	1.4	43.7	37.5	17.9	0.0
25–29	32.1	65.9	2.0	44.0	51.6	4.2	.1
30–34	16.7	79.6	3.7	37.6	61.6	.2	0.0
35–39	7.5	85.8	6.7	35.3	64.1	.1	.1
40–44	5.9	83.4	10.8	33.0	66.7	0.0	.3
45–49	4.3	78.6	17.1	36.5	60.0	.3	2.8
50–54	4.6	69.6	25.8	31.0	60.2	0.0	8.4
55–59	5.5	55.2	39.3	24.7	48.6	.3	25.9
60 and over	3.8	26.8	69.4	13.3	21.9	.1	64.1

Source: VQGTK (1968: 18).
Notes: See notes for previous table.

of household head. The differences between men and women lie largely in the more frequent (and more enduring) status of head of household for men. Nevertheless, a sizable number of women were heads of household and not even the dictates of Confucian filial piety kept older men from being considered parents of the household head rather than being designated as household heads themselves.[7]

As with the previous set of data, what is more interesting than the general pattern is the specific timing of the transition, especially for men and women in their twenties and early thirties. The delay in moving out of the status of "child" matches the delay in marriage, but is more pronounced. For men aged 20–24, 63 percent were still with their parents. For men aged 25–29, the figure drops to 51 percent and for men aged 30–34 to 30 percent. For women aged 20–24, 64 percent were still with their parents. For women aged 25–29, the figure drops to 40 percent and for women aged 30–34 to 21 percent. Thus, not only were people relatively slow to marry, but were even slower to set up their own households. Young couples were thus residing for at least some period of time with their parents. Given the importance of patrilineality in Vietnamese kinship, it is likely that this was generally the son and his wife living with his parents. Recent data on

Table 5.3 Male relationships to head of household; percentages by age
(Saigon, 1967)

	HEAD	SPOUSE	CHILD	PARENT	SIBLING	OTHER
Age group						
0–4	—	—	74.8	—	.1	24.8
5–9	—	—	84.2	—	.7	14.8
10–14	—	—	85.0	—	2.7	11.4
15–19	.6	.2	66.0	—	8.4	18.5
20–24	4.5	.6	62.7	—	13.3	16.6
25–29	17.6	2.7	51.3	—	14.1	10.6
30–34	43.6	6.5	29.9	.1	9.5	6.3
35–39	59.8	8.5	12.5	.1	8.5	4.5
40–44	69.5	10.7	4.8	—	7.0	4.0
45–49	76.8	7.9	3.6	.8	4.3	2.2
50–54	79.0	10.6	2.4	1.8	1.4	1.2
55–59	76.2	9.5	1.1	3.8	3.0	2.2
60–64	71.4	11.4	1.4	6.7	3.8	1.9
65–69	74.4	7.0	—	11.6	1.7	2.3
70–74	60.4	5.6	—	26.4	3.8	—
75–79	62.5	5.0	2.5	25.0	—	—
80 and over	47.4	—	—	42.1	—	—
All ages	20.7	2.8	55.7	.7	4.7	12.8

Source: VQGTK (1968: 5–6).

Notes: The categories of uncle/aunt, temporary resident, and worker as provided in the original are not included here, thus rows will not sum to 100 percent. Such categories account for only very small numbers of household members. The latter two categories do, however, have significant numbers at the young adult level, as would be expected. Also, the number of households by age groups drops off sharply for men (although less so for women) after age 69.

northern Vietnam are conclusive on that issue (Nguyen 1998), although the extent to which such patterns apply in southern Vietnam is still open to considerable debate (Bélanger 2000; Do Thai Dong 1991; Hickey 1987).[8]

Southern Vietnamese Households Compared

These data indicate a clear pattern of relatively late marriage and even later movement out of the parental household. That pattern does *not* match employment since employment comes earlier for both men and women. The result is thus that there are many households with two generations of

Table 5.4 Female relationships to head of household; percentages by age
(Saigon, 1967)

	HEAD	SPOUSE	CHILD	PARENT	SIBLING	OTHER
Age group						
0–4	—	—	74.2	—	*	25.2
5–9	—	—	84.0	—	.5	15.2
10–14	—	—	86.1	—	2.4	10.1
15–19	.4	1.1	73.6	.1	5.7	12.3
20–24	4.3	7.6	63.6	.1	8.7	10.4
25–29	10.5	27.1	39.5	—	10.6	6.9
30–34	15.0	47.2	20.6	.1	7.4	4.8
35–39	19.9	58.7	9.5	.4	5.2	1.5
40–44	22.5	62.0	5.6	.3	4.6	.7
45–49	27.5	58.5	3.6	2.2	2.7	1.2
50–54	26.2	61.4	1.5	8.6	4.4	1.9
55–59	36.0	38.5	1.8	11.6	4.3	1.5
60–64	41.6	22.4	.7	22.4	4.6	.7
65–69	39.6	15.7	1.4	30.9	5.1	1.8
70–74	27.1	8.5	—	55.1	4.2	—
75–79	22.2	4.4	—	61.1	—	3.3
80 and over	21.4	1.2	—	70.2	—	1.2
All ages	8.9	17.3	53.1	2.8	3.9	10.5

Source: VQGTK (1968: 5–6).
Notes: See notes for the previous table. In addition, the situation for the missing categories, particularly of worker/servant, is different for women. Overall, as seen in the data for totals, this category is about twice as frequent for women as for men. By the age of about 30, this category begins to have a more significant percentage effect than the category of "other" as presented in the table, a category that, however, is of relatively little importance for either men or women beyond the period when it probably reflects the grandchild/nephew/niece relationships.
*Less than .05 percent.

potential workers. The advantages of that arrangement for resettlement in a new country are great. Before considering the situation of Vietnamese refugees in the United States, however, a further (although abbreviated) review of the extent and durability of this pattern in Vietnam itself may be useful.

The first question that might be raised is whether this pattern seen in the Saigon data is representative of southern Vietnam overall. There is some research that addresses this question, although none provides as much detail as the Saigon data. Data from rural areas of Vietnam in 1971 (VQGTK 1973), for example, are provided in Table 5.5 for marital and work status

Table 5.5 Marital status and current activities; percentages by age (rural areas in Vietnam, 1971)

	MARITAL STATUS			MAJOR ACTIVITIES			
	SINGLE	MARRIED	DIV/WID	WORK	HOME	SCHOOL	OTHER
Men							
15–19	90.0	10.0	0.0	59.6	4.2	33.5	2.7
20–34	28.1	71.2	0.7	92.6	.8	2.5	4.1
35–44	2.5	95.2	2.3	96.9	.6	0.0	2.5
45–64	1.3	93.1	5.6	93.8	1.3	0.0	5.0
65 and over	3.0	57.3	39.7	62.3	1.6	0.0	36.0
Women							
15–19	85.4	13.9	.7	56.4	22.2	20.9	.5
20–34	25.0	64.4	10.6	72.0	25.3	2.1	.7
35–44	3.5	82.3	14.2	73.3	26.0	.1	.7
45–64	2.1	73.5	24.4	69.2	22.8	0.0	8.0
65 and over	3.0	36.9	60.1	29.9	14.3	0.0	55.9

Source: VQGTK (1973: 1, 5).

Notes: "Div/wid" means divorced or widowed; there was no separate category in the survey for separation per se. For major activities, work means in the labor force (i.e., working or "unemployed" in the normal sense); unemployment so defined was quite rare among respondents—only a fraction of a percent for all those (both male and female) of age 10 and older. Rows may not sum to 100 percent because of rounding.

and in Table 5.6 for relationship to head of household. The collapsing of age categories makes analysis difficult. The indication that 71 percent of all men from age 20 to 34 were married is inconclusive on the exact timing of marriage but not inconsistent with the Saigon data. The same is true of the proportion of women currently married (64 percent) or previously married (11 percent). The figure of 63 percent for both men and women aged 20–34 residing with parents is also consistent with the Saigon data. A comparison of these data with those from a survey of urban areas (VQGTK 1971) is not presented here (see Haines 2006) but suggests that issues of marital timing and household status were not sharply different among cities in southern Vietnam at that time. There is thus some support for seeing the more detailed Saigon data from 1967 as roughly representative of urban areas and at least not greatly inconsistent with data from rural areas.

A second question that might be raised is whether this pattern was a durable one, or simply an intermittent arrangement because of the war.

Table 5.6   Relationship to head of household; percentages by age (rural areas in Vietnam, 1971)

	HEAD	SPOUSE	CHILD	OTHER RELATIVE	NONRELATIVE
Men					
0–4	0.0	0.0	73.8	25.9	.3
5–9	0.0	0.0	80.8	18.9	.3
10–14	0.0	0.0	86.8	12.8	.4
15–19	.8	.2	88.4	10.0	.6
20–34	28.7	2.6	62.9	5.1	.7
35–44	75.9	3.2	18.4	2.0	.4
45–64	92.8	2.4	3.5	1.0	.3
65 and over	92.1	1.4	.2	6.1	.1
Women					
0–4	0.0	0.0	76.7	23.1	.2
5–9	0.0	0.0	81.5	18.4	.1
10–14	0.0	0.0	86.9	12.9	.2
15–19	.3	.5	89.2	9.7	.4
20–34	9.3	22.9	63.0	4.5	.3
35–44	17.2	64.2	15.8	2.6	.2
45–64	26.6	65.9	3.0	4.1	.4
65 and over	40.5	30.9	.3	27.9	.4

Source: VQGTK (1973: 2).
Notes: See notes to previous table.

One answer to that question comes from a consideration of later censuses conducted by the government of the now unified Vietnam. The 1989 census is a particularly useful benchmark since it was conducted fifteen years after reunification but before family planning programs sharply reduced fertility levels in the 1990s (CCSC 2000). Although the Vietnamese census data do not permit a comparison of household statuses, they do indicate the basic progressions of work and marital status. The data for Saigon—now Ho Chi Minh City—in 1989 are presented in Table 5.7. The basic pattern is similar to that found over twenty years earlier. Employment comes early for the large majority of men and a more modest majority of women. The percentages married at different age groups are very similar. For example, 57 percent of the men aged 25–29 were married in 1989 compared with 55 percent in 1967. Similarly, 63 percent of women of that same age were married in 1989 compared with 66 percent in 1967. There is, however, a noticeable drop in percentages married for women in their thirties and

Table 5.7 Marital status and current activities; percentages by age (Saigon 1967, Ho Chi Minh City 1989, Hanoi 1989)

	PERCENT MARRIED			PERCENT WORKING		
	SAIGON 1967	HCM 1989	HANOI 1989	SAIGON 1967	HCM 1989	HANOI 1989
Men						
15–19	3	2	2	36	35	42
20–24	20	21	32	69	70	74
25–29	55	57	67	90	84	88
30–34	81	78	89	98	88	92
35–39	89	87	95	98	89	91
40–44	94	90	97	97	87	85
45–49	92	92	97	95	83	78
50–54	92	92	96	94	75	71
55–59	88	91	95	77	60	58
60 and over	76	82	86	45	23	23
Women						
15–19	7	6	8	30	30	49
20–24	38	35	54	44	59	83
25–29	66	63	81	44	65	92
30–34	80	73	86	38	65	94
35–39	86	73	87	35	62	93
40–44	83	72	86	33	57	88
45–49	79	71	83	37	50	80
50–54	70	68	81	31	38	70
55–59	55	62	76	25	24	51
60 and over	27	38	44	13	8	18

Source: Tables 5.1 and 5.2 of this chapter; CCSC (1991: Table 3.1 and 5.4).
Notes: The greatest portion of those in W/D/S (Widowed/Divorced/Separated) were divorced. "Invalid" is the CCSC's translation of *mat kha nang lao dong* (lit: lost ability to work), which probably includes many of the people who would have otherwise considered themselves retired. Note that figures will not sum to 100 percent because of exclusion of other categories. See original for details. The format here represents an attempt to match the categories used in the 1967 Saigon survey as discussed in the text.

early forties. This doubtless represents the marriage squeeze caused by the out-migration of men (Goodkind 1997).[9] Despite that change, these data suggest considerable durability in the patterns of later marriage.

A third, and final, question that might be raised is whether this pattern in the data applies more broadly to Vietnam or is a distinctly southern pattern. Again, the 1989 Vietnamese census provides a useful comparison, specifically between Saigon (Ho Chi Minh City) and Hanoi. As also presented in Table 5.7, this comparison yields strong contrasts. For Hanoi women, the percentage married at the three critical age groups (20–24, 25–29, 30–34) climbs from 54 percent to 81 percent and then to 86 percent, while the equivalent figures for Saigon/HCM are 35 percent, 63 percent, and 73 percent. This is a sharp difference. For Hanoi men, the percentages married at the three critical age groups are 32 percent, 67 percent, and 89 percent, whereas the equivalent figures for Saigon/HCM are 21 percent, 57 percent, and 78 percent. Again, the difference is a clear one. This brief comparison thus suggests that, while *not* generalizable to all of Vietnam, there is a distinct pattern of delayed marriage and delayed household formation that applies not only to those who left when the Republic fell but also to those who continued to leave decades after that time.

Vietnamese Households in the United States

One way to assess the continuity in marital timing and household formation between Vietnam and the United States is to consider the federal government's annual surveys of refugees that have been discussed in prior chapters.[10] These surveys provide data on the Vietnamese refugees who are the specific focus of this discussion and also provide comparative data on other refugees. This permits a direct examination of the durability of Vietnamese household patterns across migration and the distinctiveness of those patterns to Vietnamese as compared with other refugees. The 1999 survey is particularly useful. It included refugees who had arrived from May 1994 to April 1999. Overall, the survey included 1,557 households with 5,590 individuals.[11] There were 1,262 individuals in the survey who were Vietnamese by ethnicity as well as nationality. These Vietnamese represent the very last years of significant flows from Southeast Asia and therefore a good test of the durability of the household patterns found in the historical material from some thirty years earlier.

Table 5.8 provides information on the marital status of Vietnamese refugees covered in the 1999 survey. The descriptive numbers suggest an even sharper delay in marriage than is seen in the country of origin data. For men, it is not until their forties that the majority are married; for women, it is not until their late thirties that the majority are married. (The greater frequency of marriage for women at most ages can be explained partially by the disproportionate number of males in the U.S. Vietnamese refugee population—52 percent of this survey population.) A similar pattern is seen in the percentages still residing with parents. For both men and women, residence with parents (or parents-in-law) continues to be the majority pattern

Table 5.8 Marital status and residence with parents by age (Vietnamese refugees, 1999)

	PERCENT MARRIED		PERCENT RESIDING WITH PARENTS	
	FEMALE	MALE	FEMALE	MALE
Age group				
15–19	0.0	1.2	97.0	97.6
20–24	13.3	3.8	98.8	86.5
25–29	12.5	12.8	82.2	82.1
30–34	25.6	11.9	74.2	70.1
35–39	52.6	17.4	61.5	62.5
40–44	72.7	44.4	31.6	22.0
45–49	94.3	86.2	12.1	0.0
50–54	93.0	93.7	0.0	0.0
55–59	97.4	89.8	0.0	0.0

Source: 1999 Annual Survey of Refugees.
Notes: Marriage specifically refers to current marriage. Residence with parents includes sons and daughters, as well as sons-in-law and daughters-in-law.

until the 40–44 age group and shows roughly the same percentages for men and women.[12] The patterns of delay in marriage and household formation seen in Vietnam are thus replicated here but at an increased degree.

There are various possible explanations for these findings. The basic premise here has been that there are distinctive patterns in southern Vietnamese household formation that can be expected to affect marriage and family formation both in the home country and in the United States. Those distinctive patterns will, for example, affect the selection and premigration experience of migrants (e.g., people may delay marriage in order to migrate) as well as their decisions about marital status and household residence after migration. One alternative argument is that the nature of refugee migration (or international migration in general) itself produces this pattern. Research on other immigrants, as varied as Mexicans in the United States (Dávila and Mora 2001) and Turks and Moroccans in Belgium (Schoenmaeckers, Lodewijckx, and Gadeyne 1999), has indicated delays in marital timing in relation to migration. The argument would thus be that the patterns seen for Vietnamese refugees simply reflect the dynamics of migration. Another alternative argument is that the patterns reflect individual characteristics of Vietnamese refugees either before migration (e.g., prior education, English competence at time of arrival) or currently (e.g., employment, current education). One might then argue that the patterns thus reflect identifiable individual characteristics of the Vietnamese in the United States rather than general cultural and historical continuities. Since the survey included refugees from other countries who have a broad range of premigration characteristics and postmigration experiences, some statistical testing of the original argument and these two alternative arguments is thus possible.[13]

To simplify a much longer argument,[14] a set of two regression analyses of selected variables from the survey both show the predictable, strong effects of age. That is expectable: age increases the chances of being married and decreases the chances of living with parents. In both regression analyses, however, being Vietnamese was the second strongest predictor. In comparison with other refugees groups, being Vietnamese decreased the chances of being married and increased the chances of residing with parents. Other variables that were significant in at least one of the analyses included length of residence, employment, education, gender, and ability to speak English.[15] Overall, the expectation that these patterns of marriage timing and household formation are distinctive to Vietnamese is not only supported in both regression analyses, but supported very strongly. These historical patterns have continued across migration to the United States; they cannot be explained away as somehow the result of migration or of individual refugee characteristics.

The situation of Vietnamese—and of those from southern Vietnam in particular—is thus distinctive compared with other recent refugees. But there are other sets of immigrants (if not refugees) who might have an analogous distinctiveness of household formation patterns, similar durability in these patterns over time, and some equivalent range of options that those patterns imply for adapting to a new country. Research on other East Asian groups, particularly Koreans (Park 1997) and Chinese (Song 1999), for example, has suggested similar patterns in the specific area of family businesses. That would suggest some similarity among East Asian groups—and there are good reasons to include Vietnam as part of East Asia on cultural and historical grounds. Data from the 2000 U.S. census provide the basis for a quantitative comparison among these groups. Considering simply the proportion of those who are married at different age groups, the differences are modest (see Table 5.9). Migrants from Japan, Korea, and Vietnam all have relatively low percentages married during their early twenties, ranging from 10 percent to 15 percent and, during their late twenties, ranging from 40 percent to

Table 5.9 Percent of adults married by age (selected countries of origin)

	20–24	25–29	30–34	35–39
China	18	59	79	88
Japan	10	40	65	77
Korea	13	42	71	84
Vietnam	15	41	61	76

Source: U.S. 2000 census (PUMS).

42 percent. All three groups, however, are quite different from those coming from China.

The more interesting data concern the percentages of adults living with their parents. Here, the Vietnamese case again emerges as quite distinctive (see Table 5.10). For those in their early twenties, over half were still residing with their parents. The second highest figure was for Koreans and that was a full 10 percentage points lower. For Vietnamese in their late twenties, a third were still residing with their parents. Again, the Koreans had the second highest figure, but this was now some 13 percentage points lower than the Vietnamese figure. That the Vietnamese figure for those in their early thirties was not particularly high suggests that this is indeed a delay in marriage rather than non-marriage per se. It is also interesting that the percentages of adult Vietnamese residing with siblings is also noticeably high. That figure remains at roughly 10 percent for those throughout their twenties and early thirties (see Table 5.11). Residing with siblings has much

Table 5.10 Percent of adults residing with parents by age (selected countries of origin)

	20–24	25–29	30–34
China	42	13	7
Japan	16	5	4
Korea	44	19	13
Vietnam	54	32	15

Source: 2000 U.S. census (PUMS).

Table 5.11 Percent of adults residing with siblings by age (selected countries of origin)

	20–24	25–29	30–34
China	6	6	4
Japan	2	0	0
Korea	5	3	2
Vietnam	9	11	11

Source: U.S. 2000 census (PUMS).

the same effect as residing with parents: more adults to share both income generation, family care, and educational investment expenses.

Change and Continuity

The suggestion that there is some continuity in household patterns between Vietnam and the United States may seem a modest one. Nevertheless, it is an important reiteration of the way that basic patterns of household formation persist even when the conditions of migration are, as they are for refugees, relatively disorderly. It is also an important point that what is seen here is not a generic "Vietnamese" pattern but one that is lodged within a particular area of the country under specific historical conditions. Some of those conditions have indeed changed—particularly a sharp decline in fertility. That there are these continuities despite such demographic change is crucial for the understanding of Vietnamese both at home and abroad.

What is more interesting and more problematic is the distinctiveness of this pattern compared with other populations. The data examined here strongly support that distinctiveness compared with other legally admitted refugees during early resettlement in the United States, and to other immigrants from East Asia. Compared with these other refugees—and even compared with other areas of Vietnam—there is for southern Vietnamese at home and abroad a significant delay in marriage and a significant delay in creating new households. Those findings have implications for understanding Vietnamese refugee adaptation in the United States.[16] In particular, the findings suggest an area of analysis that lies between the conventional categories of cultural and socioeconomic. In discussions either of Vietnamese cultural characteristics (such as a generic East Asian valuing of education) or of the socioeconomic background of individual refugees (such as occupational background or English language competence), these household dynamics can be overlooked. Yet, if people live in households that include two generations of working adults—households that hold their children through their twenties and sometimes even into their thirties—then their options are greatly expanded. Indeed, the household is then well positioned for what has become the American government's criterion for refugee success: economic self-sufficiency.

Perhaps more importantly, these households can accommodate a flexible allocation of roles. Mothers, for example, need not inevitably be the household's second wage earner. A son or daughter can provide that role. Furthermore, those who are working need not necessarily work full-time; instead, the combination of part-time wages among more people may equal full-time wages among fewer people. Adult children, in particular, may not have to work full-time since contributing to their parents' household is likely to be less expensive than creating their own. Continuing their education will thus be easier. If all the household members do decide to work full-time, then they can accumulate capital. The range of options is impressive: from freeing a family member from work for education or parenting, to putting everybody to work to accrue funds for some joint goal—such as owning a home.

What is clear from this Vietnamese case is that an understanding of the household in refugee adaptation can only be achieved through analysis that bridges home and new country experiences and that locates household dynamics in specific sociohistorical contexts. The fact that the patterns of delay in marriage and new household formation are not Vietnamese in a universal cultural sense[17] is indeed a useful reminder that migrants are rarely representative of their overall societies and, in the case of refugees, are almost never so. Yet, this Vietnamese case does suggest that sociohistorical comparisons are possible and can yield indications of distinctive and durable social arrangements among particular sets of refugees. That, in turn, permits a more balanced appreciation of what things change and what may yet remain the same across the dislocations of refugee flight and resettlement.

This Vietnamese case also suggests the need to consider how refuge in America is structured and whether program goals are consistent with the resources refugees bring with them, including these issues of household structure. In the Vietnamese case, for example, one can see some unique strengths that deserve attention not only in academic terms, but in policy terms as well. Perhaps above all, the Vietnamese case is a reminder of the very long story of migration—the unabridged and unexpurgated version—and how it extends over multiple generations in ways that are sometimes predictable and sometime unpredictable, sometimes reflecting change and sometimes durability.

Notes

1. As one alternative, people fleeing danger to the United States may be granted Temporary Protected Status. That makes them legal residents and provides work permits, but is granted only for limited periods of time (although often extended). Many of those fleeing to the United States, however, end up as part of the larger pool of illegal immigrants. They may eventually be approved for asylum (giving them a status equivalent to that of refugees), but that is often a very long process with an uncertain outcome.

2. See Caplan, Whitmore, and Bui (1991) for the classic elaboration of the argument about the cultural valuation of education.

3. This issue of family connections is often viewed differently by refugees and service providers. For example, an extensive early survey of Southeast Asian refugees in Illinois found that 77 percent of those questioned believed that broken families (as a result of exodus) were a "very serious" problem (Kim 1980: 110). It was, from the point of view of the refugees, their most serious problem, even more than English language difficulties. Confirming data come from another early survey in California in which "worry about family or friends still in homeland" was rated as the second most serious problem by the refugees interviewed (Human Resources Corporation 1979). In both these surveys, however, service providers were also asked to assess the seriousness of various problems facing refugees and in both cases rated such family problems as much less serious.

4. Ironically, the New Orleans Vietnamese again were displaced by Hurricane Katrina. Yet that resulted in another variant story of refugee perseverance. The MSNBC story included this commentary from Stone Phillips: "And I came away deeply impressed. No matter what our cultural background, we Americans have always taken pride in our ingenuity and initiative in times of crisis. The faith-based, grassroots recovery of these Vietnamese–Americans amidst all the damage inflicted by Katrina is a can-do, feel good story that all Americans can applaud" (http://insidedateline.msnbc.msn.com/archive/2007/06/15/142251.aspx).

5. The numbers remain uncertain, but it is clear that the major portion of the refugees leaving from northern areas of Vietnam were ethnic Chinese who fled to China itself or to Hong Kong (Amer 2009). Many of those coming from southern Vietnam, of course, were themselves northern in origin, having fled to the south after armistice in 1954. They are disproportionately represented among Vietnamese refugees in the United States (Dunning and Greenbaum 1982). That the southern Vietnamese pattern described here includes "Northerners" as well underlines the argument that these are not cultural values but social arrangements located in specific conditions. Li Tana's (1998) work on the early history of southern Vietnam

provides useful background, as does Woodside's (1995) discussion of what the southern frontier areas looked like to a northern court official.

6. The dynamics of Chinese-Vietnamese exodus (especially from northern Vietnam) are rather different from those for ethnic Vietnamese. It was the crackdown on ethnic Chinese in the late 1970s (and the border war with China) that increased the flows of ethnic Chinese from both northern and southern Vietnam.

7. Female household headship reflected both the temporary and permanent absence of spouses. However, it was often the case that women served as household heads even when their husbands were present. One particularly extensive survey in Vietnam in the 1990s, for example, showed that fully one-third of female household heads had a spouse present (FAO 2002). This doubtless reflects in part the fact that household headship in Vietnam has formal administrative duties in relation to the state; there are thus good reasons to avoid it.

8. This issue of continued residence with parents *after* marriage is not pursued in the rest of the paper. The number of people residing with parents-in-law was very small. Given the even sharper delays in marriage that will be noted for Vietnamese refugees in the United States, a quicker creation of a new household at the time of marriage would make much sense.

9. Such differences in sex ratios (and thus marriage patterns) are hardly unique to Vietnamese refugees in the United States. Lievens (1999) provides a useful comparison from Belgium.

10. As noted in previous chapters, these annual surveys had their origin in 1975 with what had become by 1979 a set of nine surveys of Southeast Asian refugees conducted published by Opportunity Systems, Incorporated. In 1981, the survey was substantially redesigned and in 1984 transformed into a panel design.

11. Other major sets of refugees by their ascribed ethnicity were Bosnians (724); Cuban or other Hispanic (286); Hmong (219); Jews (816); Russians (379); Somali (263); and Ukranians (448). For some of these groups the identifiers are ambiguous: for example, there were an additional 108 persons who identified themselves as Bosnian-Muslim (see discussion in Chapter 4). There were also, as would be expected from that discussion in Chapter 4, some other identities. For example, 89 people identified themselves as "white," 8 as "black," and 3 as "Christians."

12. Note that residence with parents-in-law is also included in this category—although the numbers are very small.

13. This discussion is limited to early arrivals in the United States and is based on organizational patterns rather than cultural values. There are longer-term issues in marital timing (Arias 2001) and the selection of spouses (Qian, Blair, and Ruf 2001). There are also questions that lie more with the meaning associated with marriage and family than with the actual organizational forms (Foner 1997).

14. A longer explanatory discussion of these regression analyses follows here. The actual tables can be found in Haines (2006: 210–211).

The discussion of household formation in the text focused on two specific issues: the frequency of marriage at different ages and the frequency of co-residence with parents at different ages. The two critical questions, then, are whether or not people are married and whether or not they are co-residing with their parents. These two issues (delay in marriage and co-residence with parents) were the outcome variables in two separate regression analyses. Since these outcome variables were dichotomous, logistic regression was used (forward stepwise with removal contingent on the likelihood ratio). The variables selected for input into the regression were somewhat limited by the nature of the survey—which is strongly oriented toward current economic status. However, the two crucial independent variables were readily available: age and being Vietnamese. Age could be expected to have a very powerful effect and the effect of being Vietnamese was exactly the question at issue. Thus, age at last birthday and being Vietnamese (versus any other ethnic self-identification) were included in both regressions. Other independent variables were then chosen from those available to represent both prior background and current situation. For prior background, years of education and highest degree were included, along with English at time of arrival. Length of residence in the United States and stability of residence (living in the same state a year ago or not) were also included. For current situation, the variables chosen were current employment (worked last week or not), current or recent enrollment in an educational program, and current level of English competence. Finally, gender was also included.)

The expectation was that age would inevitably be the major explanatory variable (the greater the age, the higher the likelihood of being married and the lower the likelihood of residence with parents). Vietnamese ethnicity was also expected to be significant (with being Vietnamese decreasing the likelihood of marriage and increasing the likelihood of residing with parents). The general direction of the other variables could also be predicted (e.g., that current education would have a negative relationship on marriage) but no effort was made to predict the strength of those associations compared with the effect of being Vietnamese. Finally, the cases for analysis were restricted to refugees aged 15–49. This avoids the tautological relation of age to marriage at the younger years and the separate issue of widows and widowers. (The exact cutoffs at 15 and 49 years were simply for consistency with the age categories used throughout the historical analysis.)

The results of the regression analysis of marriage showed that, as would inevitably be expected, age had a strong, positive effect on the probability of being married. The second most powerful predictor of being married was whether the person was Vietnamese. As expected, the relationship was an inverse one: being Vietnamese greatly reduced the probability of being married—all other things being equal. The third strongest effect was related to whether or not people were currently or recently in school. The direction of the relationship—being in school decreased the likelihood of being married—is expectable. Also expectable was the effect of gender: women were more likely to be married than men—other things beings equal. Length of residence was significant but in an unexpected direction. Those who had been in the country longer were less likely to be married—suggesting the influence of cohort characteristics rather than time in country per se. The normal expectation would be that length of residence would increase the chance of being married. However, in these data, the reverse was the case, suggesting that the characteristics of more recent arrivals were different in terms of marital status (more were married) and that there may have been some attrition in respondents from earlier years. Since this was an annual survey, it is possible to reconstruct the same analysis used here for those prior years. For the 1975 and 1976 surveys, length of residence had the expected effect of increasing the probability of being married; for the 1997 survey, length of residence was not a significant predictor; and for the 1998 survey, the results were similar to those presented here for the 1999 survey. Also, the negative relationship between work and marriage may initially seem surprising but reflects the great extent to which married women were less likely to work than unmarried ones. If the regression on marriage is run separately for men and women, this effect is clearly seen. Employment has an even stronger inverse effect for women and has a positive (but not statistically significant) effect for men.

The results of the analysis thus reflect the predictably strong effect of age, the implications of being Vietnamese, and an additional set of significant factors (current/recent education, gender, length of residence, and current employment) that are generally reasonable at face value. The results from the second regression analysis (continued co-residence with parents) match these results very closely, although the direction of the effects is generally the reverse. Thus, while age had a strong and positive effect on the likelihood of being married, it correspondingly had a strong and negative effect on the likelihood of residing with one's parents. In this regression, being Vietnamese was again the second most powerful predictor. Being Vietnamese had a strong and *positive* effect on the likelihood of residing with parents, just as it had a strong and *negative* effect on the likelihood of being married. Length of residence, gender, and current/recent education were significant factors in this regression as in the previous one: current/recent education significantly increased the likelihood of residing with parents, while gender (being female) decreased the likelihood. Length of residence was—again counterintuitively—a positive predictor. The difference between the two regressions lies with only the last two of the significant predictors. In the regression on co-residence, working has a more predictable effect (those residing with parents tend not to be working) and speaking English well is an additional significant and positive predictor of the likelihood of co-residing with parents.

15. For both regressions, interaction variables were also created and included in an additional set of analyses. Those interaction variables were indeed significant— as they would be expected to be. For the regression on marriage, the interactions of age with being Vietnamese, age with current education, age with gender, and length of residence with current employment were all significant at the .001 level. Nevertheless, even including those interaction variables, the original variables of age, being Vietnamese, current education, and gender all retained their individual significance at the .001 level. For the regression on co-residence, the situation is somewhat more complicated. Age remained the major predictor, followed by the interaction effect of being Vietnamese and length of residence. This makes sense given the decline in percentages of Vietnamese refugees during the periods of entry covered by these surveys, suggesting again that the length of residence variable is

polysemic. If the same analysis is conducted on an earlier version of the survey, being Vietnamese retains its individual significance—although it does not do so in the 1999 survey.

16. For the study of Vietnamese kinship more generally, the findings suggest an area for analysis that lies between the more cultural study of kinship (which has tended to emphasize such issues as patrilineality and hierarchy) and a more sociological approach that has tended to emphasize the demographics of Vietnamese households (especially fertility) and the distinction between extended and nuclear family households. Here, instead, is a different dynamic of two generations bound together not only in the rearing of the younger generation, but in the co-residence for some time of both generations when they are economically active. This may not necessarily produce extended family households since adult children may start new households before they have children—it is just that marriage and child-bearing are delayed. Nor does this dynamic necessarily produce large households. Indeed, the delay in marriage and child-bearing would be fully consistent with smaller households. Yet, this dynamic nevertheless produces the co-residence of two adult generations, does so for significant periods of time, can do so for even longer periods when necessary (as with migration), and does so for both sons and daughters. Although the resulting households might be described technically as nuclear rather than extended, they nevertheless permit exactly the enduring relations into adulthood between parents and children that are expected from extended, three-generational households. Another crucial result of the delay in marriage is that generations are relatively far apart in years. Thus, these two co-residing generations span a longer period of chronological time. This changes the very meaning of inter-generational transmission. See Haines (2006) for this broader discussion of Vietnamese households.

17. It could also be argued, however, that what is seen in the southern Vietnamese data is nothing but a variation on a broader theme in Vietnamese kinship: the continued binding of the generations even after the junior generation reaches adulthood. The delay of marriage discussed here, and the frequent postmarital residence of newlyweds with the husband's parents as described for northern Vietnam, could thus both be seen as producing the same end result: an overlap of the generations as co-residing adults. This is a line of argument that could help recreate a more unitary cultural analysis of Vietnamese kinship.

6

The Logic of Resettlement: English and Self-Sufficiency

Refuge in the United States ultimately requires adaptation to a new society that presents a variety of options and constraints, and that has its own expectations about newcomers. The refugees' "second story" of life in a new country is thus interlinked with the expectations of that country. In the United States, these expectations have generally been that refugees will become "good" immigrants, that they will value their opportunity to be in the United States, and that they will use that opportunity to advance themselves and their children. Other results of life in the United States—whether of poverty or of yearning to return to the home country—often strike Americans as inappropriate and ungrateful. This is a distinctly American story and one with roots in the Christian heritage: refuge means moving on to a new promised land, not returning to the old one. By contrast, an Islamic notion of refuge would, following Mohammed's own exile in Medina, suggest the goal of return. In that case, refuge provides the resources to endure until the time of return, not the resources to build a new life in a new country.

This American notion of a new life for refugees—that refugees are also immigrants—pervades the U.S. refugee resettlement program. It is not that the United States fails to recognize the need for temporary refuge. There is, in fact, exactly such a program in the United States. But it is not the refugee program; it is a separate program for "temporary protected status" (TPS) that permits people of designated national origins to remain in the United States, but only for specified periods of time. It is not convertible into other kinds of legal status. That can be a problem when the status ends. In 2007, for example, TPS for Liberians officially ended, leaving many long-time U.S. residents with the difficult choice of returning to a country that explicitly stated it was not yet ready to receive them or drifting into illegal status. (Ultimately, TPS for Liberians was reinstated in 2009 under the new Obama administration.)

Whether or not this particular notion of refuge as permanent settlement is correct or not, U.S. efforts at resettling refugees have at their core this notion of permanency, of a new chance, and thus of considerable pressure on refugees to prove that they are deserving of that chance. This can have effects on decisions regarding admissions since, as with regular immigrants, the more skilled the refugees are, the more likely they are to succeed in this task of becoming new Americans. Any "difficult" new case, whether because of age, health, education, or socioeconomic background, is a potential threat to the success of the resettlement program. Any "good" new case, whether because of youth, English competence, education, or economic skills, helps show that refugees are not only the dispossessed but deserving of a new life in America. This is a difficult dynamic: true refugees must thus be in need, but not needy; without resources, but still resourceful.

The refugee resettlement program is forever at the mercy of this quandary and, as Chapter 1 suggested, the existing research cannot resolve the issue because the course of refugee adaptation to the United States will always hinge on the starting point for each individual refugee. It is impossible, given the sheer range of variation among refugees, to design research that can establish the extent of their incremental gains in adjustment when taking into account that variation. Despite such problems, this chapter attempts a closer look at two key goals of the refugee resettlement program, the internal logic of these goals, and how they match up with the research. These two key goals are English language competence and economic self-sufficiency. The discussion will largely focus on the period from 1975 to 1985, a particularly turbulent period of large and complicated Southeast Asian arrivals; the passage of the Refugee Act of 1980; the sudden influx of a large number of Cubans and Haitians immediately thereafter; and the new Reagan administration's coordinated attack on the welfare system—into which refugees had just been placed by that very Refugee Act. Prior to that discussion, however, a brief return to the period of the DPs, Hungarians, and early Cubans helps set the stage for the shift from a relatively informal, voluntary agency-based approach to a refugee resettlement program under the tight control of the federal government.

A Program for Refugees

As the St. Louis sailed along the eastern coast of the United States in 1939, advocates for the refugees aboard noted that many of the refugees already had affidavits of support. Some person or organization had already made the commitment to support the refugees after arrival. The federal government, after all, had long been concerned that refugees (and other immigrants) not become public charges. So, in effect, there was a division of labor between the government (which decided on admissions) and non-governmental organizations (which ensured that refugees were not a public burden after arrival). There was thus, effectively, no governmental program concerned with refugee adaptation after arrival. That second refugee story of building a new life was not their business, but that of the private sector. While there might be an argument about special admissions for refugees, there could be no talk of special governmental assistance.

That lack of a formal government program for refugee resettlement was of little concern when there were not many refugee arrivals. In the years after the end of the Second World War, however, that changed. There were millions of displaced persons in Europe after the war and, with shifts in borders, it was not always clear where they should go back to. Perhaps above all, there was a growing recognition, even fear, of forcing these DPs back to countries that were now communist and, in Winston Churchill's evocative coinage of 1946, behind an "iron curtain." It was a fear jointly shared by Franklin Roosevelt's widow Eleanor and his presidential successor Harry Truman. Indeed, one of the last exchanges in the long correspondence between Eleanor Roosevelt and Harry Truman in 1959 concerned exactly this point, with the former somewhat plaintively inquiring whether somehow there had been forced returns and Truman reassuring her that forced returns had occurred only in specific and justifiable cases (Neal n.d.).

The need to provide resettlement in the United States for at least some of these DPs was first formally acknowledged with a directive from President Truman in 1945 that permitted a limited number of DPs to enter the country. Most of these were Jewish (Dinnerstein 1982: 163). Initial efforts to expand the numbers met with limited support for that reason—the anti-Semitism seen in the events of 1939 had hardly disappeared. Only as the public began to realize that most of the DPs were, in fact, Christian, did enough support develop to expand the program (Dinnerstein 1982). The result was the Displaced Persons Act of 1948 which, as subsequently amended, allowed for the entry of 415,000 DPs—and the Refugee Relief Act of 1953 authorized another 214,000 under somewhat different conditions.[1]

While it was the U.S. government that approved the entry of the DPs, it was the voluntary agencies that had the central role in post-arrival assistance. Indeed, the author of the original house bill (Representative Stratton) stressed how unlikely these people were to need assistance since they "represent a survival of the fittest, having escaped and endured what millions of their kinsmen could not survive" (quoted in Divine 1957: 116). If there was to be assistance, then, it would come from the voluntary agencies. Some of these, especially the Catholic and Jewish agencies, were large and well-funded. Others were smaller and with more limited resources. The Polish American Immigration and Relief Committee, for example, was dependent on rather small amounts of money, which may have sparked its interest in innovative group employment projects for the refugees it sponsored (Cizek 2006).

In 1956, in the wake of the crushed Hungarian uprising, some 200,000 refugees (the CIA's estimate was 188,000—Coriden 1958) streamed across the border into Austria, and ultimately 38,000 of them were resettled in the United States. This time, however, the government was more actively involved. Refugees were processed through an actual military base on U.S. soil (Camp Kilmer in New Jersey) and post-arrival assistance received some-what greater attention. But still the emphasis was on how readily self-reliant these refugees would be. Bon Tempo (2008: 75), for example, notes the gov-ernment's "feverish efforts to reassure Americans" that these refugees were like them, that they were "good Americans" in terms of family, gender roles, and employment.[2] A classified CIA memo at the time noted the "happy" fact that these refugees were young and well-educated and with relevant occupational backgrounds (Coriden 1958). They would, it seemed, fit in quickly and well.

Less than four years later, a much larger refugee influx began from Cuba. The influx occurred in distinct phases, reflecting the degree to which the Cuban government under Fidel Castro would allow people to leave and, if so, whether they could go directly to the United States.[3] There was also a major change in the U.S. government's involvement in post-arrival assistance for the refugees. Perhaps the two key initiatives were the establishment of a federal government presence directly in Miami in 1960 and legislation two years later (the Migration and Refugee Assistance of 1962) that directly authorized federal funds for assistance to refugees, including cash assistance, health care, education and training (including refresher courses for professionals). Transportation costs and other assistance for refugees willing to resettle away from Miami were also available.[4] This assistance was, at least until the end of the 1970s,[5] open-ended in terms of how long refugees could receive the assistance and how long the federal government would reimburse state and local governments for their costs in assisting Cuban refugees.

Over the next decade and a half, there were continued Cuban arrivals, an increasing number of refugees from the Soviet Union, and occasional smaller groups—for example, the Chileans who fled after the 1973 coup against then President Salvador Allende. By and large, these arriving refugees could count on strong community support in the United States, from the Cuban community in Miami (with a helping hand from the Catholic Church) and from the very well-organized Jewish community (such as the Hebrew Immigrant Aid Society [HIAS]). Both communities were well organized, had their own resources, and had the political heft to ensure that federal funding continued. While refugees might be receiving public assistance from the federal government, they were thus not a burden on state and local governments.

The influx of refugees from Southeast Asia posed, at least initially in 1975, a situation somewhat like the Hungarian case, although on a bigger scale. This time there were multiple processing centers and the need for a far larger number of sponsorships. Thus, again, the federal government was handling processing and the voluntary sector was handling actual resettlement (although in both cases state governments could also sign as sponsors). There was also, however, the precedent of the Cuban case with direct federal funding of post-arrival assistance. The legislation regarding assistance to these refugees (the Indochinese Migration and Refugee Assistance Act of 1975) thus granted the same kinds of assistance and services, and the same reimbursement of state and local government costs, that already existed for Cuban refugees.

The Southeast Asian refugee influx after 1975, however, posed some different problems. One was simply that a one-time crisis had developed into a continuing one. The number of refugees was increasing by the end of the decade to crisis proportions (around 81,000 in 1979 and 167,000 in 1980 versus 130,000 in 1975). The arriving refugees were also increasingly diverse in national and ethnic origins, and in the language, educational, and occupational background that would so strongly influence the course of their new lives in America. These new refugees also lacked a strong community base in the United States. That presented some positive policy options, for example, in dispersing the refugees across the country and thus avoiding the kind of refugee concentration that existed in Miami. It also, however, meant that it would be some time before there was an active refugee community that could work in cooperation with the government and the voluntary agencies.

There was also uncertainty about how the Southeast Asian refugee exodus would develop over time and how the program for these particular refugees should be integrated with other existing refugee programs. There were administrative complexities with different agencies responsible for different aspects of post-arrival assistance (and different program offices responsible for different refugee groups) and with different legislation for the various refugee groups, each with its own kind, level, and duration of support. There were also long-lingering questions about why the United

States had still not incorporated the formal U.N. refugee definition into its own laws and why U.S. refugee admissions were so restricted to particular areas of the world (e.g., almost entirely excluding Africa). There was no single "refugee program" that accounted for all refugees in terms of admissions or in terms of post-arrival assistance. It was time to get organized.

When Senator Edward Kennedy opened hearings in 1979 on comprehensive refugee legislation, he remarked for the record, "I believe our national policy of welcome to the homeless has served our country and our traditions well. But we are here this morning to explore how we can do this job better" (U.S. Senate 1979: 1). The final version of that legislation, the Refugee Act of 1980, was passed the next year and remains the U.S. refugee program of today in administrative ways (as in the division of responsibility between the Department of State and the Department of Health and Human Services), in how refugee admissions are decided (through annual consultations with the Congress), and in the weaving together of the public and private sectors (and of government at the federal, state, and local levels).

In terms of the post-arrival situation, the Refugee Act was clear on the need for transitional assistance. However, the actual nature of that transitional assistance was the subject of considerable debate during the hearings and in the years immediately preceding and following its passage. The picture was also clouded by the influx of Cubans and Haitians a few months after the passage of the Act. They received an entirely new legal status of "entrant." Although they were ultimately given the same kinds of support that refugees received, they did not have the same legal status. Perhaps more importantly, the new Reagan Administration moved to limit the time periods for much refugee assistance, doing so just as the country slipped into a major recession. Meanwhile, the flow of refugees from Southeast Asia continued at a high rate.

This effort to make the refugee program more orderly and more effective came in the middle of a period of remarkable turbulence. This period was the crucible in which the future of refugee admissions and the futures of refugees after arrival were reconfigured. There would now be a very clear and central role of the government in post-arrival assistance as well as in admissions and processing. Because of that central role, there was also during this period an unusually broad range of research on refugee adaptation, especially a series of strong research initiatives from the new Office of Refugee Resettlement in the Department of Health and Human Services. In considering the policy development of refugee resettlement in the years bracketing the new Refugee Act of 1980, it is thus also possible to invoke a degree of research on refugee resettlement probably unmatched either before or since.

In addressing this fortunate pairing of policy and research, the remainder of this chapter examines the two core goals that emerged in this newly revised and integrated resettlement program: English language competence and economic self-sufficiency.[6] Both goals seem reasonable at face value, but they also illustrate the difficulties—and dangers—in specifying narrow goals for very broad social programs, particularly given the fundamental dilemma of whether refugees are admitted because of humanitarian need or because they have the characteristics that will help them prosper after arrival in America. Because this issue is so fundamental to refugee resettlement, the following discussion is rather detailed and focuses specifically on this critical period bracketing the Refugee Act of 1980.

English Language Training

On the face of it, knowledge of English would seem to be a prerequisite for successful adaptation to the United States, not only through the economic advantages it confers (inarguable at all but the most limited occupational levels) but also in its implications for absorption into, and commitment to, mainstream American social, cultural, and political life. English language competence, it would appear, is a good thing all around. The Refugee Act of 1980 itself stipulated English language competence as a program goal in its own right, not simply as something conducive to economic adjustment.

The essential reasonableness of this emphasis on English language competence was strongly supported by the early research on Southeast Asian refugees in the United States. A very wide range of research demonstrated that the ability to speak English was closely correlated to economic success, including obtaining jobs, the salary and wage levels of those jobs, and the overall economic situation of refugee households. Table 6.1 provides illustrative data on such correlations. Suffice it to say that the better the level of English, the more frequent the search for work, the more successful that job search, and the better the job obtained.

Furthermore, the research also indicated that refugees themselves perceived English as a crucial skill. In surveys that included questions regarding key needs, problems, or barriers to successful resettlement, English consistently emerged as of great perceived importance, indeed, often as the greatest perceived need (e.g., Dunning and Greenbaum 1982; Human Resources Corporation 1979; Kim 1980). This emphasis on the importance of English language competence partially reflected the lack of such competence among many early Southeast Asian refugees. National survey data (ORR 1985a: 96), for example, suggested that throughout the first ten years of Southeast

Table 6.1 Some consistent correlates of English language competence
(selected sources)

	LEVEL OF ENGLISH LANGUAGE COMPETENCE			
	NONE	SOME	GOOD	FLUENT
1975 Vietnamese arrivals in 1976				
Labor force participation rate		26.3	66.4	76.2
Unemployment rate		27.7	12.5	9.6
1975 Vietnamese arrivals in 1978				
Labor force participation rate		18.0	65.9	69.2
Unemployment rate		3.9	6.4	3.6
Percent in white-collar occupations		11.4	19.4	50.0
Percent with wages over $200 per week		8.8	29.4	39.8
All Southeast Asian arrivals in 1984				
Labor force participation rate	19.6	55.3	63.3	64.4
Unemployment rate	32.3	18.5	9.1	4.4
Average weekly wages	$194	$197	$224	$275
1975–1977 Vietnamese arrivals in 1980				
Overall employment ratio	25	57	69	70
Percent with cash assistance	63	34	22	12
Median monthly personal income	$455	$595	$828	$944

Sources: For 1975 Vietnamese arrivals, OSI (1976: Tables 38, 39; 1979: Tables 4, 5, 11, 14); for all Southeast Asian refugees in 1984, ORR (1985a: 94); for the 1975–1979 Vietnamese arrivals, Dunning and Greenbaum (1982: 110, 154, 160).

Note: For 1975 Vietnamese arrivals in 1976 and in 1978, only three levels of competence were used. For the 1975–1977 Vietnamese arrivals in 1980 (Dunning and Greenbaum 1982), the categories were somewhat different than as listed at the column headings: (1) hardly at all or none, (2) not very well, (3) fair, and (4) well or very well.

Asian refugee resettlement, over two-fifths of each year's arrivals spoke no English, rising to roughly two-thirds for those arriving in the peak years of 1979–1981.[7]

English language competence was thus not only an explicit goal of the refugee program, but one whose reasonableness was virtually unquestionable. The research supported its frequent co-occurrence with economic success, there was wide demand for it, and there was a demonstrable lack of such competence among the arriving refugees. Not only was the emphasis on English language competence reasonable, but it involved a desired client effect that was potentially measurable, and a quite definable service that was relevant to that desired effect: English language training. Thus, the goal of increased English language competence led without any great paroxysms of policy analysis to a program based on the transfer of funds from the federal government to a very wide range of organizations that, in turn, provided training in order to improve the English language competence of their refugee clients.

The high degree of reasonableness, precision, and implementability of English language competence as a program goal was matched by the relative simplicity in assessing program outcomes. Only three central questions needed to be asked: (1) whether the service was being provided; (2) whether it achieved its goal of increasing English language competence; and (3) whether it did so at reasonable levels of effectiveness and cost. Not only were these questions straightforward, but there was sufficient research to provide preliminary answers to them, and sufficient funding to pursue additional more refined research.

In answer to the first question of whether the service was being provided, the answer was a strong yes. Unlike many programs that aim at small service groups, English language training for refugees was so pervasively used that it could be measured in very general survey work. Such data showed very large numbers of adults in English language training classes. The federal government's 1982 and 1983 annual surveys (ORR 1983a: 25; 1984: 111), for example, indicated proportions of about one in two for those in the United States less than a year, declining to around one in three for those in their third year of U.S. residence. Other survey data showed the very high proportions of those who had been in such classes at some point since arrival in the United States: generally in the range of three out of four adults (see Caplan, Whitmore, and Bui 1985; Dunning and Greenbaum 1982; ORR 1984: 99; Strand and Jones 1985). The frequency of English language training for all segments of the refugee population is illustrated by the data presented in Tables 6.2 and 6.3, the former based on a survey of training providers, the latter on a survey of refugees in four sites (see Reder and Cohn 1984; Reder et al. 1984; Reder, Nelson, and Arter 1982). While women were less frequently enrolled than men, still two-thirds of them had received some training. While those with limited education were less frequently enrolled than those with more education, still two-thirds of them had received some training. Thus, the reasonable emphasis on English language competence was coupled with very impressive enrollment in English language training.

The second question was whether refugees actually learned English from the English language training. Probably the best documentation comes from the federally funded study of English language training for refugees conducted by the Northwest Regional Educational Laboratory

Table 6.2 Some characteristics of English language students and programs (survey of programs, 1982)

	%
Type or organization	
Secondary school adult education program	26.1
Community college	23.0
Voluntary or resettlement agency	14.6
Other nonprofit agency	13.7
Vocational–technical school	10.6
University or college	3.5
Other type of agency	8.5
Hourly cost of training	
Less than $1.00	10
$1.00–$1.99	27
$2.00–$2.99	22
$3.00–$3.99	9
$4.00–$4.99	7
$5.00–$5.99	2
$6.00–$6.99	1
$7.00–$7.99	2
$8.00 or more	21
Program size	
Small (50 or less)	19
Medium (51–150)	27
Large (151–300)	19
Very large (301 and over)	35
Students' educational background	
None	15.2
1–3 years	19.6
4–6 years	29.5
7–12 years	31.5
13 years and over	4.2
Students' length of U.S. residence	
0–6 months	30.5
7–12 months	27.1
13–18 months	15.1
19–24 months	16.6
25–30 months	5.3
31–36 months	2.7
37 months and over	2.6

Source: Reder, Nelson, and Arter (1982: 18, 43, 47, 49, 101).

Note: The source for the data is a survey of English language programs (including small numbers of non-Southeast Asian refugee clients) conducted in 1982. Percentages related to refugee characteristics and to program size are computed on the basis of the total refugee student population in the programs. Rounding in the table follows the original; figures do not always sum to 100 percent because of that rounding.

Table 6.3   English language training for Cambodians, Hmong, and Vietnamese (four sites, 1982)

	PER CAPITA HOURS OF TRAINING	PERCENT RECEIVING TRAINING	MEAN HOURS FOR THOSE RECEIVING TRAINING
In refugee camps			
Cambodian	18	12	150
Hmong	5	5	101
Vietnamese	29	12	242
Female	5	5	
Male	23	14	
Age			
20–29	21	14	
30–39	11	8	
40–49	11	8	
50–59	10	3	
60+	1	2	
In the United States			
Cambodian	535	76	700
Hmong	512	74	692
Vietnamese	486	72	675
Female	390	67	
Male	622	81	
Age			
20–29	573	79	
30–39	567	82	
40–49	558	78	
50–59	303	61	
60+	83	18	
By years of education prior to entry			
None	364	67	
1–3 years	476	67	
4–6 years	561	75	
7–11 years	659	84	
12+ years	588	79	

Source: Reder and Cohn (1984: 180, 181, 183, 185, 186).
Note: By design, all respondents were adults who had been in the United States from one to three years.

(Reder et al. 1984). That study (the source of the data in Tables 6.2 and 6.3) included a general survey of English language training programs, site reviews of specific programs, surveys of refugees to assess the extent and effects of the language training, and pre- and post-testing of refugees in selected programs. The results, although indicating wide variation in language acquisition, showed the positive effects of English language training even when the effects of longer residence in the United States were considered. The wide provision of English language training thus resulted in the gain in English language competence that was the originating program goal.

In answering the third question about relative effectiveness and costs, the research provided less clear-cut answers. As indicated in Table 6.2, the range in cost per hour of training in 1982 was rather large. While the mean cost was barely above $2 per hour, for one in five programs the hourly instructional cost was over $8. Such cost figures have limited meaning without considering the relative level of success of the training. That is, it is necessary to link the cost of training to measurable units of service and of outcome to be able to define the cost per unit of defined quality. This is not an insurmountable problem. Reder et al. (1984), for example, provided projective cost assessments for bringing specific kinds of refugees to specified levels of competence. English language competence is, after all, testable; changes in it can be quantified, matched against program costs, and broken down in terms of client characteristics, curricula, institutional contexts, and other program features.

All this seems to suggest that the emphasis on English language training was eminently sensible. Yet, even with this straightforward program goal, there were some problems. Many refugees (then and now) lack much competence in English yet also achieve some measure of economic progress in the United States. That suggested that English language competence might not be an inevitable prerequisite for economic success, perhaps particularly for Spanish speakers in places such as Miami. English, of course, might remain an important cultural goal, in the sense that people who live in America should speak English as a matter of sharing a common culture and communication system. But English as a means to promote economic adjustment might have more questionable value, especially since extensive language training might take people away from work.

Furthermore, the research failed to demonstrate that the strong correlation between English language competence and economic situation was the effect of English as a specific teachable skill after arrival rather than simply a reflection of the general educational levels of refugees or their English competence at the time of arrival. Several multivariate statistical analyses of refugee economic status during that crucial 1975–1985 period (see Aames et al. 1977; Caplan, Whitmore, and Bui 1985; Dunning and Greenbaum 1982; Starr et al. 1979; Strand and Jones 1985) indicated that English language competence was *not* statistically significant when the analysis was controlled for refugees' occupational and educational background. Data from one five-site survey further suggested that, insofar as English was a predictor of current economic status, the better such predictor was not current English but English at time of arrival (Caplan, Whitmore, and Bui 1985). Thus, even if English language competence appears as statistically significant in its effects on economic status, it remains far from convincingly documented that the acquisition of *additional* language competence through formal programs makes any strong difference in economic status. Even if one maintains, despite such analytic problems, that training does improve language competence and that improved language competence improves refugees' economic situation, the amount of variation in economic situation explained by this English language acquisition appeared to be small at best.

The apparently reasonable emphasis on the value of English language training for English language competence for a population that clearly needed it no longer seems quite so reasonable. This is not to suggest that English language training was not worth providing then, or is not worth providing now. The caution has more to do with the plausible extent of the effects. Perhaps part of the problem is an American tendency to underestimate the amount of time and effort needed to achieve a fully functional level in a foreign language. The research might be suggesting that the levels of English language training that are provided are simply too limited to have any substantial effect. Instead, a more massive educational effort is needed—one that would require keeping refugees out of work for a period long enough to provide full facility with spoken and written English. The period of transitional assistance for refugees would then have to be reconceptualized as a much longer period of time. Such a potential delay in refugee employment was often discussed in the period leading up to the Refugee Act. However, it inevitably came into conflict with a second primal goal that emerged during this crucial period of program restructuring: the emphasis on refugee self-sufficiency.

Economic Self-Sufficiency

Like English language competence, the refugee program goal of self-sufficiency seems eminently reasonable in principle and it too was embedded as a primary goal in the Refugee Act of 1980—indeed, probably, the single most important program goal and the one on which the U.S. General Accounting Office (now the Government Accountability Office) would chastise the program only three years later (GAO 1983b). Yet, this idea of self-sufficiency poses some problems. The problems begin at the definitional level. The term "self-sufficiency" has very broad potential reference. At the broadest level, self-sufficiency (or self-reliance) might be seen as a core American value that applies to all areas of economic, social, cultural, and political life. While this helps explain its appeal as a program goal, it does not provide much precision to its meaning. Another troublesome question is whose self-sufficiency is of concern. If self-sufficiency is limited strictly to economic issues, for example, it is not really individuals who are self-sufficient, but the households in which they live. Thus a problem of unit definition is introduced into any implementation of this goal; self-sufficiency necessarily refers to transitory sets of persons many of whom are, by definition, not self-sufficient as individuals—children, for example.

One solution to these ambiguities in the refugee program was to define self-sufficiency as the absence of receipt of cash assistance by a household. It is a minimalist kind of governmental definition. Its advantage is that it goes to the heart of public concern about whether refugees are costing anybody any money. Missing, of course, in such a formulation are such broader questions as whether a household is rising above poverty or how it is doing given its specific advantages (such as good education) or its specific needs (such as numerous children, lost spouses). Should there not be a separate standard (or timetable) for the well-educated versus those whose education has been limited or interrupted? Should there not be a separate standard (or timetable) for refugee groups that are disproportionately old, or with large numbers of children? The minimalist governmental definition thus tended to elide the complexities of the refugee situation.

Compared to English language competence, then, self-sufficiency as a program goal is more diffuse in meaning, complicated by analytic problems in unit definition, and lacking in easy calculability as a program effect— other than as a minimalist on/off public assistance. This difficulty in goal definition is matched by the administrative complexity of the refugee program that was formalized in the Refugee Act of 1980. Cash assistance to refugees, for example, was tied directly in eligibility, benefit levels, and administrative procedures to cash assistance provided to other Americans. There was also a special refugee cash assistance program that reflected the disruption of refugee flight, especially the obvious fact that refugees did not have a normal work history.[8] The costs of that assistance were also paid by states and localities but were to be reimbursed by the federal government. That provision of reimbursement provided a very clear tracking of the exact costs of assistance to refugees. States and localities had to identify assistance recipients as refugees in order to obtain federal reimbursement. Refugee cash assistance thus became a subset of mainstream assistance programs rather than a special transitional assistance program for a unique population. Implicitly, then, there was thus no longer any basis for thinking about cash assistance as a way to enhance self-sufficiency, for example, by using cash assistance as a way to remedy an interruption of education, or provide a multiyear attempt at true English language education. Cash assistance was no longer a tool to be used proactively toward refugee self-sufficiency, but only an indication of a lack of self-sufficiency, of a dependence on the welfare system that the new Reagan administration would attack so strongly.

Such cash assistance, of course, was only one part of a broad range of assistance and services for refugees, including training toward that other core goal of English language competence. These other kinds of support were also provided through rather complex administrative procedures, with funding from both the Department of State and the Office of Refugee Resettlement— and other mainstream programs as well. The result for refugees was often confusion; the result for refugee agencies was often a frenetic pace of grant applications to different sources trying to patch together a coherent and stable program. There were thus multiple funding channels; multiple grant awards within these channels; a mix (and sometimes overlap) of public and private involvement; complicated federal, state, and local relationships; and more detailed congressional interest than would seem to be justified by the program's size.

During this crucial period from 1975 to 1985, there were also major changes in the context in which the refugee program operated—and to which refugees were adapting. Consider how tumultuous were the formative years of the program both immediately before and after the Refugee Act of 1980. First, there was a very large influx of refugee in the 1979–1981 period (predominantly of so-called boat people) that inevitably stretched resettlement resources. Flows during that period dwarfed the 1975 influx, the management and results of which had always been treated as great accomplishments. It is hardly surprising that such a large and continuing influx, handled without the special provisions available in 1975, may have left many arrivals with less than necessary services and assistance, leaving problems for future years. There could not help but be a backlog. The Mariel exodus of some 125,000 Cubans in 1980, and the arrival of some 25,000 Haitians during that same year, placed additional stress on the refugee program since it became eventually responsible for assistance and services to the Cuban/Haitian entrant population as well as to legally designated refugees.

Second, refugees arriving during those years presented some special problems in resettlement. While the common discussions of drastically different "waves" of refugees from Southeast Asia are ill-advised (the best data show rather moderate changes in occupational and educational background over this period), nevertheless the arriving population included increased numbers of occupational groups (such as farmers) likely to face difficulties in finding relevant work, and a wider range of national and ethnic groups each with its own special problems (e.g., Khmer holocaust survivors; non-literate Hmong). Thus, not only was the arriving population large, but it was also extremely diverse and with some groups likely to have significant post-arrival adjustment problems.

Third, the early 1980s witnessed a deep recession that greatly affected the employment opportunities of refugees who were arriving or had recently arrived in the United States. The survey data at the time indicated the problems faced by even the earliest arrivals, those who had generally been held up as models of success in adapting to American society. Comparison of annual survey findings from the Office of Refugee Resettlement across the early 1980s, for example, shows not only the effects of the recession on these early arrivals but also their subsequent recovery as the economy moved out of the recession.

Fourth, the early 1980s witnessed not a stabilization of the refugee program, but an additional series of key program changes. Some derived from the Refugee Act of 1980, but others from amendments to that Act and from non-legislatively driven changes in program policy. One that merits attention is the institution of a cut-off of federal reimbursement of cash assistance to refugees, making the post-three-year costs a state responsibility, thus ensuring the states' very active involvement in refugee policy debates. Subsequent limitations of special refugee cash assistance to an eighteen-month period (which greatly affected states that lacked strong general assistance programs), and later shifts away from policy alignment with Aid to Families with Dependent Children (AFDC) created further instability both for refugees and for the state and local governments that now found themselves paying more of the cost for refugee assistance. (Those periods of reimbursement and special assistance were further limited in the late 1980s; by 1990, the special assistance available to refugees was limited to nine months and there was no federal reimbursement at all of state costs for that assistance [Holman 1996].)

Given the complex web of new and existing programs, and this complex, shifting context, the hope of assessing refugee program effects might seem slight indeed. However, the federal government's restriction of the notion of self-sufficiency to a binary on/off public assistance did offer one simple resolution. It represented an evolution of the concept of self-sufficiency from a broad, multifaceted, and self-sustaining self-sufficiency to a minimalist on/off public assistance kind of self-sufficiency. That minimalized goal clearly required rapid employment at whatever future cost. Out of the maze of questions about what self-sufficiency might mean emerged two specific goals: rapid employment (more people employed more quickly) and "reducing dependency" (fewer households on assistance—and quickly for that as well).

Reducing Dependency

This narrow definition of self-sufficiency eased some of the analytic difficulties in assessing how refugee program resources should be used. Although the refugee program in the early 1980s was closely tied to existing mainstream cash and medical assistance programs, yet there was latitude for program innovation and modification, and still quite extensive funding. Virtually all aspects of the program, then, could be explicitly directed toward the goal of "reducing dependency." Thus, one reason tighter management of voluntary agencies was instituted by the Department of State was the concern that these agencies were involving refugees too soon or too easily in cash assistance programs. Relatively liberal provisions within the refugee legislation that might be seen as encouraging use of public assistance were also removed. For example, there had originally been a two-month waiver of the obligation to seek work—hardly unreasonable for newly arriving refugees. That was eliminated.

There were also a variety of more procedural changes. Policies were tightened to provide "incentives" for refugees to get off assistance and to provide sanctions when they failed to do so. Demonstration projects were funded to provide alternative mechanisms for provision of assistance to refugees who were more removed from the mainstream system (especially in California, which, like most liberal assistance states, tended to have large numbers of refugees on assistance), and special "targeted assistance" funds were provided to address the backlog of clients previously underserved because of high refugee "impact" on particular localities. Efforts were also made to focus on "harder" services such as job placement rather than "softer" services such as counseling or services related to mental health. There was frequent emphasis on "case management" as a method to more effectively control refugee clients in general, and to keep them from becoming "dependent" on the welfare system. To that end, assistance was in some cases reduced by fiat (as occurred with the reduction of the refugee cash assistance program to ever shorter periods of time). There were also extensive efforts at designing and evaluating program options, not only by the federal government (e.g., ORR 1982b, 1983b) but also by state and local governments, voluntary agencies, foundations, and other organizations and individuals. Throughout, there was also a kind of ideological campaign that chastised refugees (to some extent) and those who served them (to a greater extent) for the development of an "entitlement mentality" and for the self-serving creation by voluntary agencies and service providers of a "refugee industry."

There was thus in the early 1980s no lack of action and no lack of funding toward the realization of this program goal of "reducing dependency." Some of these program efforts were quantifiable as units of service (such as intake assessments, job referrals, medical services provided), while others showed at least the possibility of being rendered as measurable outcomes (such as jobs retained for ninety days, assistance cases closed). With this vast, pervasive, and explicit program thrust, what effects were actually to be seen at the client level?[9] Since virtually all program activities were putatively geared toward reducing the use of cash assistance, one plausible measure of program success would be the overall rate of such cash assistance utilization by refugees. This was exactly the approach the federal government itself chose under the new Reagan administration. The key measure of how refugees were doing became the "dependency rate" and the key measure of refugee program success became the reduction of that dependency rate.

Initially there was some cause for relief as this newly constructed dependency rate (including Southeast Asian and non-Southeast Asian groups as well) declined from 67 percent in 1981 to 54 percent in 1982 (as calculated on the basis of refugees in the United States for three years or less). However, that rate was to remain essentially the same through the end of 1985 (ORR 1983a, 1986). The refugee program had chosen as its prime measurement one of failure (dependency) rather than one of success (refugee improvement), and itself failed at that measure of failure. In a sense, then, the purpose of the refugee program became to overcome its own failure, rather than the simpler, older goal of simply helping refugees by providing transitional assistance so that they could get back on their feet. The notion of "dependency" was thus not only an insult to the many refugees who were trying very hard to adjust but also a rather backward, even self-destructive phrasing for the program as a whole. The refugee program, the dependency rate seemed to suggest, was a failure. Its main job, then, was to reduce its own failure.

Despite those problems, the question of how refugees were actually doing during the early 1980s remains an important one. Some relatively useful data come from the annual federal government surveys of Southeast Asian refugees (not including other refugees at that time) conducted from 1982 to 1985. While the surveys provide only cross-sectional data, the consistency of the survey design and sampling procedures suggests that they are a relatively solid base for assessing shifts in the economic situation of refugees. The data, presented by six-month periods of residence in Table 6.4, address the specific

Table 6.4 Employment patterns by length of residence (Southeast Asian refugees, 1982–1985)

	IN 1982	IN 1983	IN 1984	IN 1985
Labor force participation rate				
0–6 months	21.6	12.0	30.0	24.7
7–12 months	33.3	33.9	38.5	38.5
13–18 months	36.6	42.5	37.6	40.6
19–24 months	54.6	38.0	45.2	41.9
25–30 months	48.9	45.4	48.0	45.5
31–36 months	59.0	52.5	42.4	42.9
Over 36 months	68.4	63.9	74.4	41.6*
Unemployment rate				
0–6 months	75.0	83.6	48.6	42.5
7–12 months	49.7	47.5	35.5	24.4
13–18 months	40.8	28.4	35.9	13.3
19–24 months	41.0	29.8	19.4	12.2
25–30 months	29.3	18.1	12.7	15.1
31–36 months	26.4	17.7	17.7	18.7
Over 36 months	14.8	15.5	09.0	16.4*
Average weekly wages ($)				
0–6 months	150.10	151.50	190.44	161.72
7–12 months	156.43	116.88	143.32	170.18
13–18 months	153.92	153.77	156.24	171.47
19–24 months	180.66	134.49	151.93	185.15
25–30 months	157.74	163.50	167.04	191.30
31–36 months	184.71	166.10	176.79	208.56
Over 36 months	236.32	223.70	249.37	243.09*

Sources: ORR (1983a: 25; 1984: 111; 1985a: 99; 1986: 111).

Note: Figures on labor force participation and unemployment refer to the population age 16 and over; data on salary and wage income refer to those employed (very small numbers for some categories). Because of the sampling procedures, figures for the 0-to-6-month category are based on few cases and should be treated with particular caution. Interpretation of the figures for over 36 months should take into consideration the fact that this residual population has an increasing proportion of post-1978 arrivals. In 1985, this category was limited specifically to the 37-to-60-month resident population (see figures with asterisks).

question of whether, given the well-documented improvement in economic situation that is typical over time for refugees (see Haines 1985, 1987), the situation of Southeast Asian refugees improved overall from 1982 to 1985. That is to say, there is almost an inevitable improvement in economic status over time for refugees, so the specific refugee program question is whether that improvement is enhanced in degree or in speed.

The data do not provide a simple answer to the question, but several distinct patterns do emerge in terms of labor force participation, unemployment, and wages. In terms of labor force participation, the data show no improvement from 1982 to 1985. While there are some changes from year to year for different length-of-residence categories, they do not suggest any general pattern. The clearest changes are for those in the first six months of residence but, because of the survey design, this category tends to have very few cases. (The decline for those in the over-36-month length-of-residence category reflects a change in survey design: in 1985, this category included those who had been in the United States from 37 to 60 months, whereas in prior years it included refugees whose arrival was as early as 1975.) If any pattern is to be extracted here (other than the lack of change) it would be a decline in labor force participation among those in their second eighteen months of U.S. residence. This is apparent from the first to the last of the surveys, if not equally across all four surveys.

The data on unemployment, on the other hand, show unequivocal improvement. Unemployment rates for almost all length-of-residence categories are halved between 1982 and 1985. The exceptions involve longer-term residents whose unemployment rates were modestly less bad in the 1982 and 1983 surveys. However, it is also worth noting that much of the improvement was at the end of the period, especially for the shorter length-of-residence categories. Average weekly wages of those employed show a similar improvement for all length-of-residence categories. As with unemployment data, it is striking the extent to which the improvement occurs between 1984 and 1985. It is also striking that, particularly for longer-resident refugees, the net gains from 1982 to 1985 are quite unimpressive, even though the specific 1984–1985 gains are substantial. That is, and quite unlike the situation for unemployment rates, the later improvement is partially a rebound from the net downward shift between 1982 and 1983. The findings are quite consistent with the status of the economy, although with the rebound for refugees coming well after the official end of the recession. (The overall U.S. unemployment rate climbed above 8.0 percent in late 1981, reached 10.8 percent in late 1982, and did not drop below 8.0 percent until early 1984.)

While labor force participation was relatively steady, unemployment was falling, and wages were increasing (to some extent only offsetting previous decline), cash assistance utilization showed different patterns for three groups. For those in their first eighteen months of residence, the percentage receiving cash assistance declined noticeably and (more or less) incrementally through the four surveys. For those in the second eighteen-month period, however, despite the vacillation from survey to survey, the situation in 1985 was similar to that in 1982: a decline from 67 to 63 percent for the 19-to-24-month category, an increase from 54 to 56 percent for the 25-to-30-month category, and an increase from 46 to 52 percent for the 31-to-36-month category. Finally, for the population resident over 36 months, there was a gradual increase in the percentage on assistance (although the large increase in 1985 reflects the restriction of that category to those in the United States no more than 60 months).

Finally, data on service usage (presented in Table 6.5) suggest some other distinct shifts that occurred during these years. The changes are most

Table 6.5 Patterns in the use of services and assistance by length of residence (Southeast Asian refugees, 1982–1985)

	IN 1982	IN 1983	IN 1984	IN 1985
Percent in English language training				
0–6 months	58.5	57.9	28.5	38.3
7–12 months	47.4	53.1	43.0	25.8
13–18 months	54.5	35.6	45.8	23.7
19–24 months	39.7	38.5	18.3	17.1
25–30 months	30.0	32.6	22.0	19.7
31–36 months	25.6	35.9	20.4	15.2
Over 36 months	11.5	14.6	11.1	34.8*
Percent in other education/training				
0–6 months	23.4	23.7	37.1	29.0
7–12 months	27.4	15.9	30.4	31.5
13–18 months	26.4	33.7	25.9	27.4
19–24 months	27.1	35.0	29.7	31.6
25–30 months	35.9	24.0	42.0	35.6
31–36 months	30.1	31.7	39.2	34.1
Over 36 months	31.6	30.4	23.7	19.6*
Percent receiving cash assistance				
0–6 months	82.7	77.0	70.1	61.4
7–12 months	81.7	81.3	74.1	49.2
13–18 months	75.6	64.0	61.6	54.5
19–24 months	67.3	61.6	52.8	62.8
25–30 months	54.0	67.7	44.6	56.3
31–36 months	46.3	49.4	57.0	51.4
Over 36 months	22.7	32.0	38.8	50.3*

Sources: ORR (1983a: 25; 1984: 111; 1985a: 99; 1986: 111).

Note: Figures on receipt of services refer to the adult population age 16 and over; figures on cash assistance refer to the percentage of the entire population residing in households that receive cash assistance. See notes to prior table regarding cautions about the numbers of respondents in particular categories, and changes in the 1985 sampling design.

compelling in regard to English language training: for all but the over-36-month population, there is a sharp drop in enrollment in such training from 1982 to 1985, a reduction of at least a third for all groups. For those in other than English language training, percentages tended to remain fairly constant across the surveys, suggesting a steady pattern in use of such training. The difference lies with the over-36-month population, which shows both an increased use of English language training and a decreased use of other kinds of education and training (neither of these seemingly traceable to the methodological changes for the 1985 survey).

These data thus show limited overall improvement in the economic situation of Southeast Asian refugees from 1982 to 1985, although the reduction in unemployment is impressive, and the reduction in assistance utilization among 0-to-18-month refugees would be impressive, were there not countervailing increases in assistance utilization among longer-resident refugees. Although it may be difficult to trace particular client outcomes to specific aspects of the refugee program, one might expect that the totality of the refugee program effort at reducing dependency ought to have been reflected in some improvement in the situation of refugees. Thus, the relative lack of improvement suggests a relative lack of program effectiveness.[10]

There are, however, some alternative explanations. For example, the high "dependency rate" in 1981 reflected not only a population with some potential difficulties but also one that was disproportionately in its early years in the United States. Since refugee employment and use of assistance usually show a consistent improvement over time, the simple "aging" of this population in terms of length of residence could be expected to cause an increase in employment and a decrease in the receipt of cash assistance. The effects of the recession on refugees also merit consideration. While the recession was at its worst in 1982, refugees were clearly still suffering from it in 1983. Thus, the improved employment situation of refugees in 1984 and even more so in 1985 could be construed as the result of the improvement in the economy rather than as an effect of the program. Finally, it is possible that the kinds of shifts in background characteristics that caused problems for some 1979–1981 arrivals provided some additional benefits for those arriving in later years. One change during that period was the increase in the percentage of those with some English language competence at arrival. Based on retrospective refugee assessments, for example, only about a third of 1979–1981 arrivals spoke some English whereas the figure increased to about three in five by 1984 (ORR 1985a: 96). The data are thus inconclusive although, insofar as it is possible to assess the reasons for improvement in refugees' economic situation, refugee characteristics at arrival and current economic conditions seem at least as important as actual program effects.[11]

At the very least, it is difficult to see such contextual factors as dampening an otherwise more impressively effective program effort.[12]

Lessons From a Cautionary Tale

This review of the logic of refugee program goals provides a cautionary tale. Despite the reasonableness of English language competence as a program goal and its direct translation into a specific, measurable service, its ultimate economic effect remains unclear. An examination of that other seemingly straightforward goal of economic self-sufficiency presents more severe problems. There seems little possibility that the success, level of success, and duration of success of such a general program goal as self-sufficiency can ever be documented in more than an illustrative or extremely inferential way. It is easy to understand why programs take on broad goals, choosing to simplify reality, whether for ideological, political, or simply practical reasons. Yet problems inevitably occur when it comes time to see if those goals are met. Program effects will be found to be unmeasurable, untraceable to the program, or simply too modest to match the scope of the goal. Program "success" or "failure" must thus be arbitrarily determined, breeding a constant stream of programmatic corrections and ideological reconstructions. Here, then, is the source of that understandable confusion about refugee resettlement that was noted in Chapter 1: Why is it not possible to know how this program is doing?[13]

In some ways, the lessons from this cautionary tale from the formative period of the U.S. refugee program are simply historical ones, but in other ways they continue as crucial dilemmas in the post-arrival adjustment of refugees today. The "problem" of use of cash assistance by refugees has to a great extent been resolved over the years by simply offering less cash assistance. If there is not any (or much) cash assistance, then refugees cannot very well be dependent on it. Initial refugee employment rates in recent years, as a result, are indeed much higher than they were twenty or thirty years ago. Immediate employment is the only option, no matter what the ultimate costs. If one income is not enough, then there must be multiple incomes. If household income is still low, refugees must live in poor housing, in dangerous neighborhoods, with poor transportation to jobs, and with poor schools for their children. It is "welcome to the other America."

Knowing that the protestations of refugee success or refugee failure can never be documented with "hard" quantitative data remains a vital lesson today. Success and failure can only be illustrated in particular cases and the meaning of these cases is not always clear. Some refugees have done well in America and some have not. Many are in between. Furthermore, those refugees who have not, it seems at first glance, done very well still have done quite well in a relative sense—factoring in the difficulties they have faced in gaining refuge and then adjusting, in this their second life, to an unknown, unpredictable, and sometimes dangerous new country. Indeed, an abundance of stories of refugee success might suggest that American refugee policy was starting to look a bit too much like American immigration policy: the young, strong, and educated are welcomed warmly but no longer welcome are—as the Statue of Liberty inscription would have it—the "poor . . . the homeless, tempest-tosst."

Notes

1. The actual mechanisms used in the two laws were slightly different. The 1948 legislation mortgaged these admissions against future regular immigration quotas for the countries in question. The 1952 legislation, by contrast, created new slots for the refugees. See CRS (1979a, 1979b, 1980) and LeMay and Barkan 1999).

2. General reviews of these early issues of refugee policy and program can be found in Loescher and Scanlan (1986) and Zucker and Zucker (1987, 1996). Divine (1957) provides a very lucid overview of the DP program, although Dinnerstein (1982) provides much more detail. A recent review of the politics of DP, Hungarian, and Cuban programs is provided by Bon Tempo (2008). A wide range of those in both public and private sectors were rethinking refugee policies and programs in the late 1979 period, so there is a wealth of governmental reports, congressional hearings, and independent reports, perhaps especially the Taft, North, and Ford (1979) volume *Time for a New Focus*. Note also the work of the Select Commission on Immigration and Refugee Policy, both its overall report in 1981 and the various papers commissioned for it.

3. See Garcia (1996) and Grenier and Pérez (2003) for succinct reviews of the major refugee flows from Cuba. Note also that there has long been migration between Cuba and the United States and that the word "refugee" is often used in a general rather than specific sense. Most arrivals from Cuba have had their legal status revised to permanent resident under legislation specifically for Cubans— and that does not invoke legal refugee status. Furthermore, beginning with the Mariel exodus of 1980, those arriving from Cuba are largely classified as "entrants." Furthermore, many Cubans would be more comfortable with the label "exile" rather than "refugee."

4. The concentration of Cubans in Miami had many positive outcomes, but it did cause concern. One result was the attempt to resettle Cubans away from Miami. However, the greater effect was to create a later policy to disperse Southeast Asian refugees as widely as possible across the country. The initial results were impressive in that regard. Program data indicated that some of the 1975 arrivals were resettled in *all* states; only one state (California, which had a major processing center) had a

particularly high percentage of the arrivals (21 percent); and only four other states (Florida, Pennsylvania, Texas, and Washington) had more than 3 percent of the total. Refugees subsequently did move, producing greater concentrations, but certainly nothing like the Miami situation. One effect was to make refugees a vanguard for diversity in many smaller communities. Even in more recent decades, there are still places in which refugees provide that role as the vanguard in establishing cultural diversity (Singer and Wilson 2006).

5. There was subsequently in the late 1970s an attempt to phase out such assistance, but that plan was overtaken by the passage of the Refugee Act of 1980, which did provide limits both for refugee assistance and for reimbursement to states and localities for their costs.

6. There was a subsequent improvement in the English competency of refugees at the time of arrival. That can be at least partially explained by increased efforts at pre-arrival English language training in refugee processing centers overseas.

7. This special cash assistance was, in effect if not in explicit construction, a federally provided equivalent to the AFDC unemployed-parent programs that were available in some states. The logic was that refugees had been unemployed even if they did not have a normal work history by the standards of regular public assistance programs.

8. Instead of the positive goal of self-sufficiency, there was also throughout this period an increasing emphasis on the reduction of refugee "dependency." While some aspects of this change are subsequently discussed in the text, the implications of this inversion deserve additional attention. This emphasis on "dependency" introduced a note of negativity: the core program goal was no longer to facilitate a natural process of increasing economic (and social/political) capacity among a transitionally dislocated population; rather it was to reduce the failure of a program characterized by a high "dependency rate." The use of assistance by refugees was no longer to be viewed as transitory and a result of the inherent disjunctions of refugee exodus and resettlement, but rather as a potentially addictive client state, one that required rigorous monitoring and sanctioning. "Dependency" inevitably raised the question of blame, and there were always sufficient candidates: refugees who lacked ambition or willingness to work, sponsors who had led refugees down the path into dependency, and indeed legislators who had "sent the wrong message" to refugees. Romano Mazzoli, cosponsor of what would eventually become the Immigration Reform and Control Act of 1986, was fond of talking about "Refugee, Inc.": a "great industry that spans the globe" and is based on public and private sector "careers that have been created over refugees" (Refugee Reports 1982).

9. As the English language example suggested, it is unlikely that any radical transformation of the client population could be expected. Furthermore, no single identifiable service (such as language training) was likely to emerge as the basic "unit of service" for reducing dependency.

10. The discussion in the text is phrased in terms of the effectiveness of the program during the early 1980s. That discussion suggests a very weak case for indicating any *improvement* in the effectiveness of the program during the early

1980s. Restricting assistance may be an effective budget strategy, but not necessarily an effective assistance strategy.

11. It is also possible that different program components may not only offset each other, but that they may even offset their own effects. Consider the policy changes of 1982 in which, with extremely limited time for implementation, the eligibility period for the special program of refugee cash assistance was reduced from thirty-six to eighteen months of residence in the United States. Such a move is the most direct way to reduce "dependency," for if assistance is provided to fewer people by reason of regulatory restriction, then more people are inevitably "independent" of such assistance. Thus, the eighteen-month policy could automatically be expected to reduce "dependency." However, the potential reduction was offset by a number of factors. For example, subsequent legal action forced additional funding for two states (Washington and Oregon) greatly affected by the change. That undermined the immediate fiscal benefits. In many other states, those removed from this kind of assistance were then eligible for other kinds of assistance, particularly state-based general assistance (Worthington et al. 1983). That also undermined the immediate fiscal benefits. Finally, in some cases people subsequently moved to other jurisdictions with more favorable assistance policies. That effect might have been less immediate but certainly undermined the general intent of the changes. Thus the specific policy change was partially undercut by its own side-effects. There was also, predictably, intense aggravation about the changes and their effects on refugees and on those involved in refugee resettlement. That too is a kind of cost.

12. If these data indicated a clearer "reduction of dependency" that seemed beyond explanation in terms of contextual variables, additional questions would be necessary. For example, the relative significance of the effects would require attention. Effects might become so thin as to be irrelevant in program terms. Another question that would need to be addressed would be the summability of program effects. Given the wide variety of program efforts directed toward speeding up refugee self-sufficiency (or reducing "dependency"), it would be necessary to ask whether any effects were the additive results of these different elements, the result of some particular elements, or a positive result of some elements despite the negative effects of others. This is an especially tortuous problem for the refugee program because of the wide variety of organizations involved, the great economic and sociocultural diversity of the client population, and the large number of individual program components. If "dependency rates" did decline, would it be the result of employment services or cash assistance policy changes? Of regular social service funds which provide to initial employment counseling, or targeted assistance funds which provide the same client on-the-job training? Of a solid initial orientation by a voluntary agency, or the intermediate haven of an English language class?

13. This is not to say that research efforts are somehow irrelevant to policy analysis. Research may be able to provide some increased precision about some elements of some programs that have discernible and relatively isolatable effects. Research may also be able to help clarify the inherent limitations in program goal formulation and elucidate the contextual factors that must be considered in

visualizing plausible levels of program effect. But such research requires a recognition that program effects are not only complex as questions about client status but are also complex in requiring an understanding of the logic of policy formulation and of the mechanisms (logical and practical) by which general policy is transformed into specific program actions. Since the refugee program is such a broad one, touching nearly all aspects of refugee lives, it provides a particularly good example of these problems.

7

Refuge in America

The story of refuge in America is a complicated one that includes both refugees and the United States. It is a universal story of loss, hope, and a new life, but also a narrower story of one particular country's history of both providing and refusing refuge. It is also a story of the many local communities in which refugees have been resettled. A walk along the pathways of refugee resettlement is also a walk along the highways, byways, and backways of America.

Rather than providing a chronological discussion of refugees in America or a political history of the U.S. refugee program, I have opted in this book to present some different aspects of the relationship between refugees and America that can illustrate the universal story, the national story, and the local one. Chapter 1 sketched the historical outlines of the relationship between refugees and America, the implications for admissions levels, and some of the inherent challenges in post-arrival adjustment. Subsequent chapters then turned to general patterns in refugee adjustment after arrival (phrased largely in terms of what refugees bring with them and what they find in America); an analysis of how Americans view refugees and how these refugees fit into American society (using the example of press accounts in one particular city); a consideration of the dynamics of refugee identity (with an emphasis on racial, ethnic, national, and religious options); an examination of the family and its role in resettlement (with the extended example of Vietnamese households); and an analysis of the development and internal logic of the government's program of post-arrival assistance for refugees. A brief review of important lessons learned may be helpful before considering two final issues: how refugees are to be defined and what is the status of safe haven for them in America.

Some Lessons

In historical terms, as discussed in Chapter 1, there are many places from which the story of refugees and America could be traced. Here, I have emphasized the last seventy years, beginning not with the provision of refuge, but with its denial. I have suggested that over the years what has made the difference between acceptance and denial has been a moral consideration of relative complexity. That moral consideration has not hinged on some formal, idealized definition of what a refugee is, but a more additive consideration of the kinds of connections between America and particular refugees. This is an "on-the-run" morality, anchored in the personal not the abstract, the parochial not the universal. It is a morality that is simultaneously self-serving and generous, both regressive (refuge to our kin, friends, coreligionists) and progressive (expanding refuge to those beyond these personal connections). It is thus not about whether people are "for" or "against" refugees, but how different connections cumulatively make particular refugees morally significant to America.

A consideration of the actual experience of refugees in America, as in Chapter 2, suggests that the reasons for refuge in America and the dynamics of life after that refuge is provided are quite distinct. The experience of loss and flight that lies at the heart of the refugee experience has lingering effects on refugees, but life in a new country has its own requirements. An extremely broad range of research on different refugees at different times suggests a fairly predictable set of patterns. As with immigrants in general, educational and occupational background and English language skills make an enormous positive contribution. Lack of educational experience and language competence (particularly nonliteracy) are forbidding obstacles. Yet, much of this post-arrival experience still retains a distinctly refugee flavor. Political sentiments, for example, often continue to run very hot, and the psychological after-effects of refugee loss and flight can be severe. Lack of social resources—fractured families and weak community structures— makes matters worse. Perhaps the broadest lesson is that it is often very difficult to distinguish which aspects of refugee life after arrival reflect the predictable patterns of immigrant life and which reflect more specifically the refugee experience. Refugees are both refugees and immigrants and their post-arrival lives a mesh of the two.

This tension between life as a refugee and life as an immigrant becomes even clearer in a consideration, as in Chapter 3, of the historical and cultural meaning of "refugee" in America. The durability in the Richmond press accounts regarding the "refugee story" is impressive, and quite similar to other popular and scholarly accounts of refugees. The sequence is consistent—refugees are persecuted in some way, they flee to some temporary refuge, and finally they find permanent refuge: a new life in a new country. The story is both Biblical and quintessentially American. The final stage of new life in a new country is not, however, easy. The requirements and rules for that new life are forbidding. Refugees must give up some aspects of their prior lives, for example, when involvement in home country politics may implicate one in supporting "terrorism." They must also actually succeed in some demonstrable way in this new life. If they do not, it challenges the very notion of America as land of opportunity. Refugees are supposed to validate America as good, not stand as witnesses to its limitations, and this is an additional burden on them.

Refugees are often different in fundamental ways (lifestyles, beliefs, family structures) from Americans and, unlike most regular immigrants, are comparatively ill-prepared for life in the United States. In that sense, they are much more fully "foreign" than most immigrants, and the United States is correspondingly often very foreign to them. The discussion in Chapter 4 on ethnic identities provides one example of that foreignness. Ethnicity is one of the more benign ways that Americans categorize people. It is a kind of "good" diversity. It is not, however, inherently sensible to refugees. They have much to learn about American identities. Many of them are affected particularly sharply by issues of race, but issues of religion, nationality, and language (both content and accent) may confuse them or immediately place them in a stigmatized category. Refugees pose such a strong diversity challenge because they often do not fit very well in these American schemes. Their children will be acted on with more force in this regard, creating potential lines of schism within the home.

Despite the challenges and disruptions of a new life in America, there is nevertheless much durability in refugee life after arrival in the United States. Sometimes that durability lies in broader community structures, in churches, for example, or in economic mutual aid. Perhaps the most crucial domain of durability involves the family. Family forms often endure across the generations despite changes in religion, occupation, residence, or even language. Sometimes these family forms can cause problems, perhaps especially very large families in a country in which children are very expensive. Yet, sometimes, as in the Vietnamese case described in Chapter 5, families can be extraordinarily helpful in surviving migration, adjusting to a new country, and investing (often quite strategically) in the further progress of later generations. Perhaps the broadest lesson here is how much of what America can be as a refuge is conditioned by families whose capacities may not even be known until they are activated in the disruption, uprooting, and relocation that refugees know all too well.

The practical problems of adjusting to a new country, the dual requirements of being both a refugee and an immigrant, a strange set of identity
categories that mask their identities rather than clarifying them, all these
suggest that designing an effective program for resettling refugees is unlikely
to be easy. As discussed in Chapter 6, much of the research indicates that
refugees who do well could be expected to do well based on their background before arrival. That suggests that refugee program efforts—at least
those beyond the immediate essentials of placing people in good locations
and providing for their first few months—are not understandable in the
normal sense of a client population. In this case, the clients vary too greatly.
Some post-arrival assistance, for example, might benefit those relatively well-
off, so they can do even better; other assistance might benefit those whose
prospects in the United States are far more limited. Perhaps the broadest
lesson here is that the refugee program makes most sense when it is not "the
refugee program" but rather a set of calibrated responses to particular refugee
groups, and indeed to particular refugee individuals.

But What is a Refugee?

One issue that has received only occasional mention in this book is the
specific legal definition of a refugee. Often the formal U.N. refugee definition
is the first order of business, as if the subject of refugees could not be
discussed without having that definition in place. Yet the relative omission
of that definition makes good sense in the context of this book. Instead, the
starting point has been that the relationship between America and refugees
hinges on a range of moral commitments, some abstract and universal,
some quite concrete and personal. The U.N. definition of refugee, and the
international humanitarian effort that it represents, has been—as a matter
of historical fact—only one of those connections. That may be fortunate
since it permits navigation around the technicalities of international refugee
law when people are clearly in need. But the issue of definition does deserve
some attention.

"Refugee" is a word. Specifically, it is an English language word with
strong historical and cultural connotations in the English-speaking world
and also with a lengthy legal and diplomatic history because of the primacy
of English in global affairs. This simple linguistic (and political) comment
might seem unnecessary were one not to consider what words are used in
other languages to talk about refugees. In German and Dutch, for example,
refugees are "ones who fled" (*fluctelingen*; *vluchtelingen*) rather than, as in
English, ones who have arrived. In Japanese, the equivalent word is *nanmin*,
which simply means people who have difficulties, with perhaps a shade of

meaning that these people also pose difficulties. Here the emphasis is neither on flight nor on refuge, but simply on the bad conditions that might cause people to move. The Japanese word may seem colder, but if one would like to see the formal legal notion of "refugee" expand beyond its emphasis on persecution and to people who have been displaced for a wide range of reasons, such as natural disasters and environmental change, the Japanese version has some advantages. In Arabic, there are various possible terms (see Peteet 1995) that can emphasize either the destitution of those who are displaced or the moral obligation to provide them refuge, so that they can meet their moral obligation of returning to the place they had to leave. To be a "refugee" in that sense is to accept refuge as only a temporary expedient.

Yet there is also that abstract humanitarian standard represented by the U.N. definition, and it is an important one. Its central premise is that refugees are those who flee because of fear of persecution. That fear of persecution must be on the basis of one of five specific grounds: race, religion, nationality, political opinion, or membership in a particular social group. Furthermore, that persecution must have led to flight across a national border, and it must also not be possible for the person to return. There are additional complexities to the definition, but even this abridged version shows both the strength and limitations of the definition. The strength lies in the clear evocation of people who flee for very serious reasons (fear of persecution) and who have to flee very far in both geographical and national terms (across national borders). The major weaknesses lie in the requirement that there be a specific reason for flight (e.g., how can one prove that flight was from persecution specifically based on race?); that the flight be across a national border (e.g., why is fleeing into the remote hills not enough?); and that return not be possible (e.g., how can you prove after the fact that you cannot go back when the government in your former home says you can).[1]

Furthermore, there are some significant procedural problems in assessing this legalistic aspect of refugee status. For example, how do you document a refugee case when documents are one of the things that refugees often lack? How does a refugee contest a representative from the original home government who says it is a bogus claim? How can one document a reasonable "fear" of something happening and that what is feared is the result of "persecution"?[2] At the very least, this determination takes time, which refugees often do not have. At its worst, it is hopelessly subject to political tampering. Thus, as has often happened, refugees from countries to which the United States is opposed are awarded refugee status, while those from countries that are allied to the United States do not gain refugee status.

Despite such problems, this formal legal definition often works reasonably well in those cases in which people manage to reach the United States, obtain legal counsel, and make a claim. In such cases, those people who are approved become "asylees" in legal terms rather than "refugees," even though the legal standard is the same. This particular path to legal refuge in America has expanded greatly in recent years, doubling in absolute numbers to about 30,000 per year over the last decade, and thus rising even more in relative proportion to the declining annual admissions of "regular" refugees, which dropped sharply in the last decade. This is not bad in itself, but it is a shift toward those who have the resources to make it to the United States on their own. The result is a tendency toward the young, toward individuals and very small family groups, and toward the use of increasingly criminalized border-crossing networks.

Refuge in America

One can, with much justification, claim that the relationship between refugees and America is a successful one. Many, many refugees have prospered in new lives in America. They have more than repaid in their economic and cultural productivity the amounts of money and effort expended on their behalf. Many, many refugees have had more modest lives in America, but have in the process received a permanent refuge for themselves and their families now, and for their descendants in the future. Furthermore, if one measures the United States by global standards, the per capita acceptance of refugees may not match a few other countries (particularly Australia, Canada, and Sweden in recent years) but the sheer size of the United States still makes it the major haven for new refugees, and for earlier refugees who have been left eking out their lives in refugee camps and settlements.

If one thinks in terms of the 1980 Refugee Act and Senator Edward Kennedy's intent to create a better resettlement system, more fully open to all regions of the world, and more fully integrated with international conventions on refugees, the U.S. refugee program today seems a clear success. Even the adjudication of asylum claims within the United States, for example, is now regularized in terms of international law, and a great number of committed lawyers have helped make the approval rates for different countries far more equivalent than they were in the past. That international standard is also used in the greater portion of overseas screening for refugees. The commitment to global representativeness is also strong. Refugees from Africa, for example, were a tiny fraction in 1980 but have become a major component of refugee admissions over the last two decades. The United States has also, despite the risks to program success, been willing to admit many refugees likely to pose serious resettlement problems: those with limited education and English, and lack of exposure to industrial, urban societies.

There is, inevitably, a bleaker side to this portrait of America and refugees. There are three main causes for concern. First, despite these positive features, the net number of refugees admitted to the United States has indeed declined greatly. From 1975 to 2000, roughly 97,000 refugees per year were admitted. In the last decade, however, the number of refugees shrank by about half (to a little over 50,000).[3] Even if asylees are included, this is still a reduction in overall admissions, and the shift from refugees to asylees does have the effect of selecting for those most able to reach the United States rather than those who may be in even greater need. Some of this decline may be understandable, and some of it may very well be cyclical. Refugee admissions, after all, have always been quite erratic from year to year. Nevertheless, the numbers have been lower in the last decade and that merits concern.[4]

Second, and relating to post-arrival assistance, American program efforts and cultural assumptions have often put refugees in the difficult position of being both true refugees and paragons of immigrant success. That tension between being refugees and being immigrants, in both practical requirements and American expectations, can be difficult for refugees but also for those trying to help them, who often lose patience when the expected "success" does not appear. As Carol Mortland has suggested from her long experience with Cambodians and with the refugee program, when refugees "remain outside American notions of success" they are relegated to the very worst of the stereotypes of immigrants: "unwanted harbingers of threatening difference, welcome only after their difference is no longer evident" (Mortland 2001: 86–87). This too merits concern.

Third, the overall balance in U.S. immigration has shifted to the detriment of refugees. During the first decade of the Southeast Asian influx, for example, refugees were a significant component of overall immigration. By the 1990s, that proportion was reduced, but still significant: refugees represented about 10 percent of annual legal immigration. By the mid-2000s, that percentage had shrunk to about 5 percent. At the other end of the spectrum, what was once a relatively modest level of undocumented immigration has swelled from perhaps a tenth of overall immigration to perhaps a quarter—at least before the economic down jolt of 2008. That undocumented segment of immigration is, to simplify a more detailed discussion (Haines 2007b; Haines and Rosenblum 1999), very profitable for many employers and also relatively risk free for them (if not for the migrants). This is the segment of immigration that produces the quickest profit for the least commitment, while refugees represent the segment of immigration with the least profit for the greatest commitment. The enormous imbalance in these two ends of the immigration spectrum raises again the primal question about whether America is a land of refuge or opportunity, faith or profit.

Three decades ago, after Senator Kennedy opened the hearings for the Refugee Act with his evocation of refugees as "one of the oldest and most important themes in our Nation's history," Senator Strom Thurmond proposed a different standard that also "has served us well." We should, he cautioned, "weigh the cultural and demographic impact of the refugee problem" and "be guided by enlightened interest tempered with compassion." Thirty years later, the United States seems to have something of each of these two positions: following Kennedy, a refugee program that reaches out to all; following Thurmond, a refugee program small enough that it is but a "tempering" of the self-interest that rules most American immigration policy, whether it be the economic self-interest of using pliable undocumented labor, the social and cultural self-interest of basing most immigration on family ties, or a cognitive self-interest in avoiding the uncertainties posed by refugees, their unknown (and often unknowable) experiences, and their unpredictable futures.

Notes

1. The specific U.N. definition is that a refugee is any person who, "owing to well-founded fear of being persecuted for reasons of race, religion, nationality, membership of a particular social group or political opinion, is outside the country of his nationality and is unable or, owing to such fear, is unwilling to avail himself of the protection of that country; or who, not having a nationality and being outside the country of his former habitual residence, is unable or, owing to such fear, is unwilling to return to it." While there is much merit to that definition—and to its wide acceptance—concerns about its limitations are widespread. Those concerns are acknowledged by the United Nations High Commissioner for Refugees (UNHCR) in its commitment to help other "populations of interest." Those limitations are also avoided in some other regional refugee definitions, particularly that of the Organization of African Unity (OAU). The OAU definition includes the U.N. definition, but adds: "The term 'refugee' shall also apply to every person who, owing to external aggression, occupation, foreign domination or events seriously disturbing public order in either part or the whole of his country of origin or nationality, is compelled to leave his place of habitual residence in order to seek refuge in another place outside his country of origin or nationality." The U.N. definition was incorporated into U.S. law with the Refugee Act of 1980, although actual U.S. refugee admissions are not limited to that definition. Some of those admitted as refugees, for example, have not actually fled across national borders; others have presumptive refugee status because of special legislation on their behalf.

2. There is also the practical question of how one determines which relatives of a refugee can claim derivative refugee status. Nuclear family claims are easily accepted, but what about parents? Adult married children? In-laws?

3. These averages are from Department of State data on admissions up through December 31, 2009. Data include Amerasian and ODP (Orderly Departure Program) admissions from Vietnam but do not include asylees or entrants. As indicated in the text, the number of asylees has been rising, and the number of entrants (especially because of in-country processing in Cuba) has been significant in this past decade (roughly 17,000 Cubans per year). There might be some reason to consider whether these other categories should be considered to offset the decline in refugee numbers. There are two main reasons for not doing so: first, asylum is actually a domestic determination, not in any sense a reaching out by the American government and, second, most of the current entrants are Cuban and—especially given that the processing occurs in Cuba—do not constitute "refugees" in the usual sense. Also note, however, that if entrants are included in all calculations since 1980, the decline in combined numbers would still be similar since there were large numbers of such entrants in 1980 (roughly 125,000 Cubans and 25,000 Haitians).

4. Although the average for the decade was low, admissions in 2008 (about 60,000) and 2009 (about 74,000) were promising. The Obama administration has indicated that such levels will be maintained in 2010—see the presidential determination on refugee admissions of September 30, 2009. For published versions of the data underlying the estimates of overall decade numbers, see Hoefer, Rytine, and Baker (2009) for refugees and asylees, and Martin and Hoefer (2009) for estimates of the unauthorized population. Also, for a review of the admissions side of the refugee program, see Martin (2005).

References

Aames, Jacqueline S., Ronald L. Aames, John Jung, and Edward Karabenick. 1977. *Indochinese Refugee Self-Sufficiency in California: A Survey and Analysis of the Vietnamese, Cambodians and Lao and the Agencies That Serve Them*. Report submitted to the State Department of Health, State of California.

Abe, Jennifer, Nolan Zane, and Kevin Chun. 1994. Differential Responses to Trauma: Migration-Related Discriminants of Post-Traumatic Stress Disorder Among Southeast Asian Refugees. *Journal of Community Psychology* 22(2): 121-135.

Adams, Stacy Hawkins. 1995. A True Community Effort: Complex Sets Aside Center for its Refugee Families. *Richmond Times-Dispatch*, March 24: A1, A5.

Airriess, Christopher A., and David L. Clawson. 1991. Versailles: A Vietnamese Enclave in New Orleans, Louisiana. *Journal of Cultural Geography* 12(1): 1-13.

――――. 1994. Vietnamese Market Gardens in New Orleans. *Geographical Review* 84(1): 16-31.

Alba, Richard D. 1990. *Ethnic Identity: The Transformation of White America*. New Haven, Connecticut: Yale University Press.

Alexander, Abigail, Stacie Blake, and Michael A. Bernstein. 2007. The Staying Power of Pain: A Comparison of Torture Survivors from Bosnia and Colombia and Their Rates of Anxiety, Depression and PTSD. *Torture* 17(1): 1-10.

Amer, Ramses. 2009. The "Boat People" Crisis of 1978–1979: Examined through the Ethnic Chinese Dimension. Paper presented at the workshop *Refugee Politics and the Chinese/Vietnamese Diaspora*. Organized by Yuk Wah Chan. City University of Hong Kong, October.

Arias, Elizabeth. 2001. Change in Nuptiality Patterns Among Cuban Americans: Evidence of Cultural and Structural Assimilation? *International Migration Review* 35(2): 525-556.

Ashabranner, Brent, and Melissa Ashabranner. 1987. *Into a Strange Land: Unaccompanied Refugee Youth in America*. New York: G.P. Putnam's Sons.

Bach, Robert L. 1985. Labor Force Participation and Employment of Southeast Asian Refugees in the United States. Pp. 1-96 in Allan R. Gall (Ed.), *Aspects of Refugee Resettlement in the United States*. Washington, DC: Office of Refugee Resettlement (U.S. Department of Health and Human Services).

Bach, Robert, and Rita Carroll-Seguin. 1986. Labor Force Participation, Household Composition and Sponsorship Among Southeast Asian Refugees. *International Migration Review* 20(2): 381-404.

Bach, Robert, Linda Gordon, David Haines, and David Howell. 1983. The Economic Adjustment of Southeast Asian Refugees in the U.S. *World Refugee Survey* 1983: 51-55.

———. 1984. Geographic Variations in the Economic Adjustment of Southeast Asian Refugees in the U.S. *World Refugee Survey* 1984: 7-8.

Baker-Cristales, Beth. 2004. Salvadoran Transformations: Class Consciousness and Ethnic Identity in a Transnational Milieu. *Latin American Perspectives* 31(5): 15-33.

Banks, Marcus. 1996. *Ethnicity: Anthropological Constructions*. New York: Routledge.

Bankston, Carl L., III. 1995. Gender Roles and Scholastic Performance Among Adolescent Vietnamese Women: The Paradox of Ethnic Patriarchy. *Sociological Focus* 28(2): 161-176.

Basch, Linda, Nina Glick Schiller, and Christina Szanton Blanc. 1994. *Nations Unbound: Transnational Projects, Postcolonial Predicaments, and Deterritorialized Nation-States*. Basel, Switzerland: Gordon and Breach.

Bass, Thomas A. 1996. *Vietnamerica: The War Comes Home*. New York: Soho Press.

Baxter, Dianne. 1997. Idealized and Devalued: Images of Identity Among Palestinian Camp Refugees in the West Bank. Pp. 146-165 in Dianne Baxter and Ruth Krulfeld (Eds.), *Beyond Boundaries: Selected Papers on Refugees and Immigrants V*. Arlington, Virginia: American Anthropological Association.

Baxter, Dianne, and Ruth Krulfeld (Eds.). 1997. *Beyond Boundaries: Selected Papers on Refugees and Immigrants V*. Arlington, Virginia: American Anthropological Association.

Behrouzan, Orkideh. 2005. Homeless Mind: The Fate of Persian Identity in Exile. *The Discourse of Sociological Practice* 7(1-2): 275-294.

Bélanger, Danièle. 2000. Regional Differences in Household Composition and Family Formation Patterns in Vietnam. *Journal of Comparative Family Studies* 31(2): 171-189.

Benson, Janet E. 1994. The Effects of Packinghouse Work on Southeast Asian Refugee Families. Pp. 99-126 in Louise Lamphere, Alex Stepick, and Guillermo Grenier (Eds.), *Newcomers in the Workplace*. Philadelphia: Temple University Press.

_____. 2001. Garden City, Kansas: Vietnamese Refugees, Mexican Immigrants, and the Changing Character of a Community. Pp. 39-54 in David W. Haines and Carol A. Mortland (Eds.), *Manifest Destinies: Americanizing Immigrants and Internationalizing Americans*. Westport, Connecticut: Praeger.

_____. 2005. South Asian Identity in the Midwest: University and Community Factors. Paper presented at the Annual Meeting of the Society for Applied Anthropology, Santa Fe, New Mexico.

Berman, Myron. 1979. *Richmond's Jewry, 1769–1976: Shabbat in Shockoe*. Charlottesville: University Press of Virginia.

Bhuyan, Rupaleem, Molly Mell, Kirsten Senturia, Marianne Sullivan, and Sharyne Shiu-Thornton. 2005. Women Must Endure According to Their Karma: Cambodian Immigrant Women Talk About Domestic Violence. *Journal of Interpersonal Violence* 20(8): 902-921.

Birman, Dina, and Nellie Tran. 2008. Psychological Distress and Adjustment of Vietnamese Refugees in the United States: Association with Pre- and Postmigration Factors. *American Journal of Orthopsychiatry* 78(2): 109-120.

Bixler, Mark. 2006. *The Lost Boys of Sudan: An American Story of the Refugee Experience*. Athens: University of Georgia Press.

Bon Tempo, Carl J. 2008. *Americans at the Gate: The United States and Refugees during the Cold War*. Princeton, New Jersey: Princeton University Press.

Boone, Margaret S. 1980. The Uses of Traditional Concepts in the Development of New Urban Roles: Cuban Women in the United States. Pp. 235-269 in Erika Bourguignon (Ed.), *A World of Women*. New York: Praeger.

————. 1994. Thirty Year Retrospective on the Adjustment of Cuban Women. Pp. 179-201 in Linda A. Camino and Ruth M. Krulfeld (Eds.), *Reconstructing Lives, Recapturing Meaning*. Basel, Switzerland: Gordon and Breach.

Bourdieu, Pierre. 1990. *The Logic of Practice*. Translated by Richard Nice. Stanford: Stanford University Press.

Bowes, Mark. 1989. Refugee's Murder is "Story of Good Gone Bad." *Richmond News-Leader*, May 6: M1.

Bozorgmehr, Mehdi. 1996. Iranians. Pp. 213-231 in David W. Haines (Ed.), *Refugees in America in the 1990s*. Westport, Connecticut: Greenwood Press.

Bozorgmehr, Mehdi, and Georges Sabagh. 1991. Iranian Exiles and Immigrants in Los Angeles. Pp. 121-144 in Asghar Fahti (Ed.), *Iranian Refugees and Exiles since Khomeini*. Costa Mesa, California: Mazda Publishers.

Breitman, Richard, Barbara McDonald Stewart, and Severin Hochberg. 2009. *Refugees and Rescue: The Diaries and Papers of James G. McDonald (1935–1945)*. Bloomington: Indiana University Press.

Breslow, Marilyn, David W. Haines, Dirk Philipsen, and Jan Williamson. 1997. Richmond's Refugees: Understanding the Interaction Between Refugees and Their New Communities. *Migration World* 25(1/2): 30-34.

Briggs, E. (Ed). 1979. Despite Danger, Refugee to Help. *Richmond News-Leader*, November 2: B1, B3.

Burchstead, Karen. 1983. Polish Families Adopted by Richmond Sponsors. *Richmond Times-Dispatch*, April 18: A1, A6.

Burns, Allan F. 1993. *Maya in Exile: Guatemalans in Florida*. Philadelphia: Temple University Press.

Burns, Bethany. 2002. Eleanor Roosevelt and the American People in the Refugee Crisis of 1938–41. Unpublished paper, George Mason University.

Burton, Eve. 1983. Surviving the Flight of Horror: The Story of Refugee Women. *Indochina Issues* No. 34.

Campbell, Tom. 1995. VA Expecting Some Refugees. *Richmond Times-Dispatch*, May 3: A6.

Caplan, Nathan, John K. Whitmore, and Quang L. Bui. 1985. *Southeast Asian Refugee Self-Sufficiency Study: Final Report*. Ann Arbor, Michigan: Institute for Social Research.

Caplan, Nathan, Marcella H. Choy, and John K. Whitmore. 1991. *Children of the Boat People: A Study of Educational Success.* Ann Arbor: University of Michigan Press.

Capps, Lisa L. 1994. Change and Continuity in the Medical Culture of the Hmong in Kansas City. *Medical Anthropology Quarterly* 8(2): 161-177.

Catanzaro, Antonino, and Robert John Moser. 1982. Health Status of Refugees From Vietnam, Laos, and Cambodia. *Journal of the American Medical Association* 247(9): 1303-1308.

CCSC (Central Census Steering Committtee). 1991. *Population and Housing Census-1989: Completed Census Results.* Hanoi.

_____. 2000. *1999 Population and Housing Census: Sample Results.* Hanoi: The Gioi.

Chen, Chuansheng, Kari Edwards, Brandy Young, and Ellen Greenberger. 2001. Close Relationships Between Asian American and European American College Students. *Journal of Social Psychology* 141(1): 85-100.

Chiswick, Barry R., and Paul W. Miller. 1995. The Endogeneity Between Language and Earnings: International Analyses. *Journal of Labor Economics* 13(2): 246-288.

_____. 2007. Immigrant Enclaves, Ethnic Goods, and the Adjustment Process. Pp. 80-93 in Elliott R. Barkan, Hasia Diner, and Alan M. Kraut (Eds.), *From Arrival to Incorporation: Migrants to the U.S. in a Global Era.* New York: New York University Press.

Chock, Phyllis P. 1991. Illegal Aliens and Opportunity: Myth-Making in Congressional Testimony. *American Ethnologist* 18(2): 279-294.

Chung, Rita Chi-Ying, and Keh-Ming Lin. 1994. Help-Seeking Behavior Among Southeast Asian Refugees. *Journal of Community Psychology* 22(2): 109-120.

Cichon, Donald J., Elzbieta M. Gozdziak, and Jane G. Grover. 1986. *The Economic and Social Adjustment of Non-Southeast Asian Refugees.* Dover, New Hampshire: Research Management Corporation.

Cizek, Janusz. 2006. *Polish Refugees and the Polish American Immigration and Relief Committee.* Translated by Alfred Juszczak. Jefferson, North Carolina: McFarland.

Clark, Greg, William H. Sack, and Brian Goff. 1993. Three Forms of Stress in Cambodian Adolescent Refugees. *Journal of Abnormal Child Psychology* 21(1): 65-77.

Cohen, Lucy M. 1984. *Chinese in the Post-Civil War South: A People Without History*. Baton Rouge: Louisiana State University Press.

Conde, Yvonne. 1999. *Operation Pedro Pan: The Untold Exodus of 14,048 Cuban Children*. New York: Routledge.

Conquergood, Dwight. 1992. Life in Big Red: Struggles and Accommodation in a Chicago Polyethnic Tenement. Pp. 95-144 in Louise Lamphere (Ed.), *Structuring Diversity*. Chicago: University of Chicago Press.

Cooke, Joseph R. 1968. *Pronominal Reference in Thai, Burmese, and Vietnamese*. Berkeley: University of California Publications in Linguistics #52.

Coriden, Guy. 1958. Report on Hungarian Refugees (U.S. Central Intelligence Agency). https://www.cia.gov/library/center-for-the-study-of-intelligence/kent-csi/vol2no1/html/v02i1a07p_0001.htm.

Corvo, Kenneth, and Jaia Peterson. 2005. Post-Traumatic Stress Symptoms, Language Acquisition, and Self-Sufficiency: A Study of Bosnian Refugees. *Journal of Social Work* 5(2): 205-219.

Coutin, Susan B. 1998. From Refugees to Immigrants: The Legalization Strategies of Salvador Immigrants and Activists. *International Migration Review* 32(4): 901-925.

―――. 2000. *Legalizing Moves: Salvadoran Immigrants' Struggle for U.S. Residency*. Ann Arbor: University of Michigan Press.

―――. 2003. Cultural Logics of Belonging and Movement: Transnationalism, Naturalization, and U.S. Immigration Politics. *American Ethnologist* 30(4): 508-526.

Coutin, Susan B., and Phyllis P. Chock. 1995. "Your Friend, the Illegal": Definition and Paradox in Newspaper Accounts of U.S. Immigration Reform. *Identities* 2(1/2): 123-148.

CRS (Congressional Research Service). 1979a. U.S. Immigration Law and Policy: 1952–1979. [Report prepared for the Committee on the Judiciary, U.S. Senate; May.] Washington, DC: U.S. Government Printing Office.

―――. 1979b. Review of U.S. Refugee Resettlement Programs and Policies. [Report prepared for the Committee on the Judiciary, U.S. Senate; July.] Washington, DC: U.S. Government Printing Office.

―――. 1980. Review of U.S. Refugee Resettlement Programs and Policies. [Report prepared for the Committee on the Judiciary, U.S. Senate; July.] Washington, DC: U.S. Government Printing Office.

Dabney, Virginius. 1990. *Richmond: The Story of a City* (orig 1976). Charlottesville: University Press of Virginia.

Daniel, E. Valentine, and John Chr Knudsen (Eds.). 1995. *Mistrusting Refugees*. Berkeley: University of California Press.

Dau, John Bul (with Michael S. Sweeney). 2007. *God Grew Tired of Us*. Washington, DC: National Geographic.

Dávila, Alberto, and Marie T. Mora. 2001. The Marital Status of Recent Mexican Immigrants in the U.S. in 1980 and 1990. *International Migration Review* 35(2): 506-524.

Davis, Carla P. 2004. Beyond Miami: The Ethnic Enclave and Personal Income in Various Cuban Communities in the United States. *International Migration Review* 38(2): 450-469.

DeLuca, Laura. 2009. Transnational Migration, the Lost Girls of Sudan and Global "Care Work." *Anthropology of Work Review* 30(1): 13-15.

Deng, Benson, Alephonsion Deng, and Benjamin Ajak (with Judy A. Bernstein). 2005. *They Poured Fire on Us From the Sky: The True Story of Three Lost Boys From Sudan*. New York: Public Affairs.

Der-Martirosian, Claudia. 2008. *Iranian Immigrants in Los Angeles: The Role of Networks and Economic Integration*. New York: LFB Scholarly Publications.

Dewey, John. 1938. *Logic: The Theory of Inquiry*. New York: Holt, Rinehart and Winston.

Diamond, Jeff. 1998. African-American Attitudes Towards United States Immigration Policy. *International Migration Review* 32(2): 451-470.

Dillon, John. 1980. Refugees are Finding Success. *Richmond Times-Dispatch*, March 28: C1, C4.

Dinnerstein, Leonard. 1982. *America and the Survivors of the Holocaust*. New York: Columbia University Press.

Divine, Robert A. 1957. *American Immigration Policy, 1924–1952*. New Haven, Connecticut: Yale University Press.

Do Thai Dong. 1991. Modifications of the Traditional Family in the South of Vietnam. Pp. 69-83 in Rita Liljestrom and Tuong Lai (Eds.), *Sociological Studies of the Vietnamese Family*. Hanoi: Social Sciences Publishing House.

Do Thi Binh. 1999. Gender Relation in the Vietnam Family: Traditional and Modern. *Vietnam Social Sciences* 6(74): 47-53.

Donnelly, Nancy D. 1992. The Impossible Situation of Vietnamese in Hong Kong's Detention Centers. Pp. 120-132 in Pamela A. DeVoe (Ed.), *Selected Papers on Refugee Issues*. Washington, DC: American Anthropological Association.

Dunford, Earle. 1995. *Richmond Times-Dispatch: The Story of a Newspaper*. Richmond, Virginia: Cadmus Publishing.

Dunnigan, Timothy. 1982. Segmentary Kinship in an Urban Society: The Hmong of St. Paul-Minneapolis. *Anthropological Quarterly* 55(3): 126-134.

Dunning, Bruce B., and Joshua Greenbaum. 1982. *A Systematic Survey of the Social, Psychological and Economic Adaptation of Vietnamese Refugees Representing Five Entry Cohorts, 1975–1979*. Washington, DC: Bureau of Social Science Research.

Earle, Duncan. M. 1999. Border Crossings, Border Control: Illegalized Migrants From the Other Side. Pp. 396-411 in David W. Haines and Karen E. Rosenblum (Eds.), *Illegal Immigration in America*. Westport, Connecticut: Greenwood Press.

Ebihara, May. 1985. Khmer. Pp. 127-147 in David W. Haines (Ed.), *Refugees in the United States: A Reference Handbook*. Westport, Connecticut: Greenwood Press.

Eckstein, Susan. 2006. Cuban Emigrés and the American Dream. *Perspectives on Politics* 4(2): 297-307.

Egerton, Douglas R. 1993. *Gabriel's Rebellion: The Virginia Slave Conspiracies of 1800 and 1802*. Chapel Hill: University of North Carolina Press.

Erikson, Erik. 1968. *Identity: Youth and Crisis*. New York: Norton.

Espenshade, Thomas J., and Charles A. Calhoun. 1993. An Analysis of Public Opinion Toward Undocumented Immigration. *Population Research and Policy Review* 12(3): 189-224.

Espenshade, Thomas J., and Katherine Hempstead. 1996. Contemporary American Attitudes Toward U.S. Immigration. *International Migration Review* 30(2): 535-570.

Evans, Karen G. 2001. More Democracy, Not Less, in Twenty First Century Governance: Dewey's Ethics and the New Public Management. *Public Integrity* 3: 262-276.

Evans, Mariah Debra Ruperti. 2005. Do Ethnic Enclaves Benefit or Harm Linguistically Isolated Employees? *Research in Social Stratification and Mobility* 22: 281-318.

Fadiman, Anne. 1997. *The Spirit Catches You and You Fall Down*. New York: Noonday Press.

Fagen, Richard R., and Richard A. Brody. 1964. Cubans in Exile: A Demographic Analysis. *Social Problems* 11(4): 389-401.

Fagen, Richard R., Richard A. Brody, and Thomas J. O'Leary. 1968. *Cubans in Exile: Disaffection and the Revolution.* Stanford, California: Stanford University Press.

Fahti, Asghar (Ed.). 1991. *Iranian Refugees and Exiles since Khomeini.* Costa Mesa, California: Mazda Publishers.

Fairbanks, Robert B., and Kathleen Underwood (Eds.). 1990. *Essays on Sunbelt Cities and Recent Urban America.* Arlington, Texas: Texas A&M University Press.

FAO (U.N. Food and Agriculture Organization). 2002. *Gender Differences in the Transitional Economy of Viet Nam.* Bangkok, Thailand, and Hanoi, Vietnam.

Feldman, William. 1977. Social Absorption of Soviet Immigrants: Integration or Isolation. *Journal of Jewish Communal Service* 54(1): 62-68.

Ferreé, Myra Marx. 1979. Employment Without Liberation: Cuban Women in the United States. *Social Science Quarterly* 60: 35-50.

Finnan, Christine Robinson. 1980. A Community Affair: Occupational Assimilation of Vietnamese Refugees. *Journal of Refugee Resettlement* 1(1): 8-14.

Finnan, Christine, and Rhonda Ann Cooperstein. 1983. *Southeast Asian Refugee Resettlement at the Local Level: The Role of the Ethnic Community and the Nature of Refugee Impact.* Menlo Park, California: SRI International.

Fitzgerald, Randy. 1991. Teens Travel a Long Way Looking for a Home. *Richmond News-Leader*, February 20: M4.

Foner, Nancy. 1997. The Immigrant Family: Cultural Legacies and Cultural Changes. International Migration Review 31(4): 961-974.

_____. 2000. *From Ellis Island to JFK. New York's Two Great Waves of Immigration.* New Haven: Yale University Press.

Foner, Nancy (Ed.). 1987. *New Immigrants in New York.* New York: Columbia University Press.

Frederickson, George M. 1999. Models of American Ethnic Relations: A Historical Perspective. Pp. 23-34 in Deborah A. Prentice and Dale T. Miller (Eds.), *Cultural Divides: Understanding and Overcoming Group Conflict.* New York: Russell Sage Foundation.

Frelick, Bill. 1996. Hardening the Heart: The Global Refugee Problem in the 1990s. Pp. 372-382 in David W. Haines (Ed.). *Refugees in America in the 1990s.* Westport, Connecticut: Greenwood Press.

Gallagher, Dennis (Ed.). 1986. *Refugees: Issues and Directions*. Special issue of *International Migration Review* 20(2).

Gallaher, Robin. 1979a. Family Shares Modest Home With Laotians. *Richmond Times-Dispatch*, August 24: C1.

———. 1979b. Cambodians' Adjustment is Remarkable. *Richmond Times-Dispatch*, November 11: H1-2.

Gammeltoft, Tine. 1999. *Women's Bodies, Women's Worries: Health and Family Planning in a Vietnamese Rural Community*. Richmond, England: Curzon Press.

GAO (U.S. General Accounting Office [now U.S. Government Accountability Office]). 1983a. *Improved Overseas Medical Examinations and Treatment Can Reduce Serious Diseases in Indochinese Refugees Entering the United States*. Washington, DC

———. 1983b. *Greater Emphasis on Early Employment and Better Monitoring Needed in Indochinese Refugee Resettlement Program*. Washington. DC

———. 1991. *Soviet Refugees: Processing and Admittance to the United States Has Improved*. Washington, DC

———. 1995. *Welfare Reform: Implications of Proposals on Legal Immigrants' Benefits*. Washington, DC

Garcia, María Cristina. 1996. *Havana USA: Cuban Exiles and Cuban Americans in South Florida, 1959–1994*. Berkeley: University of California Press.

Geddes, William R. 1976. *Migrants of the Mountains*. Oxford: Clarendon Press.

Gentemann, Karen M., and Ying Zhou. 2005. The Expectations and Attitudes of Native- and Foreign-Born University Students. Paper presented at the Annual Meeting of the Society for Applied Anthropology, Santa Fe, New Mexico.

Gilison, Jerome M. 1979. *Summary Report of the Survey of Soviet Jewish Emigres in Baltimore*. Baltimore, Maryland: Baltimore Hebrew College.

Gilman, Sander. 1991. *The Jew's Body*. New York: Routledge.

Gitelman, Zvi. 1978. Soviet Immigrants and American Absorption Efforts: A Case Study in Detroit. *Journal of Jewish Communal Service* 55(1): 72-82.

Global Health. 2008. Background on Potential Health Problems for Somali Bantu. U.S. Department of Health and Human Services. http://www.globalhealth.gov/refugee/refugees_health_bantu.html.

_____. 2009. Background on Potential Health Problems for Burmese Refugees. U.S. Department of Health and Human Services. http://www.globalhealth.gov/refugee/refugees_health_burmese.html.

Gold, Steven J. 1992. *Refugee Communities: A Comparative Field Study.* Newbury Park, California: Sage Publications.

_____. 1994a. Chinese-Vietnamese Entrepreneurs in California. Pp. 196-226 in Paul Ong, Edna Bonacich, and Lucie Cheng (Eds.), *The New Asian Immigration in Los Angeles and Global Restructuring.* Philadelphia: Temple University Press.

_____. 1994b. Soviet Jews in the United States. *American Jewish Yearbook* 1994: 3-57.

_____. 1997. Soviet Jews. Pp. 59-84 in David W. Haines (Ed.), *Case Studies in Diversity: Refugees in America in the 1990s.* Westport, Connecticut: Praeger.

Gold, Steven, and Nazli Kibria. 1993. Vietnamese Refugees and Blocked Mobility. *Asian and Pacific Migration Journal* 2(1): 27-56.

Gonzales, Diana H. 1980. Sociocultural Adaptations Among Cuban Emigre Women in Miami, Florida. Paper presented at the annual meetings of the Caribbean Studies Association, Curacao, Netherlands Antilles.

Gonzalez, Manny J., Jose J. Lopez, and Eunjeong Ko. 2005. The Mariel and Balsero Cuban Immigrant Experience: Family Reunification Issues and Treatment Recommendations. *Journal of Immigrant & Refugee Services* 3(1-2): 141-153.

Goode, Judith. 1998. The Contingent Construction of Local Identities: Koreans and Puerto Ricans in Philadelphia. *Identities* 5(1): 33-64.

Goodkind, Daniel. 1997. The Vietnamese Double Marriage Squeeze. *International Migration Review* 31(1): 108-127.

Goodkind, Jessica R. 2005. Effectiveness of a Community–Based Advocacy and Learning Program for Hmong Refugees. *American Journal of Community Psychology* 36(3/4): 387-408.

Gordon, Linda W. 1989. National Surveys of Southeast Asian Refugees: Methods, Findings, Issues. Pp. 24-39 in David W. Haines (Ed.), *Refugees as Immigrants: Cambodians, Laotians, and Vietnamese in America.* Totowa, New Jersey: Rowman & Littlefield.

Gordon, Milton M. 1964. *Assimilation in American Life.* New York: Oxford University Press.

Gourevitch, Philip. 1999. *We Wish to Inform You That Tomorrow We Will Be Killed With Our Families: Stories From Rwanda*. New York: Farrar, Straus & Giroux.

Gozdziak, Elzbieta M. 1996. Eastern Europeans. Pp. 121-146 in David W. Haines (Ed.), *Refugees in America in the 1990s*. Westport, Connecticut: Greenwood Press.

Gozdziak, Elzbieta M., and Dianna J. Shandy (Eds.). 2002. *Religion and Forced Migration*. Special issue of *Journal of Refugee Studies* 15(2).

Grant, Bruce, and others. 1979. *The Boat People: An "Age" Investigation*. New York: Penguin Books.

Grantham, Dewy W. 1983. *Southern Progressivism: The Reconciliation of Progress and Tradition*. Knoxville: University of Tennessee Press.

Granville Corporation. 1982. *A Preliminary Assessment of the Khmer Cluster Resettlement Project*. Washington, DC.

Gray, Maryann Jacobi, Georges Vernez, and Elizabeth Rolph. 1996. Student Access and the "New" Immigrants: Assessing Their Impact on Institutions. *Change* 28(5): 41-47.

Green, Barbara. 1995. Aftershocks of War Continue. *Richmond Times-Dispatch*, April 23: A10.

Greenbaum, Susan D. 2002. *More Than Black: Afro-Cubans in Tampa*. Gainesville: University Press of Florida.

Greenberg, Martin. 1976. Agency Concerns: The Special Problems Confronting Agencies in Providing Services to Immigrants From the USSR. P. 140 in Jerome Gillison (Ed.) *The Soviet Jewish Emigre*. Baltimore, Maryland: Baltimore Hebrew College.

Grenier, Guillermo J., and Lisandro Pérez. 2003. *The Legacy of Exile: Cubans in the United States*. Boston: Allyn and Bacon.

Grillo, Evelio. 2000. *Black Cuban, Black American: A Memoir*. Houston, Texas: Arte Público Press.

Grosfoguel, Ramon. 2004. Race and Ethnicity or Racialized Ethnicities? Identities within Global Coloniality. *Ethnicities* 4(3): 315-336.

Grubb, W. Norton, Norena Badway, and Denise Bell. 2003. Community Colleges and the Equity Agenda: The Potential of Noncredit Education. *The Annals of the American Academy of Political and Social Science* 586(March): 218-400.

Gunawardena, Sandarshi, and Julia Findlay. 2005. Alike but Very Different: Comparing Cultural Identities of International and Immigrant Students

From India. Paper presented at the Annual Meeting of the Society for Applied Anthropology, Santa Fe, New Mexico.

Hackett, Beatrice N. 1996a. *Pray God and Keep Walking: Stories of Women Refugees*. Jefferson, North Carolina: McFarland & Company.

————. 1996b. "We Must Become Part of the Larger American Family": Washington's Vietnamese, Cambodians, and Laotians. Pp. 276-291 in Francine Curro Cary (Ed.), *Urban Odyssey: A Multicultural History of Washington, D.C.* Washington, DC: Smithsonian Institution Press.

Hagan, Jacqueline Maria. 1994. *Deciding to Be Legal: A Maya Community in Houston*. Philadelphia: Temple University Press.

Hagan, Jacqueline Maria, and Nestor P. Rodriguez. 1992. Recent Economic Restructuring and Evolving Intergroup Relations in Houston. Pp. 145-171 in Louise Lamphere (Ed.), *Structuring Diversity*. Chicago: University of Chicago Press.

Haines, David W. 1980. Mismatch in the Resettlement Process: The Vietnamese Family versus the American Housing Market. *Journal of Refugee Resettlement* 1(1): 15-19.

————. 1983. Southeast Asian Refugees in the United States: An Overview. *Migration Today* 11(2/3): 8-13.

————. 1984. Reflections of Kinship and Society under Vietnam's Le Dynasty. *Journal of Southeast Asian Studies* 15(2): 307-314.

————. 1986. Vietnamese Refugee Women in the U.S. Labor Force: Continuity or Change? Pp. 62-75 in Rita J. Simon and Caroline B. Brettell (Eds.), *International Migration: The Female Experience*. Totowa, New Jersey: Rowman and Allenheld.

————. 1987. Patterns in Southeast Asian Refugee Employment: A Reappraisal of the Existing Research. *Ethnic Groups* 7: 39-63.

————. 1990. South Vietnamese Households: Some Reconstructions of the 1954–1975 Period. *Vietnam Forum* 13: 192-217.

————. 1991. Southeast Asian Refugees in Western Europe: American Reflections on French, British, and Dutch Experiences. *Migration World* 19(4): 15-18.

————. 2002. Binding the Generations: Household Formation Patterns Among Vietnamese Refugees. *International Migration Review* 36(4): 1194-1217.

————. 2006. *The Limits of Kinship: Vietnamese Households*. DeKalb, Illinois: Northern Illinois University, Southeast Asia Publications.

_____. 2007a. Crossing Lines of Difference: How College Students Analyze Diversity. *Intercultural Education* 18(5): 397-412.

_____. 2007b. Labor, Migration, and Anthropology: Reflections From the Work of Philip L. Martin. *City & Society* 19(1): 60-71.

_____. 2009. Rethinking the Vietnamese Exodus: The Politics of Migration and the Migration of Politics. Keynote paper presented at the workshop *Refugee Politics and the Chinese/Vietnamese Diaspora*. Organized by Yuk Wah Chan. City University of Hong Kong, October.

Haines, David W. (Ed.). 1985. *Refugees in the United States: A Reference Handbook*. Westport, Connecticut: Greenwood Press.

_____. 1989. *Refugees as Immigrants: Cambodians, Laotians, and Vietnamese in America*. Totowa, New Jersey: Rowman & Littlefield.

_____. 1996. *Refugees in America in the 1990s: A Reference Handbook*. Westport, Connecticut: Greenwood Press.

Haines, David W., Dorothy A. Rutherford, and Patrick A. Thomas. 1981a. Family and Community Among Vietnamese Refugees. *International Migration Review* 15(1): 310-319.

_____. 1981b. The Case for Exploratory Fieldwork: Understanding the Adjustment of Vietnamese Refugees in the Washington Area. *Anthropological Quarterly* 54(2): 94-102.

Haines, David W., and Karen E. Rosenblum (Eds.). 1999. *Illegal Immigration in America: A Reference Handbook*. Westport, Connecticut: Greenwood Press.

_____. 2005. Moratorium and Crucible: Reconfiguring Identity in the American University. Paper presented at the Annual Meeting of the Society for Applied Anthropology, Santa Fe, New Mexico.

Haines, David W., Marilyn Breslow, Dirk Philipsen, and Jan Williamson. 2001. Richmond, Virginia: Refugee Resettlement and Community Reaffirmation. Pp. 89-100 in David W. Haines and Carol A. Mortland (Eds.), *Manifest Destinies: Americanizing Immigrants and Internationalizing Americans*. Westport, Connecticut: Praeger Publishers.

Hall, Kari Rene. 1992. *Beyond the Killing Fields*. Hong Kong: Asia 2000.

Hamilton, Don. 1977. Refugees' Concept of Freedom is Reflected in All He Says. *Richmond Times-Dispatch*, August 22: B4.

Handlin, Oscar. 1973. *The Uprooted: The Epic Story of the Great Migrations That Made the American People* (2nd ed.). Boston: Little, Brown and Company.

Hansen, Peter. 2009. Thanh Loc: Inside the Hong Kong Immigration Department's Refugee Screening System From a Refugee Perspective. Paper presented at the workshop *Refugee Politics and the Chinese/Vietnamese Diaspora*. Organized by Yuk Wah Chan. City University of Hong Kong, October.

Harklau, Linda. 1999. Representations of Immigrant Language Minorities in US Higher Education. *Race, Ethnicity and Education* 2(2): 257-279.

Harmon, Robert. 1995. Intergenerational Relations Among Maya in Los Angeles. Pp. 156-173 in Ann M. Rynearson and James Phillips (Eds.), *Selected Papers on Refugees Issues: IV*. Arlington, Virginia: American Anthropological Association.

Harvey, Toni. 1989. Smiling Faces Graduation Testimony of Asia Refugees' Enormous Desire to Survive and Succeed. *Richmond News-Leader*, June 27: M27.

Hecht, Joan. 2005. *The Journey of the Lost Boys*. Jacksonville, Florida: Allswell Press.

Heidegger, Martin. 1962. *Being and Time*. Translated by Joan Stambaugh. New York: Harper and Row.

Hein, Jeremy. 2006. *Ethnic Origins: The Adaptation of Cambodian and Hmong Refugees in Four American Cities*. New York: Russell Sage Foundation.

Helton, Arthur C. 2002. *The Price of Indifference: Refugees and Humanitarian Action in the New Century.* New York: Oxford University Press.

Henken, Ted. 2005. Balseros, Boteros, and El Bombo: Post-1994 Cuban Immigration to the United States and the Persistence of Special Treatment. *Latino Studies* 3(3): 393-416.

Hernandez, Andres R., Ed. 1974. *The Cuban Minority in the U.S.* Washington, DC: Cuban National Planning Council.

Hepner, Tricia Redeker. 2009. *Soldiers, Martyrs, Traitors, and Exiles: Political Conflict in Eritrea and the Diaspora*. Philadelphia: University of Pennsylvania Press.

HIAS (Hebrew Immigrant Aid Society). 1980. *Statistical Abstract*. New York.

Hickey, Gerald C. 1964. *Village in Vietnam*. New Haven, Connecticut: Yale University Press.

————. 1987. The Vietnamese Village through Time and War. *Vietnam Forum* 10: 1-25.

Hinton, Devon E., Dara Chhean, Vuth Pich, Mark H. Pollack, Scott P. Orr, and Roger K. Pitman. 2006. Assessment of Posttraumatic Stress Disorder in Cambodian Refugees Using the Clinician–Administered PTSD Scale: Psychometric Properties and Symptom Severity. *Journal of Traumatic Stress* 19(3): 405-409.

Hirschman, Charles. 2004. The Origins and Demise of the Concept of Race. *Population and Development Review* 30(3): 385-415.

Hitchcox, Linda. 1990. *Vietnamese Refugees in Southeast Asian Camps.* London: Macmillan.

Hoefer, Michael, Nancy Rytine, and Bryan C. Baker. 2009. *Estimate of the Unauthorized Immigrant Population Residing in the United States: January 2008.* Washington, DC: Department of Homeland Security (Office of Immigration Statistics).

Holman, Philip A. 1996. Refugee Resettlement in the United States. Pp. 3-27 in David W. Haines (Ed.), *Refugees in America in the 1990s.* Westport, Connecticut: Greenwood Press.

Holtzman, Jon. 2000. *Nuer Journeys, Nuer Lives.* Boston: Allyn & Bacon.

Hoskins, Marilyn W. 1975. Vietnamese Women: Their Roles and Their Options. Pp. 231-248 in Dana Raphael (Ed.), *Being Female.* The Hague: Mouton.

Hoxby, Caroline M. 1998. Do Immigrants Crowd Disadvantaged American Natives out of Higher Education? Pp. 282-321 in Daniel S. Hamermesh and Frank D. Bean (Eds.), *Help or Hindrance: The Economic Implications of Immigration for African Americans.* New York: Russell Sage Foundation.

Human Resources Corporation. 1979. *Evaluation of the Indochinese Refugee Assistance Program in Private Agencies in California.* San Francisco, California.

Hussain, Yasmin, and Paul Bagguley. 2005. Citizenship, Ethnicity and Identity: British Parkistanis after the 2001 Years. *Sociology* 39(3): 407-425.

Ignatiev, Noel. 1995. *How the Irish Became White.* New York: Routledge.

IRAC (Indochina Refugee Action Center). 1980. *An Assessment of the Needs of Indochinese Youth.* Washington, DC.

Jacobsen, Karen. 1996. Factors Influencing the Policy Responses of Host Governments to Mass Refugee Influxes. *International Migration Review* 30(3): 655-678.

Jacobson, Gaynor I. 1978. Soviet Jewry: Perspectives on the "Dropout" Issue. *Journal of Jewish Communal Service* 55(1): 83-89.

Jacobson, Matthew Frye. 1998. *Whiteness of a Different Color: European Immigrants and the Alchemy of Race*. Cambridge: Harvard University Press.

James, David R. 1988. The Transformation of the Southern Racial State: Class and Race Determinants of Local-State Relations. *American Sociological Review* 53: 191-208.

Jamieson, Neil L. 1986a. The Traditional Village in Vietnam. *Vietnam Forum* 7: 89-126.

————. 1986b. The Traditional Family in Vietnam. *Vietnam Forum* 8: 91-150.

Jenkins, Richard. 1997. *Rethinking Ethnicity: Arguments and Explorations*. Thousand Oaks, California: Sage.

Jo, Hye-Young. 2002. Negotiating Identity in the College Korean Language Classes. *Identities: Global Studies in Culture and Power* 9: 87-115.

Johnson, Ophelia. 1992. Finally, No Fear. Haitian Teens Find Open Arms in the United States. *Richmond Times-Dispatch*, June 29: C1.

Jordan, Ervin L., Jr. 1995. *Black Confederates and Afro-Yankees in Civil War Virginia*. Charlottesville: University Press of Virginia.

Karakayali, Nedim. 2005. Duality and Diversity in the Lives of Immigrant Children: Rethinking the "Problem of the Second Generation" in Light of Immigrant Autobiographies. *Canadian Review of Sociology and Anthropology* 42(3): 325-343.

Keely, Charles B. 1996. How Nation-States Create and Respond to Refugee Flows. *International Migration Review* 30(4): 1046-1066.

Kelly, Deborah. 1991. In Richmond, Look to the West to Find a Small Piece of the East. *Richmond Times-Dispatch*, March 23: C1.

Kelly, Gail P. 1977. *From Vietnam to America: A Chronicle of the Vietnamese Immigration to the United States*. Boulder, Colorado: Westview Press.

Kemp, Charles, and Lance A. Rasbridge. 2004. *Refugee and Immigrant Health: A Handbook for Health Professionals*. New York: Cambridge University Press.

Kibria, Nazli. 1990. Power, Patriarchy, and Gender Conflict in the Vietnamese Immigrant Community. *Gender and Society* 4(1): 9-24.

Kim, Young Yun. 1980. *Population Characteristics and Service Needs of Indochinese Refugees*. Vol. 3 of the Research Project on Indochinese

Refugees in the State of Illinois. Chicago: Travelers Aid Society of Metropolitan Chicago.

Kim, Young Yun, and Perry M. Nicassio. 1980. *Psychological, Social, and Cultural Adjustment of Indochinese Refugees*. Vol. 4 of the Research Project on Indochinese Refugees in the State of Illinois. Chicago: Travelers Aid Society of Metropolitan Chicago.

Konczal, Lisa, and Alex Stepick. 2007. Haiti. Pp. 445-457 in Mary Waters and Reed Ueda (Eds.), *The New Americans: A Guide to Immigration since 1965*. Cambridge, Massachusetts: Harvard University Press.

Knudsen, John Chr. 1992. "To Destroy You Is No Loss": Hong Kong 1991–92. Pp. 133-145 in Pamela A. DeVoe (Ed.), *Selected Papers on Refugee Issues*. Washington, DC: American Anthropological Association.

_____. 1995. When Trust Is on Trial: Negotiating Refugee Narratives. Pp. 13-35 in E. Valentine Daniel and John Chr Knudsen (Eds.), *Mistrusting Refugees*. Berkeley: University of California Press.

Koehn, Peter H. 1991. *Refugees From Revolution: U.S. Policy and Third World Migration*. Boulder, Colorado: Westview Press.

Kogan, Deborah, and Mary Vencill. 1984. *An Evaluation of the Favorable Alternate Sites Project*. Berkeley: Berkeley Planning Associates.

Kunz, E.F. 1973. The Refugee in Flight: Kinetic Models and Forms of Displacement. *International Migration Review* 7(2): 125-146.

Kurien, Prema A. 2005. Being Young, Brown, and Hindu: The Identity Struggles of Second-Generation Indian Americans. *Journal of Contemporary Ethnography* 34(4): 434-469.

Lafontant, Jewel S. 1990. Crafting a U.S. Refugee Policy for Asia and the World. Washington, DC: The Heritage Foundation.

Lamphere, Louise (Ed.). 1992. *Structuring Diversity: Ethnographic Perspectives on the New Immigration*. Chicago: University of Chicago Press.

Lamphere, Louise, Alex Stepick, and Guillermo Genier (Eds.). 1994. *Newcomers in the Workplace: Immigrants and the Restructuring of the U.S. Economy*. Philadelphia: Temple University Press.

Lash, Joseph P. 1971. *Eleanor and Franklin*. New York: W.W. Norton & Co.

Le Thi. 1999. *The Role of the Family in the Formation of Vietnamese Personality*. Hanoi: The Gioi.

LeBar, Frank, Gerald Hickey, and John Musgrave (Eds.). 1964. *Ethnic Groups of Mainland Southeast Asia*. New Haven, Connecticut: Human Relations Area Files Press.

Lee, Jonathan H. X. 2009. Chinese Vietnamese Refugees in America: Then and Now. Paper presented at the workshop *Refugee Politics and the Chinese/Vietnamese Diaspora*. Organized by Yuk Wah Chan. City University of Hong Kong, October.

Lee, Stacey J. 1997. The Road to College: Hmong American Women's Pursuit of Higher Education. *Harvard Educational Review* 67(4): 802-827.

LeMay, Michael, and Elliott Robert Barkan. 1999. *U.S. Immigration and Naturalization Laws and Issues: A Documentary History*. Westport, Connecticut: Greenwood Press.

Lemons, Teresa. 1993. She Helps Because She's Been There. *Richmond Times-Dispatch*, August 28: A9.

Li Tana. 1998. *Nguyen Cochinchina: Southern Vietnam in the Seventeenth and Eighteenth Centuries*. Ithaca, New York: Cornell University Southeast Asia Program.

Lievens, John. 1999. Family-Forming Migration From Turkey and Morocco to Belgium: The Demand for Marriage Partners From the Countries of Origin. *International Migration Review* 33(3): 717-744.

Light, Ivan, Georges Sabagh, Mehdi Bozorgmehr, and Claudia Der-Martirosian. 1993. Internal Ethnicity in the Ethnic Economy. *Ethnic and Racial Studies* 16: 581-597.

Liljestrom, Rita and Tuong Lai (Eds.). 1991. *Sociological Studies of the Vietnamese Family*. Hanoi: Social Sciences Publishing House.

Lin, Keh-Ming, Laurie Tazuma, and Minoru Masuda. 1979. Adaptational Problems of Vietnamese Refugees: Health and Mental Health Status. *Archives of General Psychiatry* 36: 955-961.

Lipson, Juliene G., and Patricia A. Omidian. 1995. Health and the Transnational Connection: Afghan Refugees in the United States. Pp. 2-17 in Ann M. Rynearson and James Phillips (Eds.)*Selected Papers on Refugee Issues: IV*. Arlington, Virginia: American Anthropological Association.

_____. 1996. Afghans. Pp. 63-80 in David W. Haines (Ed.), *Refugees in America in the 1990s*. Westport, Connecticut: Greenwood Press.

Liu, William T., Maryanne Lamanna, and Alice Murata. 1979. *Transition to Nowhere: Vietnamese Refugees in America*. Nashville, Tennessee: Charter House.

Loescher, Gil. 1993. *Beyond Charity: International Cooperation and the Global Refugee Crisis*. New York: Oxford University Press.

Loescher, Gil, and John Scanlan. 1986. *Calculated Kindness: Refugees and America's Half-Open Door.* New York: Macmillan.

Long, Lynellyn D. 1993. *Ban Vinai: The Refugee Camp.* New York: Columbia University Press.

Luong, Hy V. 1990. *Discursive Practices and Linguistic Meanings: The Vietnamese System of Person Reference.* Philadelphia: John Benjamins Publishing Company.

Mabe, Ann. 1994. Taking Care of People Through Culture: Zimbabwe's Tongogara Refugee Camp. Pp. 78-97 in Jeffery L. MacDonald and Amy Zaharlick (Eds.), *Selected Papers on Refugee Issues: III.* Arlington, Virginia: American Anthropological Association.

MacDonald, Jeffery L. 1997. *Transnational Aspects of Iu-Mien Refugee Identity.* Hamden, Connecticut: Garland Publishing.

_____. 1998. "We Are the Experts": Iu-Mien (Yao) Refugees Assert Their Rights as Scholars of Their Own Culture. Pp. 97-122 in Ruth M. Krulfeld and Jeffery L. MacDonald (Eds.), *Power, Ethics, and Human Rights: Anthropological Studies of Refugee Research and Action.* Lanham, Maryland: Rowman & Littlefield.

Malkki, Liisa H. 1995a. Refugees and Exile: From "Refugee Studies" to the National Order of Things. *Annual Review of Anthropology* 24: 447-470.

_____. 1995b. *Purity and Exile: Violence, Memory, and National Cosmology Among Hutu Refugees in Tanzania.* Chicago: University of Chicago Press.

_____. 1996. Speechless Emissaries: Refugees, Humanitarianism, and Dehistoricization. *Cultural Anthropology* 11(3): 377-404.

Markowitz, Fran. 1993. *A Community in Spite of Itself: Soviet Jewish Emigres in New York.* Washington, DC: Smithsonian Institution Press.

Marrow, Linda. 1981. Six Years After the Fall, the Trinhs are Independent. *Richmond Times-Dispatch,* July 2: C2.

Marsh, Robert E. 1980. Socioeconomic Status of Indochinese Refugees in the United States: Progress and Problems. *Social Security Bulletin* 43(10): 11-20.

Martin, Daniel C., and Michael Hoefer. 2009. *Refugees and Asylees, 2008.* Washington, DC: Department of Homeland Security (Office of Immigration Statistics).

Martin, David A. 2005. *The United States Refugee Admission Program: Reforms for a New Era of Refugee Resettlement.* Washington, DC: Migration Policy Institute.

Martinez, Charles R., Jr. 2006. Effects of Differential Family Acculturation on Latino Adolescent Substance Use. *Family Relations* 55(3): 306-317.

McGehee, Overton. 1984. Refugees Adjusting to Culture. *Richmond Times-Dispatch*, July 15: D1-2.

McKelvey, Robert S. 1999. *The Dust of Life: America's Children Abandoned in Vietnam*. Seattle: University of Washington Press.

McSpadden, Lucia A. 1998. "I Must Have My Rights": The Presence of State Power in the Resettlement of Ethiopian and Eritrean Refugees. Pp. 147-172 in Ruth M. Krulfeld and Jeffery L. MacDonald (Eds.), *Power, Ethics, and Human Rights*. Lanham, Maryland: Rowman & Littlefield.

Meisner, James. 1992. From Khmer Rouge War Camps VMI Student Make His Way in "A Pretty Impressive Country." *Richmond Times-Dispatch*, October 8: E1.

Melville, Margarita B. 1985. Salvadoreans and Guatemalans. Pp. 167-180 in David W. Haines (Ed.), *Refugees in the United States: A Reference Handbook*. Westport, Connecticut: Greenwood Press.

_____. 1988. Hispanics: Race, Class, or Ethnicity? *Journal of Ethnic Studies* 16: 67-83.

Menjívar, Cecilia. 1999. Salvadorans and Nicaraguans: Refugees Become Workers. Pp. 232-253 in David W. Haines and Karen E. Rosenblum (Eds.), *Illegal Immigration in America*. Westport, Connecticut: Greenwood Press.

_____. 2006. Liminal Legality: Salvadoran and Guatemalan Immigrants' Lives in the United States. *American Journal of Sociology* 111(4): 999-1037.

Miller, Randall M., and George E. Pozzetta (Eds.). 1988. *Shades of the Sunbelt: Essays on Ethnicity, Race, and the Urban South*. New York: Greenwood Press.

Model, Suzanne. 1992. The Ethnic Economy: Cubans and Chinese Reconsidered. *Sociological Quarterly* 33(1): 63-82.

Moeser, John V., and Rutledge M. Dennis. 1982. *The Politics of Annexation: Oligarchic Power in a Southern City*. Cambridge, Massachusetts: Schenkman Publishing Company.

Montero, Darrel. 1979. *Vietnamese Americans: Patterns of Resettlement and Socioeconomic Adaptation in the United States*. Boulder, Colorado: Westview Press.

Moorehead, Caroline. 2005. *Human Cargo: A Journey among Refugees*. New York: Picador.

Mormino, Gary R. 1986. *Immigrants on the Hill: Italian-Americans in St. Louis, 1882–1982*. Urbana: University of Illinois Press.

Mormino, Gary R., and George E. Pozzetta. 1987. *The Immigrant World of Ybor City: Italians and Their Latin Neighbors in Tampa, 1885–1985*. Urbana: University of Illinois Press.

Morris, Thomas R. 1980. Refugee Curbs Favored Here. *Richmond Times-Dispatch*, June 29: A1-2.

Mortland, Carol A. 1994a. Cambodian Refugees and Identity in the United States. Pp. 5-27 in Linda A. Camino and Ruth M. Krulfeld (Eds.), *Restructuring Lives, Recapturing Meaning*. Basel, Switzerland: Gordon and Breach.

_____. 1994b. Khmer Buddhists in the United States: Ultimate Questions. Pp. 72-90 in May Ebihara, Carol Mortland, and Judy Ledgerwood (Eds.), *Cambodian Culture since 1975*. Ithaca, New York: Cornell University Press.

_____. 2001. Tacoma, Washington: Cambodian Adaptation and Community Response. Pp. 71-88 in David W. Haines and Carol A. Mortland (Eds.), *Manifest Destinies: Americanizing Immigrants and Internationalizing Americans*. Westport, Connecticut: Praeger Publishers.

Mortland, Carol A. (Ed.). 1998. *Diasporic Identity: Selected Papers on Refugees and Immigrants VI*. Arlington, Virginia: American Anthropological Association.

Mortland, Carol, and Judy Ledgerwood. 1988. Refugee Resource Acquisition, the Invisible Communication System. Pp. 286-306 in Young Yun Kim and William P. Gudykunst (Eds.), *Cross-Cultural Adaptation: Current Approaches*. Newbury Park, California: Sage Publications.

Mosselson, Jacqueline. 2006. *Roots and Routes: Bosnian Adolescents in New York City*. New York: Peter Lang.

_____. 2007. Masks of Achievement: An Experiential Study of Bosnian Female Refugees in New York City Schools. *Comparative Education Review* 51(1): 95-115.

Mostofi, Nilou. 2003. Who We Are: The Perplexity of Iranian-American Identity. *Sociological Quarterly* 44(4): 681-703.

Murdock, Elizabeth. 2006. "Trying Small": Liberian Refugees in Buduburam, Ghana. M.A. thesis, George Mason University.

Musil, Caryn McTighe, Mildred García, Yolanda T. Moses, and Daryl G. Smith. 1995. *Diversity in Higher Education: A Work in Progress*. Washington, DC: Association of American Colleges and Universities.

Nasser, Haya El. 1998. Asian Population in Southern USA Soars. *USA Today*, June 2.

Neal, Steve (Ed.). n.d. *Eleanor and Harry: The Correspondence of Eleanor Roosevelt and Harry Truman*. http://www.trumanlibrary.org/eleanor/.

Ng Shui Meng. 1974. *The Population of Indochina*. Singapore: Institute of Southeast Asian Studies.

Nguyen Dinh Hoa. 1956. Verbal and Non-Verbal Patterns of Respect Behavior in Vietnamese Society. Ph.D. dissertation, New York University.

Nguyen, Kien. 2001. *The Unwanted: A Memoir of Childhood*. Boston: Little, Brown and Company.

Nguyen Manh Hung and David W. Haines. 1996. Vietnamese. Pp. 305-327 in David W. Haines (Ed.), *Refugees in America in the 1990s*. Westport, Connecticut: Greenwood Press.

Nguyen, Minh Huu. 1998. Tradition and Change in Vietnamese Marriage Patterns in the Red River Delta. Ph.D. dissertation. University of Washington.

Norlund, Irene, Carolyn L. Gates, and Vu Cao Dam (Eds.). 1995. *Vietnam in a Changing World*. Richmond, England: Curzon Press.

Oboler, Suzanne. 1995. *Ethnic Labels, Latino Lives: Identity and the Politics of (Re)Presentation in the United States*. Minneapolis: University of Minnesota Press.

Ogata, Sadako. 2005. *The Turbulent Decade: Confronting the Refugee Crises of the 1990s*. New York: W.W. Norton.

Ogilvie, Sarah A., and Scott Miller. 2006. *Refuge Denied: The St. Louis Passengers and the Holocaust*. Madison: University of Wisconsin Press.

Omi, Michael, and Howard Winant. 1986. *Racial Formation in the United States: From the 1960s to the 1980s*. New York: Routledge & Kegan Paul.

Ong, Aihwa. 2003. *Buddha is Hiding: Refugees, Citizenship, the New America*. Berkeley: University of California Press.

Orleck, Annelise. 1987. The Soviet Jews: Life in Brighton Beach, Brooklyn. Pp. 273-304 in Nancy Foner (Ed.), *New Immigrants in New York*. New York: Columbia University Press.

ORR (Office of Refugee Resettlement). 1982a. *Report to the Congress: Refugee Resettlement Program*. Washington, DC: U.S. Department of Health and Human Services.

———. 1982b. *Special Report to Congress: Alternative Methods for the Provision of Cash Assistance, Medical Assistance, and Case Management for*

Refugees. Washington, DC: U.S. Department of Health and Human Services.

_____. 1983a. *Report to the Congress: Refugee Resettlement Program*. Washington, DC: U.S. Department of Health and Human Services.

_____. 1983b. *Special Report to the Congress: The Feasibility and Advisability of Special Refugee Reception Centers*. Washington, DC: U.S. Department of Health and Human Services.

_____. 1984. *Report to the Congress: Refugee Resettlement Program*. Washington, DC: U.S. Department of Health and Human Services.

_____. 1985a. *Report to the Congress: Refugee Resettlement Program*. Washington, DC: U.S. Department of Health and Human Services.

_____. 1985b. *Report to the Congress on Alternative Projects for Refugees*. Washington, DC: U.S. Department of Health and Human Services.

_____. 1986. *Report to the Congress: Refugee Resettlement Program*. Washington, DC: U.S. Department of Health and Human Services.

_____. 1993. *Report to the Congress: Refugee Resettlement Program*. Washington, DC: U.S. Department of Health and Human Services.

_____. 2002. *Report to the Congress: Refugee Resettlement Program*. Washington, DC: U.S. Department of Health and Human Services.

_____. 2007. *Report to the Congress: Refugee Resettlement Program*. Washington, DC: U.S. Department of Health and Human Services.

Ortner, Sherry B. 1998. Identities: The Hidden Life of Class. *Journal of Anthropological Research* 54(1): 1-17.

OSI (Opportunity Systems, Incorporated). 1976. *Third Wave Report: Vietnam Resettlement Operational Feedback*. Washington, DC

_____. 1977. *Fifth Wave Report: Vietnam Resettlement Operational Feedback*. Washington, DC

_____. 1979. *Sixth Wave Report: Indochinese Resettlement Operational Feedback*. Washington, DC

_____. 1981. *Ninth Wave Report: Indochinese Resettlement Operational Feedback*. Washington, DC

Page, J. Bryan, and Diana H. Gonzales. 1980. Drug Use Among Miami Cubans: A Preliminary Report. *Street Pharmacologist* 3(11): 1-4.

Palinkas, Lawrence A., Sheila M. Pickwell, Kendra Brandstein, Terry J. Clark, Linda L. Hill, Robert J. Moser, and Abdikadir Osman. 2003. The Journey to Wellness: Stages of Refugee Health Promotion and Disease Prevention. *Journal of Immigrant Health* 5(1): 19-28.

Park, Yoosun. 2005. Survivors: Cambodian Refugees in the United States. *Social Service Review* 79(2): 378-381.

Patel, Sujata. 2000. Modernity: Sociological Categories and Identities. *Current Sociology* 48(3): 1-5.

Peck, Jeffrey M. 1995. Refugees as Foreigners. Pp. 101-126 in E. Valentine Daniel and John Chr. Knudsen (Eds.), *Mistrusting Refugees*. Berkeley: University of California Press.

Peck-Barnes, Shirley. 2000. *The War Cradle: The Untold Story of Operation Babylift*. Denver: Vintage Pressworks.

Peek, Lori. 2005. Becoming Muslim: The Development of a Religious Identity. *Sociology of Religion* 66(3): 215-242.

Penning, Kerry. 1992. Tradition and Pragmatism: An Exploration into the Career Aspirations of Vietnamese Refugee College Students. Pp. 89-99 in Pamela A. DeVoe (Ed.), S*elected Papers on Refugee Issues*. Washington, DC: American Anthropological Association.

Perez, Lisandro. 1986. Immigrant Economic Adjustment and Family Organization: The Cuban Success Story Reexamined. *International Migration Review* 20(1): 4-20.

Peteet, Julie M. 1995. Transforming Trust: Dispossession and Empowerment Among Palestinian Refugees. Pp. 168-186 in E. Valentine Daniel and John Chr Knudsen (Eds.), *Mistrusting Refugees*. Berkeley: University of California Press.

Pham Van Bich. 1999. *The Vietnamese Family in Change*. Richmond, England: Curzon Press.

Phan Ke Binh. 1983. *Viet Nam Phong Tuc*. Fort Smith, Arkansas: Song Moi.

Phan, Tam C. 1994. Public Health Agenda Year 2000: Objectives for Vietnamese Americans. *The Bridge* 11(3): 2-3, 10.

Phillips, James. 1994. Salvadorans and Nicaraguans in Honduras: A Comparative Analysis of Community-Building, Repatriation and the Transformation of Refugee Identity. Pp. 98-115 in Jeffery L. MacDonald and Amy Zaharlick (Eds.), *Selected Papers on Refugee Issues: III*. Arlington, Virginia: American Anthropological Association.

Pho, Tuyet-Lan, Jeffrey N. Gerson, and Sylvia R. Cowan. 2007. *Southeast Asian Refugees and Immigrants in the Mill City*. Burlington: University of Vermont Press.

Pipher, Mary. 2002. *The Middle of Everywhere: Helping Refugees Enter the American Community*. New York: Harcourt, Inc.

Plaut, W. Gunther. 1995. *Asylum: A Moral Dilemma*. Westport, Connecticut: Praeger Publishers.

Portes, Alejandro. 1969. Dilemmas of a Golden Exile: Integration of Cuban Refugee Families in Milwaukee. *American Sociological Review* 34: 505-518.

_____. 1997. Immigration Theory for a New Century: Some Problems and Opportunities. *International Migration Review* 31(4): 799-825.

Portes, Alejandro, and Alex Stepick. 1993. *City on the Edge: The Transformation of Miami*. Berkeley: University of California Press.

Portes, Alejandro, Juan M. Clark, and Robert L. Bach. 1977. The New Wave: A Statistical Profile of Recent Cuban Exiles to the United States. *Cuban Studies* 1: 1-32.

Portes, Alejandro, and Robert L. Bach. 1985. *Latin Journey: Cuban and Mexican Immigrants in the United States*. Berkeley: University of California Press.

Portes, Alejandro, and Rubén Rumbaut. 1996. *Immigrant America* (2nd ed.). Berkeley: University of California Press.

_____. 2001. *Legacies: The Story of the Immigrant Second Generation*. Berkeley, California: University of California Press.

Prieto, Yolanda. 1986. Cuban Women and Work in the United States: A New Jersey Case Study. Pp. 95-112 in Rita J. Simon and Caroline B. Brettell (Eds.), *International Migration: The Female Experience*. Totowa, New Jersey: Rowman and Allenheld.

Prohias, Rafael, and Lourdes Casal. 1973. *The Cuban Minority in the U.S.: Preliminary Report on Need Identification and Program Evaluation*. Boca Raton: Florida Atlantic University.

Qian, Zhenchao. 2004. Options: Racial/Ethnic Identification of Children of Intermarried Couples. *Social Science Quarterly* 85(3): 746-766.

Qian, Zhenchao, Simpson Lee Blair, and Stacy D. Ruf. 2001. Asian American Interracial and Interethnic Marriages: Differences by Education and Nativity. *International Migration Review* 35(2): 557-586.

Rader, Victoria. 1999. Refugees at Risk: The Sanctuary Movement and Its Aftermath. Pp. 325-345 in David W. Haines and Karen E. Rosenblum (Eds.), *Illegal Immigration in America*. Westport, Connecticut: Greenwood Press.

Rahe, Richard H., John G. Looney, Harold W. Ward, Tran Minh Tung, and William T. Liu. 1978. Psychiatric Consultation in a Vietnamese Refugee Camp. *American Journal of Psychiatry* 135(2): 185-190.

Rasbridge, Lance A. 1994. Health and Illness Among Refugees: Acute and Long-Term Consequences of Resettlement. Paper presented at the annual meeting of the American Anthropological Association. Atlanta, Georgia.

———. 2001. Dallas, Texas: Enclave and Suburb: Patterns and Reactions in Refugee-Host Interactions. Pp. 25-38 in David W. Haines and Carol A. Mortland (Eds.), *Manifest Destinies: Americanizing Immigrants and Internationalizing Americans*. Westport, Connecticut: Praeger Publishers.

Reder, Stephen, and Mary Cohn. 1984. *A Study of the Extent and Effect of English Language Training for Refugees, Phase II: Classroom Observation and Community Survey*. Portland, Oregon: Northwest Regional Educational Laboratory.

Reder, Stephen, Mary Cohn, Judith Arter, and Steven Nelson. 1984. *A Study of English Language Training for Refugees: Public Report*. Portland, Oregon: Northwest Regional Educational Laboratory.

Reder, Stephen, Steven Nelson, and Judith Arter. 1982. *A Study of the Extent and Effect of English Language Training for Refugees, Phase I: Results of a Comprehensive Mail Survey*. Portland, Oregon: Northwest Regional Educational Laboratory.

Refugee Reports. 1982. House Immigration Chairman Cites "Refugee, Inc." Volume 3(16), July 16.

Reimers, David M. 1992. *Still the Golden Door: The Third World Comes to America*. New York: Columbia University Press.

Reyes, Adelaida. 1999. *Songs of the Caged, Song of the Free: Music and the Vietnamese Refugee Experience*. Philadelphia: Temple University Press.

Reynolds, Kim Lee. 1994. Vietnamese Youth Puts School, Dream on Hold to Support Family. *Richmond Times-Dispatch*, February 3: E1.

Ro, Young-Chan. 2009. Cultural Identity and Korean Disaspora: An American Phenomenon. Paper presented at the workshop *Reillumination of Korean Disasporic Societies in Asia*. Seoul: Korea University. September.

Roberts, Alden E., and Paul D. Starr. 1989. Differential Reference Group Assimilation Among Vietnamese Refugees. Pp. 40-54 in David W. Haines (Ed.), *Refugees as Immigrants*. Totowa, New Jersey: Rowman and Littlefield.

Robinson, W. Courtland. 1998. *Terms of Refuge: The Indochinese Exodus and the International Response*. New York: Zed Books.

Roediger, David R. 1991. *The Wages of Whiteness: Race and the Making of the American Working Class*. New York: Verso.

Rogg, Eleanor. 1971. The Influence of a Strong Refugee Community on the Economic Adjustment of its Members. *International Migration Review* 5(4): 474-481.

Roscigno, Vincent J., and Donald Tomaskovic-Devey. 1994. Racial Politics in the Contemporary South: Toward a More Critical Understanding. *Social Problems* 41: 585-607.

Rosen, Robert N. 2006. *Saving the Jews: Franklin D. Roosevelt and the Holocaust*. New York: Thunder's Mouth Press.

Rosenblum, Karen, Ying Zhou, and Karen Gentemann. 2009. Ambivalence: Exploring the American University Experience of Second-Generation Immigrants. *Journal of Race, Ethnicity, and Education* 12(3): 337-348.

Ross-Sheriff, Fariyal. 2006. Afghan Women in Exile and Repatriation: Passive Victims or Social Actors? *Affilia* 21(2): 206-219.

Rumbaut, Rubén. 1989. Portraits, Patterns, and Predictors of the Refugee Adaptation Process: Results and Reflections From the IHARP Panel Study. Pp. 138-182 in David W. Haines (Ed.), *Refugees as Immigrants: Cambodians, Laotians, and Vietnamese in America*. Totowa, New Jersey: Rowman & Littlefield.

———. 1999. Immigration Research in the United States: Social Origins and Future Orientations. *American Behavioral Scientist* 42(9): 1285-1301.

Rutledge, Paul James. 1985. *The Role of Religion in Ethnic Self-Identity*. Lanham, Maryland: University Press of America.

Rynearson, Ann M. 2001. St. Louis Missouri: Social Convergence and Cultural Diversity Among Immigrants and Refugees. Pp. 11-24 in David W. Haines and Carol A. Mortland (Eds.), *Manifest Destinies: Americanizing Immigrants and Internationalizing Americans*. Westport, Connecticut: Praeger Publishers.

Rynearson, Ann M., and Pamela A. Devoe. 1984. Refugee Women in a Vertical Village: Lowland Laotians in St. Louis. *Social Thought* 10(3): 33-48.

Sachs, Dana. 2010. *The Life We Were Given: Operation Babylift, International Adoption, and the Children of War in Vietnam*. Boston: Beacon Press.

Sacks, Karen. B. 1994. How Did Jews Become White Folks? Pp. 89-97 in Steven Gregory and Roger Sanjek (Eds.), *Race*. New Brunswick, New Jersey: Rutgers University Press.

Sanchez, Sylvia, and Eva K. Thorp. 2005. Journeys through a Cultural and Linguistic Maze: The Experience of Immigrant Graduate

Students Preparing to Be U.S. Teachers. Paper presented at the Annual Meeting of the Society for Applied Anthropology, Santa Fe, New Mexico.

Schmidt, Susan. 2009. Liberian Refugees: Cultural Considerations for Social Service Providers. *BRYCS Bulletin*. http://www.brycs.org/documents/liberian_cultural_considerations.pdf.

Schoenmaeckers, Ronald C., Edith Lodewijckx, and Sylvie Gadeyne. 1999. Marriages and Fertility Among Turkish and Moroccan Women in Belgium: Results From Census Data. *International Migration Review* 33(4): 901-928.

Schön, Donald. A. 1983. *The Reflective Practitioner*. New York: Basic Books.

————. 1987. *Educating the Reflective Practitioner*. San Francisco: Jossey-Bass.

Schön, Donald A., and Martin Rein. 1994. *Frame Reflection: Toward the Resolution of Intractable Policy Controversies*. New York: Basic Books.

Schulz, Priscilla M., Davorka Marovic-Johnson, and L. Christian Huber. 2006. Cognitive-Behavioral Treatment of Rape- and War-Related Post-traumatic Stress Disorder with a Female, Bosnian Refugee. *Clinical Case Studies* 5(3): 191-208.

Schwartz, Seth J., and Marilyn J. Montgomery. 2002. Similarities or Differences in Identity Development? The Impact of Acculturation and Gender on Identity Process and Outcome. *Journal of Youth and Adolescence* 31(5): 359-372.

Segal, Julius, and Norman Lourie. 1975. *The Mental Health of the Vietnam Refugees: Memorandum to Rear Admiral S. G. Morrison*. Washington, DC: U.S. Department of Health, Education, and Welfare, National Institute of Mental Health.

Siddiq, Muhammad. 1995. On Ropes of Memory: Narrating the Palestinian Refugees. Pp. 87-101 in E. Valentine Daniel and John Chr Knudsen (Eds.), *Mistrusting Refugees*. Berkeley: University of California Press.

Silver, Christopher. 1984. *Twentieth-Century Richmond: Planning, Politics, and Race*. Knoxville: University of Tennessee Press.

Simmons, Alan B., and Dwaine E. Plaza. 1998. Breaking Through the Glass Ceiling: The Pursuit of University Training Among African-Caribbean Migrants and Their Children in Toronto. *Canadian Ethnic Studies* 30(3): 99-120.

Simon, Rita J. (Ed.). 1985. *New Lives: The Adjustment of Soviet Jewish Immigrants in the United States and Israel*. Lexington, Massachusetts: Lexington Books.

Simon, Rita J. 1996. Public and Political Opinion on the Admission of Refugees. Pp. 355-371 in David W. Haines (Ed.), *Refugees in America in the 1990s*. Westport, Connecticut: Greenwood Press.

Simon, Rita J., and James P. Lynch. 1999. A Comparative Assessment of Public Opinion Toward Immigrants and Immigration Policies. *International Migration Review* 33(2): 455-467.

Simon, Rita J., and Susan A. Alexander. 1993. *The Ambivalent Welcome: Print Media, Public Opinion and Immigration*. Westport, Connecticut: Praeger.

Singer, Audrey, and Jill H. Wilson. 2006. *From "There" to "Here": Refugee Resettlement in Metropolitan America*. Washington, DC: The Brookings Institution.

Slack, Charles. 1991a. Moscow on the James. *Richmond Time-Dispatch*, June 23: F1.

Smith, Paul J. 1997. *Human Smuggling: Chinese Migrant Trafficking and the Challenge to America's Immigration Tradition*. Washington, DC: Center for Strategic and International Studies.

Smith-Hefner, Nancy J. 1994. Ethnicity and the Force of Faith: Christian Conversion Among Khmer Refugees. *Anthropological Quarterly* 67(1): 24-37.

_____. 1999. *Khmer American: Identity and Moral Education in a Diasporic Community*. Berkeley: University of California Press.

Snyder, Cindy S., J. Dean May, Nihada N. Zulcic, and W. Jay Gabbard. 2005. Social Work with Bosnian Muslim Refugee Children and Families: A Review of the Literature. *Child Welfare* 84(5): 607-630.

Snyder, Cindy S., Wesley J. Gabbard, J. Dean May, and Nihada Zulcic. 2006. On the Battleground of Women's Bodies: Mass Rape in Bosnia-Herzegovina. *Affilia* 21(2): 184-195.

Song, Miri. 1999. *Helping Out: Children's Labor in Ethnic Businesses*. Philadelphia: Temple University Press.

Starr, Paul, and Alden Roberts. 1982. Community Structure and Vietnamese Refugee Adaptation: The Significance of Context. *International Migration Review* 16(3): 595-618.

Starr, Paul, Alden Roberts, Rebecca LeNoir, and Thai Ngoc Nguyen. 1979. Adaptation and Stress Among Vietnamese Refugees: Preliminary Results

From Two Regions. Paper presented at the Conference on Indochinese Refugees, George Mason University.

Stein, Barry N. 1979. Occupational Adjustment of Refugees: The Vietnamese in the United States. *International Migration Review* 13(1): 25-45.

Stein, Barry N., and Silvio M. Tomasi (Eds.). 1981. *Refugees Today*. Special issue of *International Migration Review* Vol. 15(1/2).

Strand, Paul J., and Woodrow Jones, Jr. 1985. *Indochinese Refugees in America: Problems of Adaptation and Assimilation*. Durham, North Carolina: Duke University Press.

Suárez-Orozco, Carola, and Marcelo M. Suárez-Orozco. 2001. *Children of Immigration*. Cambridge: Harvard University Press.

Szapocznik, Jose, Mercedes A. Scopetta, and Olga E. King. 1978. Theory and Practice in Matching Treatment to the Special Characteristics and Problems of Cuban Immigrants. *Journal of Community Psychology* 6: 112-122.

Szapocznik, Jose, William Kurtines, and Norma Hanna. 1979. Comparison of Cuban and Anglo-American Cultural Values in a Clinical Population. *Journal of Consulting and Clinical Psychology* 47(3): 623-624.

Ta Van Tai. 1981. The Status of Women in Traditional Vietnam: A Comparison of the Le Dynasty (1428–1788) with the Chinese Codes. *Journal of Asian History* 15: 97-145.

_____. 1984. Women and the Law in Traditional Vietnam. *Vietnam Forum* 3: 23-54.

Taft, Jula V., David S. North, and David A. Ford. 1979. *Refugee Resettlement in the U.S.: Time for a New Focus*. Washington, DC: New TransCentury Foundation.

Takaki, Ronald. 1989. *Strangers From a Different Shore: A History of Asian Americans*. New York: Penguin.

Tanaka, Greg. 2003. *The Intercultural Campus: Transcending Culture and Power in American Higher Education*. New York: Peter Lang Publishing.

Thanh Duy. 1998. Family Culture and Market Economy. *Vietnam Social Sciences* (3/65): 35-42.

Tindall, George Brown. 1967. *The Emergence of the New South: 1913–1945*. Baton Rouge: Louisiana State University Press.

_____. 1995. *Natives and Newcomers: Ethnic Southerners and Southern Ethnics*. Athens: University of Georgia Press.

Toan Anh. 1966. *Nep Cu: Con Nguoi Viet-Nam*. Unidentified reprinting.

————. 1968. *Lang Xom Viet-Nam*. Unidentified reprinting.

Tollefson, James W. 1989. *Alien Winds: The Reeducation of America's Indochinese Refugees*. New York: Praeger.

Torres, Maria de los Angeles. 2004. *The Lost Apple: Operation Pedro Pan, Cuban Children in the U.S., and the Promise of a Better Future*. Boston: Beacon Press.

Triay, Victor Andres. 1999. *Fleeing Castro: Operation Pedro Pan and the Cuban Children's Program*. Gainesville: University Press of Florida.

Tsai, Jeanne L., Yu-Wen Ying, and Peter A. Lee. 2000. The Meaning of "Being Chinese" and "Being American": Variation Among Chinese American Young Adults. *Journal of Cross-Cultural Psychology* 31(3): 302-332.

Tyler-McGraw, Marie. 1994. *At the Falls: Richmond, Virginia and Its People*. Chapel Hill: University of North Carolina Press.

U.S. Bureau of the Census. 1993a. *The Foreign Born Population of the United States*. Washington, DC

————. 1993b. *Persons of Hispanic Origin in the United States*. Washington, DC

————. 1993c. *Asians and Pacific Islanders in the United States*. Washington, DC

U.S. Senate (Committee on the Judiciary). 1979. *Hearing on the Refugee Act of 1979, S. 642*. Washington, DC: U.S. Government Printing Office.

Uehling, Greta. 1998. Is There "Refuge" in the Refugee Category? Pp. 123-144 in Ruth M. Krulfeld and Jeffery L. MacDonald (Eds.), *Power, Ethics, and Human Rights*. Lanham, Maryland: Rowman & Littlefield.

UNHCR (United Nations High Commissioner for Refugees). 2006. Bhutanese Refugees in Nepal. In *The State of the World's Refugees 2006*. Geneva.

————. 2009a. Over 20,000 Bhutanese Refugees Resettled From Nepal. *Briefing Notes* 8 (September).

————. 2009b. Insecurity Lowers Afghan Returns. *UN News Centre*. http://www.un.org/apps/news/story.asp?NewsID = 33362&Cr = afghan&Cr1 = #.

————. 2009c. Frequently Requested Statistics. http://www.unhcr.org/pages/4a0174156.html.

University of Miami. 1967. *The Cuban Immigration 1959–1966 and Its Impact on Miami-Dade County, Florida*. Coral Gables, Florida.

Urban Associates. 1974. *A Study of Selected Socio-Economic Characteristics of Ethnic Minorities Based on the 1970 Census: Volume 1: Americans of Spanish Origin*. Washington, DC: U.S. Department of Health, Education, and Welfare.

USCR (U.S. Committee for Refugees). 1984. *Vietnamese Boat People: Pirates' Vulnerable Prey*. New York: American Council for Nationalities Service.

Vang, Chia Youyee. 2008. *Hmong in Minnesota*. Minneapolis: Minnesota Historical Society Press.

Vang, Christopher T. 2005. Hmong-American Students Still Face Multiple Challenges in Public Schools. *Multicultural Education* 13(1): 27-35.

Vasquez, Jessica M. 2005. Ethnic Identity and Chicano Literature: How Ethnicity Affects Reading and Reading Affects Ethnic Consciousness. *Ethnic and Racial Studies* 28(5): 903-924.

Vignes, A. Joe, and Richard C.W. Hall. 1979. Adjustment of a Group of Vietnamese People to the United States. *American Journal of Psychiatry* 136(4): 442-444.

VQGTK (Vien Quoc-Gia Thong-Ke). 1957. *Annuaire Statistique, 1954–1955*. Saigon: Republique du Vietnam, Secretariat d'Etat a l'Economie Nationale, Institut National de la Statistique.

———. 1958. *Annuaire Statistique, 1956*. Saigon: Republique du Vietnam, Secretariat d'Etat a l'Economie Nationale, Institut National de la Statistique.

———. 1959. *Annuaire Statistique, 1957*. Saigon: Republique du Vietnam, Secretariat d'Etat a l'Economie Nationale, Institut National de la Statistique.

———. 1960a. *Enquetes Demographiques au Vietnam en 1958*. Saigon: Republique du Viet-Nam, Secretariat d'Etat a l'Economie Nationale, Institut National de la Statistique.

———. 1960b. *Interpretation des resultats de l'enquete demographique a Saigon*. Saigon: Republique du Viet-Nam, Secretariat d'Etat a l'Economie Nationale, Institut National de la Statistique.

———. 1963. *Enquete Demographique a Saigon en 1962*. Saigon: Republique du Viet-Nam, Secretariat d'Etat a l'Economie Nationale, Institut National de la Statistique.

———. 1968. *Dieu-Tra Dan-So Tai Saigon Nam 1967*. Saigon: Viet-Nam Cong-Hoa, Phu Thu-Tuong, Nha Tong Giam-Doc Ke-Hoach.

———. 1971. *Viet-Nam Nien-Giam Thong-Ke, 1971*. Saigon: Viet-Nam Cong-Hoa, Bo Ke Hoach va Phat Trien Quoc Gia.

_____. 1973. *Dieu-Tra Gia-Dinh Vung Thon Que Nam 1971 Tai 16 Tinh o Viet-Nam.* Saigon: Viet-Nam Cong-Hoa, Bo Ke Hoach va Phat Trien Quoc Gia.

Vu, Loi Manh. 1998. Fertility Behavior in the Vietnam Red River Delta: Birth Timing and Birth Interval Dynamics. Ph.D. dissertation. University of Washington.

Wagner, Wendy. 1993. After Having Only Hope, Refugee Has It All. *Richmond Times-Dispatch*, August 26: A: 17.

Waldinger, Roger, Nelson Lim, and David Cort. 2007. Bad Jobs, Good Jobs, No Jobs? The Employment Experience of the Mexican American Second Generation. *Journal of Ethnic and Migration Studies* 33(1): 1-35.

Waters, Mary C. 1990. *Ethnic Options.* Berkeley, California: University of California Press.

_____. 1999. *Black Identities: West Indian Immigrant Dreams and American Realities.* New York: Russell Sage Foundation.

Weisskirch, Robert S. 2005. Ethnicity and Perceptions of Being a "Typical American" in Relationship to Ethnic Identity Development. *International Journal of Intercultural Relations* 29(3): 355-366.

Welaratna, Usha. 1993. *Beyond the Killing Fields: Voices of Nine Cambodian Survivors in America.* Stanford: Stanford University Press.

Wellmeier, Nancy J. 2001. West Palm Beach, Florida and Phoenix, Arizona: A Continuum of Response to the Mayan Presence. Pp. 55-70 in David W. Haines and Carol A. Mortland (Eds.), *Manifest Destinies: Americanizing Immigrants and Internationalizing Americans.* Westport, Connecticut: Praeger Publishers.

White, Tanika. 1994. Family Finds Freedom Away From Bosnia. *Richmond Times-Dispatch*, August 14: B1.

Whitmore, John K. 1984. Social Organization and Confucian Thought in Vietnam. *Journal of Southeast Asian Studies* 15(2): 296-306.

_____. 1996. Chinese From Southeast Asia. Pp. 81-101 in David W. Haines (Ed.), *Refugees in America in the 1990s.* Westport, Connecticut: Greenwood Press.

Whitmore, John K., Marcella Trautmann, and Nathan Caplan. 1989. The Socio-Cultural Basis for the Economic and Educational Success of Southeast Asian Refugees (1978–1982 Arrivals). Pp. 121-137 in David W. Haines (Ed.), *Refugees as Immigrants: Cambodians, Laotians, and Vietnamese in America.* Totowa, New Jersey: Rowman & Littlefield.

Wilson, Kenneth L., and Alejandro Portes. 1980. Immigrant Enclaves: An Analysis of the Labor Market Experiences of Cubans in Miami. *American Journal of Sociology* 86(2): 295-319.

Woldemikael, Tekle M. 1996. Ethiopians and Eritreans. Pp. 147-169 in David W. Haines (Ed.), *Refugees in America in the 1990s*. Westport, Connecticut: Greenwood Press.

Wood, Joseph. 1997. Vietnamese American Place Making in Northern Virginia. *The Geographical Review* 87(1): 58-72.

Woodside, Alexander B. 1995. Central Viet Nam's Trading World in the Eighteenth Century as Seen in Le Qui Don's "Frontier Chronicles." Pp. 157-172 in Keith W. Taylor and John K. Whitmore (Eds.), *Essays into Vietnamese Pasts*. Ithaca, New York: Cornell University Southeast Asia Program.

Woodward, C. Vann. 1971. *Origins of the New South, 1877–1913*. Baton Rouge: Louisiana State University Press.

Worthington, Mark, Deborah Kuhn, Marilyn P. Rymer, and Denise Madigan. 1983. *Refugees and General Assistance: A Short-Term Evaluation of the Effects of the Changes in Federal Refugee Assistance Policy on State and Local Governments and on Refugees*. Cambridge, Massachusetts: Urban Systems Research and Engineering, Inc.

Wust, Klaus. 1969. *The Virginia Germans*. Charlottesville: University Press of Virginia.

Wyman, David S. 1985 (orig 1968). *Paper Walls: America and the Refugee Crisis, 1938–1941*. New York: Pantheon Books.

———. 1998 (orig 1984). *The Abandonment of the Jews: America and the Holocaust, 1941–1945*. New York: The New Press.

Wyman, Mark 1998 (orig 1989). *DPs: Europe's Displaced Persons, 1945–1951*. Ithaca: Cornell University Press.

Yarborough, Trin. 2005. *Surviving Twice: Amerasian Children of the Vietnam War*. Washington, DC: Potomac Books.

Yarvis, Jeffrey, Miriam Sabin, Larry Nackerud, and Kavita Pandit. 2004. Haitian Immigrants in the United States: Intergenerational Trauma Transmission, Adaptation and Ethnic Identity. *Caribbean Journal of Social Work* 3(1): 57-73.

Yiv, Chenny, and Margaret J. Secombe. 1999. Cambodian Students and Motivation to Participate in Higher Education. *Education and Society* 17(2): 85-98.

Yu, Insun. 1990. Law and Family in Seventeenth and Eighteenth Century Vietnam. Seoul: Korea University (Asiatic Research Center).

Zehr, Mary Ann. 2007. Tussle over English-Language Learners. *Education Week* 26(21): 1,18.

Zhou, Min, and Carl L. Bankston III.

———. 1999. *Growing Up American: How Vietnamese Children Adapt to Life in the United States*. New York: Russell Sage Foundation.

———. 2001. Family Pressure and the Educational Experience of the Daughters of Vietnamese Refugees. *International Migration* 39(4): 133-151.

Zhou, Min, and Yang Sao Xiong. 2005. The Multifaceted American Experiences of the Children of Asian Immigrants: Lessons for Segmented Assimilation. *Ethnic and Racial Studies* 28(6): 1119-1152.

Zucker, Norman L., and Naomi F. Zucker. 1987. *The Guarded Gate: The Reality of American Refugee Policy*. San Diego: Harcourt Brace Jovanovich.

———. 1996. *Desperate Crossings: Seeking Refuge in America*. New York: M. E. Sharpe.

About the Author

David W. Haines is a professor of anthropology at George Mason University. His original interest in refugees stemmed from rural development work in South Vietnam and graduate studies on Southeast Asian history, followed by research and policy work at the U.S. Office of Refugee Resettlement. He is a two-time Fulbright scholar (Western Europe and South Korea), past president of the Society for Urban, National, and Transnational/Global Anthropology (SUNTA), and convener of the Wind over Water comparative project on East Asian migration. His other books include *Refugees in America in the 1990s; Cultural Anthropology: Adaptations, Structures, Meanings; The Limits of Kinship: South Vietnamese Households;* and the forthcoming *Wind over Water* (coedited with Keiko Yamanaka and Shinji Yamashita).

Index

Also from Kumarian Press...

Global Migration:

The Economic Life of Refugees
Karen Jacobsen

Hollow Bodies: Institutional Responses to Sex Trafficking in Armenia, Bosnia and India
Susan Dewey

The Immigration Debate: Remaking America
John Isbister

Inequity in the Global Village: Recycled Rhetoric and Disposable People
Jan Knippers Black

New and Forthcoming:

Dispossessed People: Establishing Legitimacy and Rights for Global Migrants
Christine Ho and James Loucky

Dual Disasters: Humanitarian Aid After the 2004 Tsunami
Jennifer Hyndman

Artisans and Fair Trade: Crafting Development
Mary Littrell and Marsha Dickson

Just Give Money to the Poor: The Development Revolution from the Global South
Joseph Hanlon, Armando Barrientos and David Hulme

Visit Kumarian Press at **www.kpbooks.com** or
call **toll-free 800.232.0223** for a complete catalog

green press
INITIATIVE

Kumarian Press, located in Sterling, Virginia, is a forward-looking, scholarly press that promotes active international engagement and an awareness of global connectedness.